A HISTORY OF THE
OGADEN (WESTI .... OMALI)
STRUGGLE FOR SELF-DETERMINATION
Part I (1300-2007)

Revised Second Edition

Mohamed Mohamud Abdi

CLEAR
PRESS

Birmingham – UK

Published by Clear Press, an imprint of Safis Publishing Limited, Birmingham, UK.
www.clear-press.net

ISBN   978-1-906342-39-5 (paperback)
           978-1-906342-40-1 (ebook)

Second Edition

Version Identifier: 21070715

Acknowledgement

I would like to thank my family for their support and understanding and my friends for their encouragement, suggestions and support.

Maps

Contents

Preface

The Ogaden region is inhabited by Somalis and is geographically part of Ethiopia, but politically the region has yet to become part of Ethiopia. The region has never seen peace since the scramble for Africa in the nineteenth century, and as a result of wars and repression by the successive Ethiopian governments the inhabitants are constantly displaced. Over a million people fled to neighbouring countries during the 1970s and 1980s and are still leaving the region because of fear of prosecution. The insecurity, displacement and repression that persist in the region profoundly affected the lives and livelihood of the inhabitants in an extremely negative manner. Since the last Ethiopian occupation of the region after the Second World War the region has been in a war or warlike situation, and as a result normal life is unknown there, and instead, hunger, refugee crises and human rights abuses became the norms.

Despite the long suffering of the Somali people in the Ogaden region, the root cause of their ordeal was not dealt with nor did the victims receive due attention from the international community. Because of, among other things, lack of awareness about the plight of the inhabitants and misconception about the conflict, the international community has not intervened so far on behalf of the victims. Ethiopia's voice has always been louder than that of the inhabitants of the Ogaden region and, as a result, it misrepresented the issue in the international forums, and the inhabitants have been unable to reach out to the wider world.

The Somali people in the Ogaden deserve a better life in which they can decide their own destiny like all other peoples and those who care about justice are expected to support that goal in the name of humanity. The Somali people in that region have been striving to regain their freedom and their basic human rights, including the right to self-determination, but so far, they have been unable to remove the occupants from their land and free themselves. They see the ending of the occupation as the key to the alleviation of their suffering and are determined to pursue the liberation goal despite the odds against them.

The Ogaden issue is the cockpit of the Horn of Africa, and resolving that problem is the key to the resolutions of the conflicts and turmoil in the Horn—a resolution that will not only alleviate the suffering of the inhabitants of that region but will also make that part of the world a better place to live in.

Although I am an amateur historian (I am an economist and sociologist by profession), I have been observing the development of the region since the 1970s and have written a book and articles about this subject in the past. The work relies on historical data, recorded by local and international historians, colonial governments, and international organizations as well as eyewitness accounts.

This book aims to contribute to the understanding of the problem and to draw to it the attention of those who could make a difference to the plight of the Somali people in the Ogaden. I recognize that this is a complex conflict and a simple book as this will have a limited influence on the present reality on the ground. Nevertheless, it is my hope that at least it will achieve its aim to shed light on some of the issues related to the conflict and thereby possibly contribute to the future resolution.

Introduction

The land this book is about is known globally as the Ogaden. The exact date the territory was named Ogaden is not known, but it has been called by that name since the eighteenth century. Despite its worldwide use, the name Ogaden is not fully endorsed by all the inhabitants of the region as the name of their land. Some sections of the Somali inhabitants feel unease about the name Ogaden because the largest clan in the region is called Ogaadeen and this name mixing arouses a sense of exclusion, which is felt by the non-Ogaadeen clans in the region. To neutralize that feeling and safeguard the unity of the people some liberation movements, like the Western Somali Liberation Front (WSLF), changed the name of the region from Ogaden to Western Somali and others such as the Ogaden National Liberation Front (ONLF) kept using Ogaden as the name of the country to avoid confusion in the international arena. The successive Ethiopian regimes also used different names for the region such as Hararghe, Ogaden and the Somali State.

The inhabitants of the region have yet to vote on a name of their own choosing for their land. The territory has been under occupation since the scramble for Africa, and for that reason, the people of the region were unable to choose a name for their land. It is to be hoped that it will not be long before they regain their sovereignty and can do that. In the meantime, in the book, we call the region both the Ogaden and Western Somali interchangeably or jointly. We use these two most popular names in the region for historical reasons as well as for inclusion considerations.

The Ogaden is situated in the Horn of Africa, and it has borders with Somalia, Djibouti, Kenya and Ethiopia, and is under the latter's administration. The area of its land is estimated at 370 000–400 000 sq. km. A genuine census has never been taken, but the population is estimated at between 4 and 5 million and is ethnically Somali. It is a semi-arid land, and the main livelihoods are pastoralism and farming. Although the region is one of the poorest in Ethiopia it is rich in natural resources such as copper, gold, oil and natural gas.

The territory was historically part of the Greater Somali Nation before the Somali Nation was divided into five parts by the colonial powers (Britain, Ethiopia, France and Italy); during the scramble for Africa and it was one of the four parts that came under British administration during the Second World War. The territory's status changed from full independence and part of the Greater Somali Nation to under attack, to partly occupied and eventually to fully occupied. After the occupation it also changed hands several times as the competing powers of Britain, Italy and Ethiopia fought for its control. During the scramble for Africa, Ethiopia and Italy competed for the control of the Ogaden and fought over it during the 1930s. Likewise, Britain and Italy fought for control of the region during the Second World War. Finally, the territory was gradually handed to Ethiopia after the Second World War, and the transfer was completed in 1955 when Britain handed over the last part of the Ogaden (Haud and Reserve Area) to Ethiopia.

But the occupation was never accepted by the Somalis in general and in particular by those living in the Ogaden. The Somali people in the Ogaden remain defiant. They resisted the occupation, and the Ogaden has been one of the hot spots of the world since the scramble for the Horn of Africa. Sayyid Mohammed Abdille Hassan started his anti-colonial military campaign in the Ogaden in 1900. In the 1960s and 1970s, Ethiopia and Somalia fought two wars over the Ogaden and the superpowers (USA and USSR/Russia) were both involved in the conflict. Moreover, the successive Ethiopian governments have remained at war with the inhabitants of the region since Ethiopia's occupation.

Despite the involvement of the big powers, the Ogaden conflict did not attract proper international attention and is one of the most misunderstood problems in the world. The misconception about that conflict is also the main reason for the lack of a resolution to it. Because of Ethiopia's misrepresentation of the conflict, a cover-up by the imperialist powers, and the inhabitants' inability to reach out to the wider world, the conflict is often erroneously seen as a dispute between Somalia and Ethiopia in international arenas, and the liberation fighters there described as aggressors or terrorists by Ethiopia and its allies. The imperialist European powers that helped Ethiopia to occupy and colonize the Ogaden covered up the tragedy and the superpowers (USA and USSR) who replaced them became the chief backers of the Ethiopian occupation policies afterwards. The superpowers not only supported the successive governments in Addis-Ababa in colonizing the Ogaden but also kept silent about the suffering, the unspeakable human rights violations and destruction that followed the occupation. Taking advantage of this support and the consequently favourable situation in which it found itself, Ethiopia pursued extremely oppressive policies towards the inhabitants and at the same time kept the international community in the dark about the plight of the people there by systematically misleading the world public opinion. The conflict in the Ogaden with its local, regional and international dimensions, negatively affected the Horn of Africa region, although the Ogaden inhabitants bore the brunt of the ensuing suffering and devastation.

The Somali people in the Ogaden, however, never gave up hope and remained defiant, despite the odds against them. They refused the subjugation and resisted the occupation with all possible means. The struggle for freedom and human dignity began as a reaction to the occupation and subsequent humiliations and gross violations of human rights. The struggle for the liberation of the Ogaden was mainly driven by two forces, namely the society's dream to take its destiny into its own hands and the often harsh realities on the ground. Both forces affected the struggle directly and indirectly by interacting with one another and in turn influencing the struggle. The dream for self-determination has itself been guided mainly by nationalism, religion and – most important of all – the need to safeguard human rights. These pillars of the dream have been the main fuel for the struggle machine; that is, they provided the rationale for the liberation struggle. Although the dream was stronger at some times than at others, it never died because of the human rights violation factor.

The struggle for the liberation of the Ogaden began as a resistance to the expansionist campaigns of the Christian kingdom of Abyssinia in the fourteenth century and that resistance was led by the Islamic emirate of Adal. After the partition of the Somali Nation, the Ogaden struggle became part of the wider Somali nationalist struggle against the colonialists until 1960 when Somalia became independent. Like the other two Somali lands still under colonial rule (Djibouti and NFD), the Somali people in the Ogaden continued their struggle on their own, but because of the Somali dream of Greater Somalia that struggle was very much aided and influenced by Somalia. During the 1980s the Somalis in the Ogaden lost connection with Somalia as the dream of Greater Somalia was coming to an end. Since then, the struggle has been going on independently inside and outside the Ogaden.

In this book, we will investigate the historical development of the society's struggle to regain its independence. The core of the investigation is how this freedom dream lived with different generations of the Somali society in the Ogaden during the occupation period, what prompted the formation of freedom fighters both armed and unarmed and how they performed. Taking armed conflicts, and political, social and human rights activism as indicators of the level of the struggle as well as the strength of the dream to live in freedom, the ups and downs of the struggle for self-determination will be examined using observation, eyewitness accounts and historical data. The history starts with the time when the people of the region largely lived in freedom in their homeland, except for some attacks on the western parts of the territory, and the different stages of the struggle will be highlighted. The history ends with the situation at the time of the writing of this book and outlines prospects for the resolution of the conflict.

1

The Adal Resistance to the Abyssinian Expansion

The root causes of the conflict; the armed resistance; the fall of Harar and the collapse of Adal

1.1 The Root Causes of the Conflict

The Somali-dominated Sultanate of Adal (*Awdal* in Somali) emerged in the fourteenth century, following the invasion of the Muslim emirate of Ifat and outlying Muslim areas by Abyssinia in the early 1320s. Ifat, which was ruled by the Walasma family, was occupied and its leader, Haqedin I, was murdered by the Christian kingdom of Abyssinia. Haqedin's son Sabredin, who succeeded him led a resistance army, established an alliance with the neighbouring Somali principality of Adal and other Muslim emirates, and confronted the invading Amhara army. Although it put up fierce resistance the Muslim alliance was eventually defeated in 1332, and both Sabredin and the king of Adal were killed.

The resistance began by Sabredin continued under the leadership of his great-grandsons Haqedin II and his younger brother Se'adedin. Haqedin transferred his political centre from Ifat to Dakkar, a place near Harar, which was under Adal influence. Later the remnant of Ifat joined Adal and the Walasma princes became rulers of the new Adal sultanate.

The Ogaden was part of Adal, which also encompassed Berbera and Zeila and most of today northern Somalia and some Danakil territories. The sultanate was a Muslim kingdom in outlook with a diverse ethnic background of Somalis, Hararis, Danakils and Arabs, but its population was predominantly of Somali origin. The Somali dominated sultanate was first based in Zeila but later moved to Harar, the capital city of the Ogaden at the time, and remained capital until its occupation in the nineteenth century except for a short period (1577–1643) in Awsa.

On the other hand, Tigray and Amhara people were the predominant ethnic groups of the Christian kingdom of Abyssinia; however, the kingdom was ruled at the time by Amhara dynasty. The Amhara dynasty (also called the Solomonic dynasty), restored in 1270 by Emperor Yakunno Amlak, was different from the other dynasties that preceded it

(Zagwe and Askum) in that it did not have a fixed capital. The Amhara kings moved from place to place, often within the central parts of the kingdom depending on the season and military campaign. Because of the decline of Askum and the northern trade routes following the shift of the dynasty from Tigray to Amhara, Zeila became the kingdom's most important trade route. Territorial acquisition was one of the main aims of the Amhara dynasty and they wanted to expand the empire eastward and southward along the trade route to Aden. Christianity was their guideline and spreading and defending Christianity was their main goal. They proclaimed to be the champions of Christianity in the Horn of Africa and on that claim always sought European support. The Europeans often responded positively, both as private individuals and as governments, to the Abyssinians' plea for help whenever they were defeated by Adal.

Before the attack on Ifat, the Muslims and the Christians largely coexisted peacefully, and the Muslims had high respect for the Abyssinian kingdom because Nejashi, the Ethiopian king who reigned during the rise of Islam, gave refuge to some of the first followers (*sahaba*) of the Prophet Mohammed, who fled from the persecution of the Mecca pagans in 616. The daughter of the prophet Rakiya, her husband Othman bin Affan (third khalif), and Ja'far bin Abu Talib (cousin of the prophet) were among the 15 followers that fled to Abyssinia. It is reported that Prophet Mohammed advised these followers to go to Abyssinia and told them that: 'In Abyssinia, there was a king in whose realm no one is wronged.'[1] Islam came to Ethiopia first through these *sahabas* and Nejashi was among the first Ethiopians who accepted Islam, although he did not reveal his faith in public.

The cause of hatred that led to the attack on Ifat and the subsequent invasion of Adal is a matter for debate. However, historians often mention two possible causes, namely the spread of Islam and trade. Islam was spreading peacefully at a high speed all over Ethiopia and the Christian kingdom felt a threat to its very existence because of this rapid spread of Islam. Abyssinia also wanted to control the trade route to the Gulf of Aden for commercial and religious reasons. Its traditional route through Eritrea became too long after the kingdom moved to Shoa and the trade route through Zeila became more important. 'The rise of the "Solomonic dynasty", and the resultant shift of the centre to southern

---

[1] Paul B. Henze, 2000, *Layers of Time, A History of Ethiopia*, Hurst & Co Ltd, page 42, 1991; *The Horn of Africa, from War to Peace*, Macmillan Academic and Professional Ltd, page 18–19.

Amhara and Shoa, gave a particular significance to the Zeila routes in which the Christian kings began to show an ever-increasing interest. Apparently motivated by these considerations, we see the first Solomonic king Yekunno-Amlak, interfering actively in the internal conflicts of the Mahzumite princes of the sultanate of Shoa as well as in the final showdown between the latter and the kingdom of Ifat.'[2] The trade route was also the Islamization route because Islam spread mainly through the traders and its control would have served both purposes, and this was probably the main reason for the aggression. Faith expansion meant also land expansion and the two things were two sides of one coin for both the Christian and Muslim kingdoms.

Whatever the reason, Abyssinia conquered several Muslim emirates – of which Ifat was the biggest – and also invaded Adal territories. Adal responded to the Abyssinian invasion by declaring jihad on it. As mentioned above, both systems of government were based on religious teachings, and religious thinking provided justification for the war. According to Islam, jihad (struggle) is obligatory for every Muslim whenever Muslim land is under attack. Adal rose to that responsibility of defending the Muslims and their land from the invading infidels.

For about six centuries Adal remained on the front line, defending itself from the Abyssinian invasions and periodical Oromo incursions. Moved by religious sentiments, the devastation left by the war and the brutality of the invaders, the inhabitants usually rallied behind their leaders and the rulers easily mobilized the population for jihad whenever attacked. Usually, the heavier the attack, the stronger the counterattack, and peaks of the resistance were often preceded by heavy attacks and vice versa.

The Abyssinian attacks were very intense in the fifteenth and sixteenth centuries but ceased in the middle of the seventeenth century and did not come back until the last half of the nineteenth century when Menelik, in collaboration with some European powers, succeeded in eliminating Adal and occupied Harar.

---

[2] Taddesse Tamrat, 1977, *Ethiopia, the Red Sea and the Horn, the Cambridge History of Africa*, Cambridge University Press, Volume 3, page143.

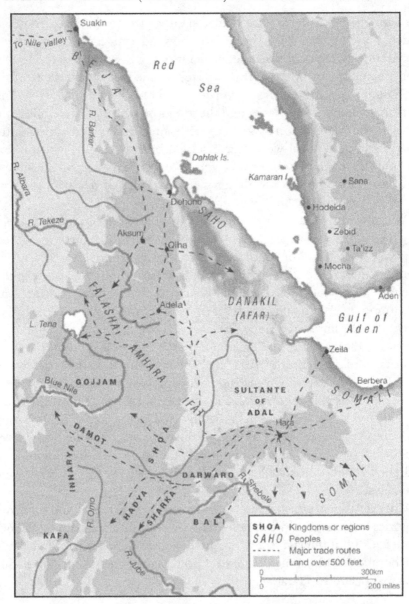

Map 1-1: North-Eastern Africa — major medieval trade routes

1.2 The Armed Resistance

As we saw in the preceding section, the resistance that Adal undertook was imposed on it by the Christian kingdom under the leadership of the Amhara dynasty that was founded by Yekunno Amlak, who reigned from 1270 to 1285. The rulers of the sultanate not only defended the Somali

16

regions under their sphere of influence, but they also contested the Abyssinian control over southern highlands by supporting the Muslim emirates there. The Abyssinian threat began in 1328 when its ruler Amda Seyon invaded Ifat and parts of Adal and captured Sultan Haqedin I of Ifat himself. His son Sabredin, who succeeded him, organized a Muslim coalition resistance, which included Adal and some other Muslim emirates. In the early stages, the coalition was successful and repulsed the Abyssinian invaders, but due to internal conflicts, the Muslim alliance was defeated by Amda Seyon in 1332. Seyon's son Sayfa-Ar'ad, who succeeded him, followed his father's hard-line policies toward the Muslims.

During the reign of Sayfa-Ar'ad's eldest son, Wurde Asfare (1372–82), a new development took place on the opposing Muslim side. What was left of Ifat joined Adal and Haqedin II, the grandson of Sabredin, became the new sultan of Adal. Soon after he took over the leadership of Adal, Haqedin reorganized the resistance forces, took- command and waged counter-offensive campaigns against the Abyssinians. He was killed in action in the end and his brother Se'adedin succeeded him. Se'adedin became a major challenger to Sayfa-Ar'ad's second son, Dawit I (1382–1412). Adal was invaded by Dawit several times and although he met strong resistance and was defeated many times, he had the final victory. In 1403 Dawit led a series of campaigns into the very heart of the Harar plateau and repeatedly defeated Se'adedin, whom he pursued as far as Zeila, where the sultan was captured and killed. Se'adedin's family fled to Yemen after his murder and stayed there some years.

The second wave of attacks happened during the years 1414–1429 when the then Abyssinian leader, Yishaq, waged a series of wars on the Somalis in the Ogaden. In those attacks many innocent people were killed, their belongings looted, their properties destroyed, and mosques were turned into churches. Despite the humiliation, the suffering and the power vacuum after the killing of Se'adedin and the subsequent self-exile of the Royal Walasma family, this Abyssinian victory did not last long. After a few years in exile in Yemen, the ten sons of Se'adedin returned, revived the Walasma power in Adal and reorganized the resistance. They conducted offensive campaigns, and in a short period, they succeed in liberating the territories occupied by the Christian kingdom after the death of their father and killed both the Amhara kings of Tewodros and Yishaq in the fighting. They drove not only the enemy from the Adal territories, but pursued the Amhara army until they crossed their original border near the Awash River:

Sabredin (1409–18), Mansur (1418–25) Jemaldin (1425–32) and Badlay (1432–45) successively took over their father's throne in Adal, and they all conducted energetic campaigns against the occupation forces of the Christian empire. It appears that they were increasingly successful in forcing the Christians to evacuate their settlements within Adali territory. The conflict had become so desperate that, in their hopeless attempts to hold on to the Adali territories acquired since Se'adedin's death, both Tewodros (1412–13) and Yishaq (1413–30) seem to have lost their lives while fighting the Walasma princes. For a period of four years after Yishaq's death, the political situation in the Christian empire was very chaotic, and Jemaldin (1425–32) took advantage of this to score a number of easy victories on the frontier. His brother Ahmed Badlay (1432–45) continued the successes of his brother.[3]

Despite the defeat, the Abyssinian raids on Adal territories resumed after Zara Ya'qob (1434–68) took over the reign of power. The new ruler, whom Edward Ullendorf the British Ethiopianist, called 'the greatest ruler Ethiopia had since Ezana'[4], reformed the kingdom. Zara Ya'qob continued the attacks against the Muslims after he reorganized both the church and the state and united them. But the Adal sultanate was ready to defend itself. Sultan Badlay regrouped the Adal army and conducted a counter-offensive against the invading forces. He attacked the Abyssinians and regained some territory lost earlier to the invading army, but he was killed while in action:

> Badlay led many raids, which were always successful and which created much havoc within the frontier provinces of the Christian empire. Finally, however, a renewed invasion of Dawaro by him was repulsed by the Christian army in 1445. Zara Ya'qob himself led the defences of Dawaro, Badlay was killed in action, and the Muslim army suffered considerable casualties.[5]

Ya'qob boasted over the defeat of the Muslims and like his predecessor Yishaq, he mentioned in particular the Somalis and listed Mogadishu among the Somali principalities that he alleged to have supported Adal in the fighting. This claim indicates the dominant position of the Somalis within Adal. Although Ya'qob's victory over Badlay relaxed the military pressure from Adal for about forty years, he

---

[3] Taddesse Tamrat, *Ethiopia, the Red Sea and the Horn*, the Cambridge History of Africa, page 154-155.

[4] Paul B. Henze, 1991, *The Horn of Africa, from War to Peace*, page 21.

[5] Taddesse Tamrat, 1977, *Ethiopia, the Red Sea and the Horn, the Cambridge History of Africa*, page 155.

could never recover the territories that had been acquired by Dawit, Tewodros and Yishaq in the Harar plateau, which was to remain completely outside the limits of the Christian kingdom until the end of the nineteenth century. However, he was able to maintain his power in the frontier provinces of Ifat, Dawaro and Bali, which has been in Christian hands since the fourteenth century.

Ya'qob's successor, Ba'eda Maryam (1468–78), followed his hardline approach against the Muslims, especially in Dawaro and Bali, until he began to suffer disastrous military reverses in his conflicts with the kingdom of Adal towards the end of his reign. The emergence of Amir Mahfuz in the 1480s as the new challenger of the highlanders, however, changed the balance of power in favour of the Muslims. Mahfuz, the Amir of Harar who became the chief of the Adal army, stepped up the frontier struggle and conducted counter-offensive campaigns against the Christian kingdom. Mahfuz often raided frontier regions, scored repeated successes, killed the Abyssinian king and destroyed the military and the economy of the Christian kingdom:

> Throughout the reigns of Eskender (1478–94) and Na'od (1494–1508), Mahfuz successfully attacked the frontier provinces. Large number of Christian military colonists were either killed or taken into slavery, and the Muslims always returned to Adal with huge spoils in slaves and cattle. The emperor, Na'od, himself died in 1508 while trying to defend the province of Ifat from one of the regular forays of Imam Mahfuz.[6]

Alarmed by the revival of the Adal power, which was indicated by the successive military successes of Amir Mahfuz, the Amhara dynasty sought European help. The Ethiopian ruler, Na'od, was killed in 1508 in Ifat in a campaign against the Muslims when his son, Lebna Dengel, was only seven years old. The Queen Mother, Eleni, who became regent for the new young Crown Prince, sent an Armenian named Mateus to Portugal to ask for help for Ethiopia in resisting the Muslim pressure. 'Mateus proceeded to Europe by way of India, had a series of misadventures, but finally reached the court of King Monoel I in Lisbon in 1514, where he was well received.'[7]

In 1516 Amir Mahfuz, the governor of Harar led an expedition to confront the Abyssinians and eliminate their threat. But another threat came from the Portuguese who responded to the Ethiopian request for

---

[6] Taddesse Tamrat, 1977, *Ethiopia, the Red Sea and the Horn, the Cambridge History of Africa*, page 167.

[7] Paul B. Henze, 2000, *Layers of Time, A History of Ethiopia*, page 84.

help and attacked Zeila. The Portuguese fleet under Lobe Soarez reached Zeila at a time when its garrison was fighting under Mahfuz in the highlands against the Abyssinians. Zeila was burnt and in a short period occupied by the Portuguese, and Mahfuz did not come back from that expedition.

The attack on Zeila and the death of Amir Mahfuz were big blows to the Somali sultanate. Morale was very low, and the decentralized emirates disintegrated. It also led to conflicts between the amirs and the army chiefs. The result of all this was the assassination of the king of the Adal sultanate, Sultan Mohammed, the fall of the royal Walasma family, and the change of the seat of the sultanate from Zeila to Harar in 1520. On the mediation of Sultan Abubakr, the capital city was changed and a new leader by the name of Imam Ahmed Ibrahim Alghazi (*Gragn*: 'left-handed' in Amharic) was also elected.

The new leader, who also held the position of Chief of Staff, reversed the balance of power in the Horn in favour of the Somalis within a short period. The man had both vision and vigour and the first thing he did was to change the old strategy of defence engagement to an offensive one. In the past, the army of the sultanate used to defend its territory, but under the new leader, the aim was not only to defend the Somalis but to liberate all the Muslim emirates under the Abyssinian rule and destroy the power base of the enemy.

Imam Ahmed first attacked the Abyssinians in 1529, inflicted a heavy defeat on Dengel, but withdrew for an internal reorganization of his sultanate. Two years later he launched a major attack on the highlanders and by 1533 he liberated all the Muslim emirates. The liberated Muslim emirates included Bali, Sidama, Dawaro and Hadiya. The Imam's army also occupied parts of Abyssinia to destroy its power base and deny them a chance to regroup. Lebna Dengel, the Abyssinian king, and his family were driven from their house and city and for some years they wandered about the country, hopeless, and suffered hunger and hardship of every kind.

By then, Lebna Dengel realized that the Imam had become master of the Horn and that he could not resist him without outside help. When the Adal army reached the northern provinces of Tigray, Lebna Dengel made a desperate appeal to Europe for help in 1535 and offered in return to accept the jurisdiction of the Pope in Rome. Japermudez, a member of the Portuguese missionary, was sent to Europe. Dengel died as a result of the hardships he had suffered before help came and his son, Galawdewos, became king in his stead.

Help from Portugal reached Abyssinia in 1541. Galawdewos

welcomed the 400 well-armed Portuguese musketeers under Christovoa da Gama, who landed in Massawa on 10 February 1541. They brought great quantities of arms, including canons, gunpowder and other supplies, and were accompanied by nearly 150 craftsmen, gunsmiths and slaves. Under the leadership of Christovoa da Gama they attacked the Adal army. Da Gama was killed and over 200 of his men were either killed or captured in the first fight with Imam Ahmed. The remaining Portuguese fighters under Galawdewos met the Imam's army at Woina-deg, near Tana Lake, and in that fierce fighting, the Imam was wounded by a Portuguese musketeer and died of his wounds.

Amir Nur Bin Mujahid, a nephew of Imam Ahmed, took over the reign of the Somali-dominated Muslim sultanate after Imam Ahmed and the new Imam was soon able to unite the population of the sultanate. Meanwhile, Galawdewos, who feared the revival of the Adal, continued the attack on it to destroy its power base:

> Galawdewos who feared the revival of Adal's power repeatedly ordered his armies to penetrate its territories, to burn its towns and villages and harass its pastoral population, with the aim of disrupting the economy of the sultanate and breaking its military power. Ironically, the resounding Ethiopian victories awakened among the different elements of the sultanate a reaction similar to that which had preceded their great irruption into Ethiopia.[8]

To the disappointment of Galawdewos, Imam Nur fought vigorously and defeated the Abyssinians in 1559. He advanced towards Shoa and met the Abyssinian army under the command of Galawdewos. In the ensuing battle, the Abyssinians were defeated and Galawdewos was himself killed on Good Friday 1559. However, instead of following his success, Imam Nur immediately returned to Harar to drive the Oromos who were attacking the town. He surrounded the town of Harar with a wall, part of which still stands to this day, to defend it from the Oromos. Imam Nur, who lived until 1567, succeeded in defending the town from both the Oromos and the Ethiopians, but after his death, the sultanate's power began to diminish because of internal differences.

Othman, who succeeded Nur, agreed with the Oromo invaders a ceasefire and tried to gain their hearts by welcoming them into the city and civilization. But the noble and religious leaders did not accept this idea, and this was the cause of the rift between Othman on the one hand

---

[8] M. Abir, 1975, *Ethiopia and the Horn of Africa, the Cambridge History of Africa,* Cambridge University Press, volume 4, page 538–39.

and Dalha and Gibril (two of his lieutenants) on the other hand. Othman's successor Nassir Bin Mohamed put the house of the sultanate in order and continued the jihad against the invaders until he was killed in 1577 in fierce fighting with the Amhara fighters on the spring points of Webe Shebele River.

The situation became exceedingly difficult for the Adal sultanate after the death of Imam Nassir, because of the unending attacks on and around the capital and its weak and unstable leadership. As a result, Mohamed Gassa, the new Imam, changed the capital temporarily in 1577 from Harar to Awsa, which was part of the sultanate:

> Following a period of confusion a member of Gragn's family Muhammad b. Ibrahim Gassa, came to power and took the title of *imam*. By then the situation in and around Harar was so precarious that in 1577 the new *imam* transferred the seat of his government from Harar to the oasis of Awsa. This move proved to be fatal mistake. Awsa was too far removed from the centre of the sultanate to control its different provinces.[9]

In the decades following the transfer to Awsa one imam followed another, the governors of Harar became autonomous, and Zeila left the sultanate and joined the Ottoman Empire, and some of the Somali tribes living in the vicinity of Harar ignored the authority of Awsa.

Amir Ali b. Dawut who took over the leadership of the Adal sultanate in 1643 brought back the seat of the kingdom to Harar. Despite the restoration of the capital, Adal did not succeed in regaining its control of the other provinces and continued to decline until it became a city-state. Further, its links with the other Somali sultanates on the coast were completely disrupted.

Despite the decline of the Adal sultanate, the Ethiopian rulers anticipated the revival of Adal's power and, because of a fear of a Somali invasion, Fasilidas (1632–67) chose Gondar in the North West as his capital. Due to the rise of the Oromo and the weakness of the Ethiopian power and internal conflicts within the Ethiopian regional kings, the Amhara attacks on the Somalis ceased from the mid-seventeenth century until the mid-nineteenth century, when Menelik II came to power in Shoa.

The advance of the Oromo started in the latter part of the sixteenth century when they began to move northward. The fighting between Imam Ahmed and the Christian empire and the subsequent pull-out of the Amhara from the south and the central parts of the highlands paved

---

[9] M. Abir, 1975, *Ethiopia and the Horn of Africa, the Cambridge History of Africa*, Cambridge University Press, volume 4, page 541.

the way for the migration of the Oromo. 'Gragn's invasion and the fighting which followed between the Christians and Muslims opened the way for the great migrations of the Oromo.'[10]

The Oromo warriors defeated the Ethiopians and also attacked Harar. They settled between Harar and the Amhara area and mixed with the Amhara. The Oromos often mixed and intermarried with Amhara and other Christian groups, after they were Christianized. Instead of imposing a new system or an ideology of their own on the defeated Amharas, they largely adopted the Abyssinian system and culture, and began to identify themselves as Ethiopians:

> Oromo leaders became major element in regional politics, but it was rare for Oromo who were intermixed among the Amhara to act together politically as Oromos above the family and clan level. After they settled and became Christianized, they often intermarried with Amhara and other Semitic peoples, and became assimilated.[11]

The Amhara kingdom got weaker after it moved its capital to Gondar, and especially during the so-called Era of the Princes (1769–1855). Before the wounds inflicted on it by Adal healed, the Oromo advanced towards its territory and defeated it. As a result of the defeat, it lost control over some of its provinces, paving the way for the formation of rival regional kingdoms, dominated by the Oromos, and eventfully lost Gondar to Yejju, an Oromo regional kingdom. The Yejju dynasty became a real power in Gondar from the last quarter of the eighteenth to the mid-nineteenth century, when Tewodros defeated it.

1.3 The Fall of Harar and the Collapse of the Adal Sultanate

After Ali bin Dawud returned the seat of the Adal sultanate to Harar in 1643 the rule of the sultanate was confined to the city of Harar and became in reality a city-state. Even though Adal was reduced to a city-state after its disintegration, Harar took its mantle and continued to function like the old sultanate. Furthermore, Harar was not only a seat of government, but it was also a commercial and religious centre:

> Moreover, Harar was the most important centre for Islamic learning in the Horn of Africa, and during the eighteenth century its caravan merchants became an important factor in the revival of Islam in southern Ethiopia. The

---

[10] Paul B. Henze, 2000, *Layers of Time, A History of Ethiopia*, page 90.
[11] Paul B. Henze, 2000, *Layers of Time, A History of Ethiopia*, page 91.

development of trade in the Red Sea in the last decades of the seventeenth century probably affected the economy of Harar and contributed to some extent to its relative political stability.[12]

After the immigration of the Oromos at the end of the sixteenth century, the demography of the area around Harar began to change. The Oromo tribes began to settle in the vicinity of Harar and became cultivators. The majority of the Oromos gradually became Muslims, especially those settled around Harar, and towards the end of the seventeenth century they accepted the Amir of Harar as their nominal master; but although they gave up some aspects of their original and socio-political organization, they still preserved their tribal system and maintained an independent political hierarchy at the side of that of the Amir.

On the other hand, some of the Somali territories that were part of the sultanate rebelled and gradually withdrew from the sultanate. Thus, the Somali influence began to decrease and that of the Oromos continued to increase because of the demographical change. Despite the increased influence of the Oromos and their acceptance of the leadership of the Amir of Harar, the Oromo pastoralists on the Harari plateau often raided Harari territories and caravans. The disregard of most of the former Somali Adal provinces for the authority of the Amir, the continuous attacks of the Oromos, and an internal power struggle within the dynasty further weakened the sultanate.

> The sultanate nonetheless, began to decline at the end of the eighteenth century. The economy of the town was no doubt affected by the stagnation of trade in the Red Sea basin, but it seems that Harar suffered even more from the internal strife in the ruling dynasty, from the unruliness of the Somali and from the continuous attacks of the Galla.[13]

The attempt by Tewodros of the revival of the old Abyssinian Empire and the crowning of Johannes IV and Menelik II as Emperor on 12 January 1872 and as king of Shoa in 1878, respectively, alarmed the Harar sultanate. By 1866 Menelik, who did not hide his southward expansionist dreams, built up a strong army, took over Shoa and even captured some territories before he was officially crowned by the new Emperor of Abyssinia, Johannes IV, as king of Shoa on 26 March 1878. The two men agreed to Christianise the Muslim and pagan population of Ethiopia and both carried out Christianisation campaigns. The Muslim officials were

---

[12] M. Abir, 1975, *Ethiopia and the Horn of Africa, the Cambridge History of Africa*, page 552.
[13] M. Abir, 1975, *Ethiopia and the Horn of Africa, the Cambridge History of Africa*, page 552.

given three months either to renounce their positions or their religion; pagan officials were to accept Christianity immediately. Menelik undertook mass conversions of Muslims and pagans in Shoa and Johannes made similar conversion efforts in Wollo.

After he officially became king of Shoa, Menelik concentrated on his southward expansion. During the next ten years, he more than tripled Shoan and thereby Ethiopian territory in the south. The annexed territories included Gurage, Kestane, and Arsi. After these conquests, Menelik planned for the elimination of the sultanate of Harar and the sultanate anticipated his invasion. But this time the Egyptians were faster than the Abyssinians. As part of the southward expansionist policies of the new Khedive, Ismail Pasha, Egyptian forces moved inland in 1875, after having occupied the Red Sea Somali coast, and took over Harar. A few years later (1879), Khedive Ismail Pasha was deposed and replaced by a young and inexperienced successor, Khedive Tawfiq Pasha. An armed rebellion led by the Mahdi also broke out in Sudan and, because of the war in Sudan and the expansionist policies of the Khedive, Egypt was financially near bankruptcy and its army disaffected. Alarmed by the development in Egypt and concerned about its lifeline in India, Britain occupied Egypt in 1882.

After the occupation of Egypt, Britain took over the northern Somali coastal towns under the Egyptian administration and encouraged Italy to take Assab and Massawa out of rivalry with France, and both Britain and Italy helped Menelik to take over Harar. Menelik made no secret of his intention to take the city and so informed King Umberto of Italy. Menelik systematically planned the takeover, and the European military and diplomatic backing enabled him to conquer the city. During the 1870s and 1880s the European powers – particularly Italy, Russia and France – provided Ethiopia with modern arms and other materials, which helped Menelik win over his rivals and later in the 1890s used against Italy itself. In his book *The Betrayal of the Somalis*, FitzGibbon wrote the following list of arms shipments to Abyssinia in the 1880s:

> Records show that in one journey on 27 June 1885 the famous French trader, Savoure, sold to Abyssinia 30 000 cartridges, 600 000 percussion caps, 3000 muskets and 24 cannons. In the same year even distant Russia contributed by furnishing 50 000 rifles, 50 000 carbines, 5000 revolvers, 40 cannon, 5000 swords and ample ammunition. On 21 January 1886 the French arms dealer, Labatut, transhipped at Aden 2,230 rifles, 194,200 cartridges, 80 000 percussion caps followed, ten days later, by 360 rifles and

4000 cartritges.[14]

He also mentioned in that book a similar report by a British official. On 27 November 1882 F. M Hunter, the First Assistant Resident, reported to the British Political Resident in Aden as follows:

> As soon as the port of Assab was opened the Italians began to pour arms through it in a steady flow into Shoa; the French did the same through their protectorate, first Obok and next at Tadjoura.[15]

In addition to the huge inflows of arms from Europe, Menelik secured the backing of Britain for his invasion plan and that support was in particular very crucial to his occupation plan of and beyond Harar.

Britain ordered the Egyptian army to leave the city in 1884 and threatened to stop wage payments to any official who might disobey. Amir Abdalla Mohammed was reinstalled as governor of the city after the Egyptian withdrawal but after the Amir took over the reign, Britain suddenly demanded that he return 18 rifles she claimed were stolen from her. Britain wanted to secure the borders of the Christian empire from the Muslims and the evacuation of the Egyptian army and the claim of the weapons were part of the plot. On 27 March 1886, an Italian commercial and scientific expedition started under Count Porro from Zeila for Harar and was ambushed and killed at Arto near Harar, and both the British and the Italians blamed the Amir of Harar for the massacre. On the pretext of that massacre, the Italians not only encouraged Menelik but also took part in the Abyssinian invasion of Harar, both militarily and politically.

The withdrawal of the Egyptian forces was completed in May 1885, but Menelik invaded the sultanate only after he secured the backing of both Britain and Italy for the invasion in 1886. In January 1887, a joint Italo-Abyssinian force descended on Harar. However, despite the huge army, the Menelik-led alliance met strong resistance. After the last battle that took place at Chalenqu, in which the Amir's army was defeated, the alliance finally occupied the city on 6 January 1887. The correspondences between Menelik and the British Consul in Aden show that Britain was not only happy about the takeover, but they also tolerated the ensuing atrocities committed by Abyssinians against the inhabitants of Harar and surrounding areas. (See Appendices 1and 2.)

The fall of Harar meant the collapse of the Adal sultanate. As a city-state, it died when its only city was annexed, its Amir fled, and its grand

---

[14] Louis FitzGibbon, 1982, *The Betrayal of the Somalis*, Rex Collins Ltd, page 20–21.
[15] Louis FitzGibbon, 1982, *The Betrayal of the Somalis*, page 14.

mosque turned into a church. Upon taking over, Menelik declared boastfully: 'This is not a Muslim country, as every one knows.'[16] Harar was his final great conquest as king of Shoa but, as emperor since 1889, he continued his southward expansion further into the Ogaden.

---

[16] Mohamed Osman Omar, 2001, *The Scramble in the Horn of Africa*, Somali Publications, page 107.

2

The Partition of the Somali Nation

Before the partition; the establishment of the European protectorates; the occupations of the Ogaden

2.1 Before the Partition

Before the partition, the Somali Nation was united by its common language, religion, culture and legal system, and its territory was also united. Despite these unifying factors, there was no political unity or common authority. In the mainland pastoralism was the dominant livelihood and the pastoral communities had no allegiance to any real power other than the loose authority of the clan leader. In the coastal areas, however, the situation was different, and even though there was no unified administration, there existed some form of local government. There were functioning sultanates in both Obbia and Majerten and, as we saw in the preceding chapter, the Adal sultanate in the northern coastal towns and Harar was replaced by Egyptian administration in the 1870s. Since the establishment of the Ajuran Sultanate in the 13th century, functioning administrations also existed in the coastal towns of the southern part.

The Sultanate of Ajuran, which was based in southern Somalia and parts of the Ogaden, ruled a large part of the Horn of Africa from the 13th century to the 17th century. The Sultanate not only defended the Somali lands from the Portuguese and Oromo invaders but also built a large empire with a relatively modern economy. In addition to the expansion of trade, it introduced new agricultural and water resource management systems and invented hydraulic techniques that enabled it to increase the production scale of farming. It also used its own currency and introduced a taxation system to improve the functioning of its economy and increase the income of the sultanate. The Sultanate disintegrated in the late 17th century due to internal conflict. Remnants of the Ajuran Sultanate formed small local kingdoms after the collapse of the central administration and continued to rule most of the south, although the coastal part of Benadir became part of the Sultanate of Zanzibar afterwards. When the partition of the Somali lands began, the

Sultan of Zanzibar exercised loose sovereignty over the principalities of Kismayo, Brava, Merca and Mogadishu:

> Ethnic solidarity was reinforced by common socio-legal institutions and by a common language, the skilful use of which was at once a powerful weapon in Somali politics and the major Somali art-form. These unifying factors had not however generated any form of political unity, or indeed of political authority, above the level of the individual clan; and even clan-leaders were usually no more than respected dignitaries, not 'chiefs' or rulers with effective institutional power. Only in the coastal 'sultanates' of Majerteyn and Hobyo (Obbia) was political authority rather more effective, probably supported by resources derived from the sea-borne trade.[1]

2.2 The Establishment of the European Protectorates

The foreign power intrusion into the Somali lands began in 1870 when Egypt hoisted its flag on the northern Somali coasts. 'By 1866 Turkey had transferred the Red Sea ports of Suakin and Massawa to the government of Khedive Ismail, and the latter claimed that this new jurisdiction also embraced the Somali coast.'[2] The Egyptian government took over Zeila, Berbera and Bulhar in the early 1870s. Having consolidated its control on most of the main ports on the Red Sea coast, it moved inland and occupied Harar in 1875. Britain and France initially opposed the Egyptian occupation and expansion, but because of other problems it faced elsewhere, Britain softened its position towards the Egyptian occupation of the Somali lands in 1875, and in 1877 it signed a convention with the Egyptian government recognizing Egyptian jurisdiction as far as Ras Hafun on the Indian Ocean. Meanwhile, Egypt faced huge political and economic problems by the end of the 1870s. Khedive Ismail Pasha was deposed and replaced by a young and inexperienced successor in 1879, and the country was near bankruptcy because of its expensive expansionist policies. Furthermore, its imperial adventures provoked a Sudanese Mahdist revolt that resulted in the collapse of Egyptian authority in northeast Africa. Taking advantage of Egypt's imperial and economic failures, Britain occupied Egypt in 1882 to protect its lifeline to India as she claimed.

As a result of the British occupation, the Egyptians were forced to abandon their administrations on the Red Sea coast. Following the evacuation of the Egyptian garrisons from the Eritrean and Somali

---

[1] G.N. Sanderson, 1985, *The Nile Basin and the Eastern Horn, The Cambridge History of Africa*, Cambridge University Press, Volume 6, pages 665–667.

[2] I.M. Lewis, 2002, *A Modern History of the Somali*, James Currey, page 41.

coasts, Britain encouraged Italy to take over the Eritrean coasts and preserved the northern Somali coasts for herself. The British took over the northern Somali coast opposite Aden (formerly administrated by Egypt) in 1884 and declared it a British protectorate, without defining the interior limits of the protectorate. Subsequently, the Italians occupied Eritrea in 1885. The British interest in the Somali lands was a secondary one and stemmed from the need to get provisions for its colony in Aden. Britain signed treaties with various Somali clans in 1884/5 and additional protocols in 1886, promising them protection (see Appendix 3). This protectorate became known as British Somaliland and remained under British rule until its independence day on 26 June 1960, except for a short period of Italian occupation in 1940.

In 1886, Britain also began to acquire the Somali regions of Jubbaland and Tannaland, which is the area around the Jubba River and the Tanna River. Britain gradually occupied the territory, and for the most part between the years 1895–1912, but it came under effective British administration for the first time in 1919. Britain ceded Jubbaland to Italy in 1925 and it became part of the former Italian Somaliland, but Tannaland, which came to be known as the Northern Frontier District (NFD), became part of Kenya. The local people in NFD were neither consulted when Britain occupied the region nor was their will respected when Kenya became independent. Despite repeated requests by the inhabitants to be reunified with Somalia, Britain handed over the territory to Kenya after its independence in 1963. Furthermore, the 'District has been isolated from the rest of Kenya by laws passed in 1902 and in 1934 which restrict the movement of all persons entering or leaving the District, and is still in operation.'[3] Not only the movement of the Somalis is restricted, but they are also treated like second-class citizens in their own region.

Italy became active in the Somali lands in 1885, when it began negotiations with the local rulers in the northeast as well as Zanzibar. Italian commercial and diplomatic agents also became active everywhere along the coast soon after. In the spring of 1889, Italy achieved its aim of bringing Obbia and Majerten under its protection after it signed protection agreements with the local rulers. In November of the same year, it declared a protectorate over the entire coast from Brava to the Majerten kingdom, though the ports were not actually transferred to Italy until 1893. Italy ended up with the largest share of the Somali coast and

---

[3] John Drysdale, 1964, *The Somali Dispute*, Pall Mall Press Ltd, page 104.

its protectorate, Italian Somaliland, was more enlarged by the incorporation of Kismayo and the rest of Jubbaland into its territory in 1925. The territory was occupied by Britain in 1941 and remained under British rule until 1950 when it became a trusteeship under the Italian administration. It became independent on 1 July 1960.

France's real involvement in the Horn of Africa started in 1862 when it signed a treaty with the chiefs of the Danakil tribes in which it bought the port of Obock on the Danakil coast. France paid 55,000 francs for the use of the port but exercised little sovereignty over it until 1881 when the Franco-Ethiopian company treaty was set up there. By 1883 Obock had three more French firms, a coaling station was set up and some French settlers arrived. The trading companies did not prosper, but the French were very keen to establish their base on the Red Sea. France needed a port to serve and protect its lifeline to the Indian Ocean and Indochina. Leonce Lagarde, who was appointed governor of the colony in 1887, took charge of the colony with vigour. After the Egyptian withdrawal, France occupied Tadjoura just as the British were preparing to move into it and signed treaties with local chiefs in the regions of Ambabo and Djibouti, pre-empting British efforts to extend their control beyond Zeila. An Anglo-French boundary was agreed in 1888. The governor persuaded the French government to build Obock as a military, and trading centre, but geographically Obock was poorly suited for this role. Lagarde realized this when he abandoned Obock in 1892 in favour of Djibouti, which the French had acquired in 1888. Djibouti grew rapidly and became the capital of French Somaliland. The territory became independent on 27 June 1977 as the Republic of Djibouti.

2.3 Occupations of the Ogaden

2.3.1 The First Ethiopian Occupation of the Ogaden

After the death of Emperor Johannes IV on 10 March 1889 at the battle of Matemma (against the Mahdist forces), Menelik acceded to the Ethiopian throne and assumed the title of King of Kings. After having consolidated his rule all over the country, Menelik turned his attention to the issue of land expansion. The new emperor's primary goals were to contain the advances of the Europeans and expand his empire, and exploitation of the Europeans was the means to achieve these goals. Menelik developed skills in diplomacy and exploited the competing European powers' willingness to provide him military aid and diplomatic support. He played the game well and all the imperial powers helped him achieve his goals in one way or another. The Italo-Ethiopian relationships in the last three decades of the nineteenth century best illustrate this point.

The military alliance between the Kingdom of Shoa and Italy in conquering Harar resulted in the formal alliance treaty of 20 October 1887, under which Italy provided large consignments of armies to Shoa. In 1890 Italy sponsored Ethiopian admission into the Brussels General Act, which permitted Ethiopia as a Christian state to import arms on an unrestricted scale. Ethiopia benefited enormously both militarily and diplomatically from the membership of the European club. Because of the military and diplomatic assistance Italy gave to Ethiopia, the relationship between the two countries was good. However, their relations became strained when the discrepancy between the two versions of the 1889 Wichale Treaty became apparent. Italy attempted to entice Ethiopia into colonial status by the Treaty of Wichale. The Amharic text of this treaty, which Menelik signed, gave Ethiopia the option of using Italian good offices in the conduct of its foreign affairs; the Italian text, which Menelik did not sign, made Ethiopia an Italian protectorate. The discrepancy between the two versions was the root of the conflict that led to the Italo-Ethiopian war in which the Italians were ultimately defeated at Adowa in 1896. In the subsequent peace treaty in Addis Ababa in 1896, Italy abandoned all the pretence of a protectorate over Ethiopia in return for Menelik's recognition of the Italian retention of Eritrea.

Menelik played all his cards with skill and held control of the game. Despite the victory over Italy and the smart way he played the game, Menelik's contribution to the Ethiopian successes is often exaggerated by historians. Although the rival European powers' dealings with Ethiopia were not the same all the time, it seems that there was a consensus among the European powers on the independence of the Christian kingdom and its defence from the Muslims. They all supported Ethiopia directly or indirectly against its Muslim opponent, gave military and political support and all of them opposed Italy in its attempt of turning Ethiopia into an Italian protectorate, by the Treaty of Wichale. For example, France, which always maintained close relations with Addis Ababa, ignored the Wichale treaty and facilitated a massive duty-free import of arms for Ethiopia through Djibouti. Two French officers also accompanied Menelik's army during the Italo-Ethiopian war. Although Britain recognized the Italian version of the Wichale treaty, its help to Ethiopia was enormous. Britain helped Menelik conquer Harar and the whole of the Ogaden. Likewise, Russia not only opposed the Wichale treaty but supported Ethiopia both militarily and diplomatically.

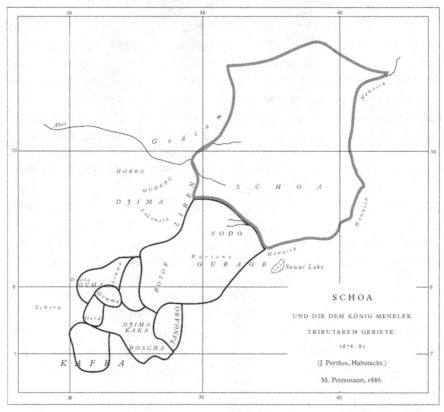

Map 2-1 Southern boundaries of Abyssinia before the scramble

Emboldened by the diplomatic support and the modern weapons he obtained from the European imperial powers, Menelik wrote his famous circular to the European powers in 1891: 'I have not the least intention of remaining a disinterested onlooker if powers from a distance come with the notion of dividing Africa between themselves, Ethiopia having been during the course of quite fourteen centuries, an island inhabited by Christians in a sea of pagans.'[4]

Menelik's southward expansionist dreams did not end with the occupation of Harar in 1887; on the contrary, the annexation of this buffer-city opened the way for further expansion into the Ogaden. In fact, Ogaden was one of the places he had in mind when he was writing the circular in 1891. He became more aggressive and took maximum

---

[4] David D. Laitin & Said S. Samatar, 1987, *Somalia, a Nation in Search of a State*, Westview Press, page 53; Louis FitzGibbon, 1982, *The Betrayal of the Somalis*, Rex Collins pages 24-25.

advantage of the extremely favourable position in which he found himself.

In the first phase of his occupation of Western Somali/Ogaden, Menelik used to send his troops from his base in Harar to the neighbouring Somali territories to terrorize the inhabitants and loot their livestock. The army undertook frequent raids into the region, killing the inhabitants indiscriminately and then returned to their base with the looted livestock. Afterwards, Menelik systematically extended his terror and robbery to the whole region.

The great famine of 1888–1892, and the wars of 1890s devastated the subsistence Ethiopian economy. Menelik's huge and hungry army was pressing hard upon the resources of Shoa, and because of this pressure, the occupation was accelerated and extended further to feed its hungry soldiers. Because of the limited resources in the region and the fact that the conquering army had to live on the conquered, the brutal Ethiopian occupation of Ogaden became more burdensome and traumatic to the inhabitants:

> Because the bulk of the Somali people lived inland as nomadic pastoralists, they were not unduly traumatized by the European intrusion, which was confined to a few coastal areas. The case was different with the Ethiopians who expanded into the heart of Somali pastureland and whose sudden eruption in the lush grazing zones of the Ogaaden constituted a disquieting presence. Furthermore, because the Ethiopian highlands were devastated by the 'succession' wars of the 1890s and by an ensuing famine, the Ethiopians descended on the lowlands to recoup their losses from the 'great herds' of the Oromos and the Somalis. Driven alike by the need to feed his growing and hungry army and by a political desire to make his occupation of the Ogaaden good, Menelik, between 1890 and 1900, allowed his warlords to raid livestock indiscriminately in the Ogaaden. These raids repeatedly despoiled the Ogaadeen Somalis.[5]

In other words, Ethiopia did not behave like a government but like a robber. Unlike the European powers who occupied the other parts of the Somali lands, it did not bring administration and service departments. All it brought was an army that acted like a gang of robbers:

> Indigenous testimony puts the number of the Ogaadeen livestock seized by Menelik between 1890 and 1897 at 100 000 head of cattle, 200 000 head of camels, and 600 000 sheep and goats. Because the Amharas, the dominant ethnic group in the Ethiopian empire, neither drink camel milk nor eat its

---

[5] David D. Laitin & Said S. Samatar, 1987, *Somalia, A Nation in Search of a State*, page 54.

meat, the seized camels were used principally as a bargaining asset with the Somalis who were invited to recover their looted camels with payment of cattle, sheep or goats.'[6]

Abyssinia was not only looting but she was killing the people too in great numbers and a cruel manner. According to the records of the British colonial authorities, not only was the level of killing high but the method of killing was even more shocking. As reported by the British authorities, the Abyssinian cruel killing included the cutting of women's breasts and skinning individuals while alive. The Somali victims were often from the clans that signed protection treaties with Britain and, at the time of the worst killing, Italy was claiming the whole of Ethiopia as its protectorate. Despite their promise of protection, these powers did not bother to condemn the atrocities, let alone intervene on behalf of the victims (See Appendix 2).

The European responses to Menelik's invasion of the Ogaden and the ensuing atrocities were to reward him with more land and legitimize the occupation, by concluding boundary delimitation agreements with him. Because of its recognition of the Italian version of the Treaty of Wichale, London negotiated with Italy in May 1894 over boundary delimitation on behalf of Ethiopia. In the Treaty, Britain ceded to Italy (and therefore ultimately to Ethiopia) part of the Ogaden. A further slice of territory in the region was abandoned directly to Ethiopia by the Rodd Treaty of 1897. The French made a similar treaty with Ethiopia two-and-a-half months earlier. In March 1897, a French mission under Leonce Lagarde signed a treaty granting Ethiopia much of the desert lowlands the French had originally considered part of their Somaliland protectorate. The treaty reduced the Somali French territory to the immediate hinterland of Djibouti. Furthermore, France continued to let arms and other goods flow into Ethiopia through Djibouti.

---

[6] David D. Laitin & Said S. Samatar, 1987, *Somalia, A Nation in Search of a State*, page 55.

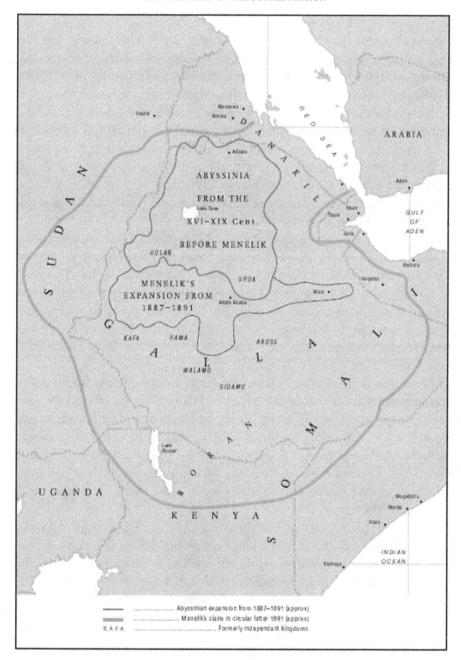

Map 2-2 Territorial claims of Menelik II (Circular Letter 1891)

The European imperialists all signed boundary delimitation agreements with Menelik on his terms, thereby giving legal sanction to what he occupied, and by the turn of the century nearly the whole of the Ogaden became part of his empire geographically. However, politically Ogaden never became part of Ethiopia. Menelik succeeded in occupying the region, but Ethiopia could win neither the hearts and minds of the inhabitants, because of the Somali intolerance to subordination, the gross human rights violation committed by the successive Ethiopian regimes, and the looting and the destruction; nor could it maintain full control of the region because of the resistance, as we will see in the next chapter.

After Menelik became incapacitated in 1909, following a series of strokes, his grandson Lij Iyasu, born in 1898, took over the reign. Iyasu's mother was a daughter of Menelik; his father was Ras Mikael, the great provincial lord of the Oromo of Wollo, who in 1878 had been forced to give up Islam for Christianity by Emperor Johannes IV. Mikael was called Mohammed Ali before he was forced to convert to Christianity. In March 1910 Iyasu was declared heir, but because of his young age, Ras Tessema of Shoa was made his regent. The regent died in 1911 more than two years before the death of Menelik (in 1913) and from that time the thirteen-year-old Iyasu began to run the country himself. However, Iyasu's reign did not last long and was overthrown by a council of ministers in 1916.

Iyasu was accused among other things of being soft on the Muslims and in particular favouring the Somalis. His opponents alleged that he gave arms to the Somali Patriot Sayyid Mohamed Abdille Hassan who, we will see in the next chapter, fought against all the colonial powers, including Ethiopia in the Somali peninsula. European powers in the region also showed concern over the appointment of Abdalla Sadiq as governor of the Ogaden alleging that he was a preacher of Pan Islam and an agent of the Sayyid.

The ruler paid frequent visits to the Ogaden region and even his overthrow was accomplished while he was on one of his visits in the region. He also appointed Abdullah Sadeq, a local personality, as governor of the Ogaden, intended probably as a gesture of goodwill and to win the hearts and minds of the Somalis. Because of their negative attitude toward the Somalis, his opponents interpreted his visits there – eating the Muslim food and his attendance at social events with Somalis – as being unnecessary and out of line with Christian beliefs.

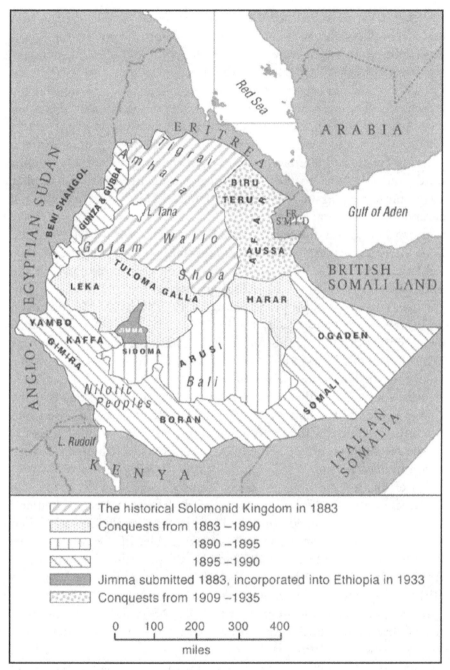

Map 2-3 Expansion stages of the Ethiopian Empire

The contact he made with Sayyid Mohammed Abdille Hassan was, however, what most alarmed the opposition, because of its internal and external implications. Ethiopia was one of the imperial powers the Sayyid was fighting to evict from the Somali lands and the contact was condemned in that context. In addition, the tripartite powers (Britain, France and Italy) interpreted the contact as inciting colonial subjects for an uprising at a time when their masters were engaged in mortal combat with Austria-Hungary, Germany and Turkey in the European and Middle Eastern theatres of war. Because of this, the allies saw Iyasu as a threat, whereas Turkey and Germany wanted to enlist him in their cause. 'A joint note from the Allies to the Ethiopian government in early September 1916, protesting against the inimical actions of Iyasu, brought the simmering opposition to the boil.'[7]

Iyasu's policies in the region made headlines in the press and alarmed both the Ethiopian establishment and the allies, but on the ground, they did not improve the situation for the inhabitants as claimed by the opposition. The killing and the subjugation continued unabated and Iyasu was as brutal as his predecessor. 'In 1913 and 1915 -16, however, he behaved with equal cruelty towards Muslims – the Afar, Ise Somali and Karayu Oromo – on his return from tours east of the capital. This behaviour hardly bears out those who accused Iyasu of showing undue favour to Muslims suffering discrimination.'[8]

It is not clear whether Iyasu was in fact a Muslim, but that was the charge made against him by the Shoan Aristocrats who opposed him when they gathered with the presence of the church to decide his future. Iyasu was deposed on 27 September 1916 after the Ethiopian Church excommunicated him.

After the overthrow of Iyasu, Menelik's daughter Zewidtu was declared empress and Iyasu's cousin, Tafari Makonnen, became heir and regent. Zewidtu remained symbolic Head of State until early 1930 when she died. Tafari Makonnen was the effective ruler of the country since Zewidtu's coronation early in 1917 and he was proclaimed emperor on 3 April 1930 with the throne-name Haile Selassie. Because of his long reign (1917–1974) and the turmoil in the Horn of Africa, Haile Selassie witnessed many historical events, which left profound effects on both the Ethiopians and the Somalis. Among these were the Italian occupation of the Ogaden and Ethiopia, his subsequent exile in England, the brief restoration of the unity of three Somali territories – following the Italian

---

[7] Bahru Zewde, 1991, *A History of Modern Ethiopia (1855–1974)*, James Currey, page 127.
[8] Richard Caulk, 1986, *Ethiopia and the Horn, the Cambridge History of Africa*, Cambridge University Press, Volume 7, page 711.

occupation of both the Ogaden and the British Somaliland, the British eviction of Italy from its Horn empire, the restoration of the Ethiopian government, the second reunification of four parts of the Somali lands under Britain and the gradual handover of the Ogaden to Ethiopia. The topic of our discussion is neither about Haile Selassie nor about his rule of Ethiopia, hence will we briefly review only those issues that have relevance for the occupation of the Ogaden which we are dealing with here.

2.3.2 The Italian Occupation of the Ogaden

Since the fascist regime came to power in 1922, Italy's imperial ambitions increased, and Mussolini like many Italians was determined to avenge the ignominy of Adowa. An incident in Walwal, Ogaden, in which an Ethiopian expedition clashed with Italian troops in December 1934, set the pretext for the Italian invasion of the Ogaden and Ethiopia in 1935.

Italy first invaded the Ogaden, and after its capture, continued westward into Ethiopia. A parallel north front from Eritrea accelerated the Italian campaign and the Italo-Ethiopian war (1935/6) ended in May 1936, when Addis Ababa fell and Haile Selassie left for England, where he lived as a refugee until 1940.

The Italian occupation of the Ogaden and the subsequent reunification with the Italian Somaliland brought some positive consequences that were not intended by the Italians. The reunification brought together for the first time in forty years families and clans that were arbitrarily separated by the Italo-Ethiopian boundaries and, for the first time, the great majority of Somalis were brought under a common rule. It also brought some social services, which the Ogaden inhabitants did not have under Ethiopia. The subsistence economy of the unified Somali land also improved as a result of the increased mobility and large-scale farming which Italy introduced in the south.

During the Second World War, Italy was on the German side. As part of the war campaign, Italy overran the British Somaliland protectorate in August 1940, shortly after it entered the war. The Italians added the British portion into their Somali colony and this incorporation further enhanced the Somali unity. The Italian victory, however, proved short-lived and the British reversed the whole saga in 1941, by taking over the whole of the Italian colony in East Africa (Eritrea, Ethiopia, and the Somali lands):

'Italy's entry into the Second World War, however, left the Italian forces in the Horn isolated from the metropolitan country, among a generally hostile population. The rout of the Italian armies in North Africa in December 1940 completed their isolation, and released Allied troops under British command for an assault on Italian East Africa. One army invaded Eritrea from the Sudan, while another attacked Somalia from Kenya, and the Emperor Haile Selassie, who had flown from exile in England to the Sudan in December 1940, entered Ethiopia through Gojjam province with a small Anglo-Sudanese and Ethiopian force. The Italian forces were swiftly defeated, though only after heavy fighting at Keren in Eritrea, and the last Italian garrison, in Gondar, surrendered in November 1941.[9]

2.3.3 The British Occupation of the Ogaden

Britain returned to the Horn and its East African division that was based in Nairobi invaded the Somali lands under Italy. The British occupation of the Ogaden and all the Somali lands except French Somaliland was complete in 1941. In April they captured Addis Ababa, and on 5 May Haile Selassie was back in Addis Ababa. The war ended when Gondar fell in November 1941.

The British occupation of the Ogaden and Ethiopia did not necessarily mean the automatic restoration of the old status quo. Haile Selassie expected, as promised to him by Britain, to be reinstalled as emperor on the territory he had ruled before the Italian invasion and his first task was to regulate his relationship with the British military forces, which effectively controlled the country pending the formation of a civil administration. Although the Anglo-Ethiopian Agreement of January 1942 gave Britain special privileges, which included the provision that no foreign advisers be appointed without British government consent and that a British judge should hear any court case involving foreigners, Britain accepted him as Head of State in that agreement, but at that stage, the Ogaden was to remain under British rule:

> The Emperor's future role was questioned by the British military administration of "occupied" Ethiopia, headed by Sir Philip Mitchell, but the Anglo-Ethiopian agreement of January 1942 confirmed Haile Selassie's position as Head of State.[10]

In the second Agreement of December 1944, the special status was abandoned, but Britain retained the Ogaden and the whole of the Somali peninsula (apart from the French Somaliland) came under British military administration, which was to continue for almost a decade. In 1946 the

---

[9] Christopher Clapham, 1984, *The Horn of Africa, the Cambridge History of Africa*, Cambridge University Press, Volume 8, page 461.
[10] Richard Caulk, 1986, *Ethiopia and the Horn, the Cambridge History of Africa*, Cambridge University Press, Volume 7, page 740.

then British foreign secretary, Ernest Bevin, proposed that the British-occupied Somali territories remain united under British rule. Despite an emotional speech in the British parliament in which he emphasised the need 'to give those poor nomads a chance to get decent living', his proposal was turned down by the other members of the four-power commission (France, the United States and the Soviet Union) responsible for the disposal of the ex-Italian colonies. After the rejection of its proposal by the big powers, Britain handed over southern Somalia to Italy to prepare for independence, made NFD part of Kenya, handed over the Ogaden to Ethiopia and retained the northern part, to which it gave independence later in 1960.

2.3.4 The Second Ethiopian Occupation of the Ogaden

As Samatar & Laitin explain in the following paragraph, the rejection of the British proposal and the consequent handover of the Ogaden were mainly the results of the diplomatic success of the Ethiopian emperor Haile Selassie:

> The rejection of Britain's proposal to reunify the Somalis by the other three members of the commission was based to some extent on their suspicion that Britain might be conniving to obtain a new colony behind the façade of Somali unity, but it was due largely to Ethiopia's successful lobby for the return of the Ogaadeen. In this Emperor Haile Selassie found useful the powerful backing of the United States with whom he was in negotiation for the provision of a U.S. military base in Eritrea, in the event of that territory's federation with Ethiopia. Additionally, Ethiopia gained considerable political mileage as a victim of fascist aggression and had been acquiring the sympathy of the world community ever since the fugitive emperor delivered his famous oration ("God and history will remember your judgement") before the League of Nations, shortly after Ethiopia's conquest by Italy. In 1897 as in 1946 the sin of European aggression against Ethiopia was atoned for by the surrender of Somali territory to Ethiopia and the consequent sacrifice of Somali interests.[11]

Whatever the cause, the final occupation was not different from the first one except that the transfer was better planned and better coordinated by the two concerned imperial powers. The occupied people were neither consulted on either occasion nor were they treated like human beings. Britain handed over most of the Ogaden in 1948 and the Ethiopian administration was resumed after thirteen years in Jigjiga and

---

[11] David D. Laitin & Said S. Samatar, 1987, *Somalia, A Nation in Search of a State*, page 64.

Dagahbour between May and July. The occupation of Qabridahare, Qalafe and Warder followed, and the Ethiopian administration reached the eastern part of the region on 23 September 1948 for the first time in its history. The rest of the territory, the portion known as Reserve Area, was transferred to Ethiopia in 1955. Since that time, the Ogaden remained under Ethiopian occupation, except for a short period during the 1977/78 Ogaden war. In that period, over 90 per cent of the Somali region regained its freedom.

The handover of the Ogaden to Ethiopia, the most backward imperialist on earth proved to be the most tragic event that took place in the region. The occupation is the main source of the instability and conflicts in the Horn of Africa, and the chief cause of the misery, suffering, underdevelopment and unspeakable human rights violations that persisted in the Ogaden since Ethiopia occupied it.

The reaction of the Western Somali people to the occupation and the consequent loss of freedom, dignity, normal life, etc., was not to surrender but to resist. Spontaneous protest demonstrations broke out throughout the region when the British surrender of the Ogaden to Ethiopia was announced; however, the occupying forces brutally suppressed the uprising. The Ethiopians were determined to suppress the national spirit and adherents and sympathizers – the Somali Youth League (SYL) – were particularly targeted. Beginning with the Harar and Dire Dawa, they continued the killing as they occupied the towns one after another. From Jigjiga, where the strongest protest took place, Drysdale reported as follows:

> The last burst of overt Somali nationalism occurred in Jigjiga when Major Demeka, the governor-designate of the Ogaden Province, requested the British military administration, which was still in charge to remove the SYL flag from flying from party headquarters. It had been run up to give offence to the Ethiopians and was in fact illegal. As the leaders refused to pull down their flag, the police brought it down with a machine gun mounted on an armoured car. Disturbances followed, during which a policeman was killed and another wounded by the explosion of a hand grenade thrown from the roof of the SYL headquarters. The police opened fire on the crowd, killing twenty-five of them and that was the end of the final act of defiance by the SYL before it was proscribed as are all political parties in Ethiopia.[12]

---

[12] John Drysdale, 1964, *The Somali Dispute,* page 70.

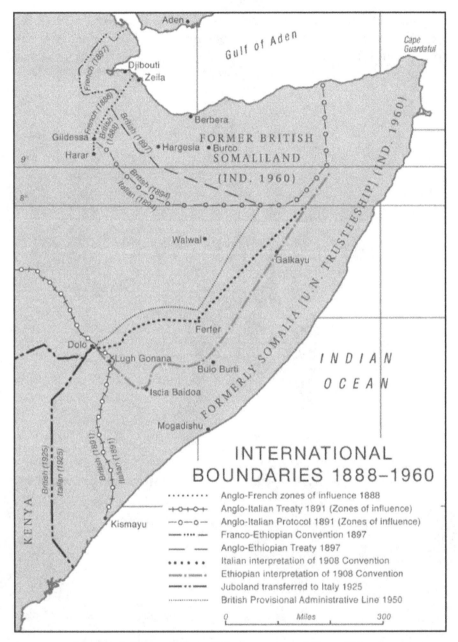

Map 2-4: Boundaries of the partitioned Somali lands

In addition, the resistance started by Adal continued over the years and centuries and took various forms, armed as well as political struggle and the resistant movement were in action all the time. In the next chapter, we will review two such resistance movements, namely the Dervish resistance led by Sayyid Mohammed Abdille Hassan and the Somali Youth League.

3

The Pan-Somali Nationalist Resistance

The Dervish Resistance Movement; the legacy of Sayyid Mohammed; the Somali Youth League (SYL)

3.1 The Dervish Resistance Movement

Sayyid Mohammed Abdille Hassan, the man who founded the Dervish Resistance Movement, was born on 7 April 1864[1] at Kob Faradod near Kirrit. He learned the Quran by heart within three years and at the age of seven, he mastered it. By the age of ten, he became his teacher's assistant. At an early age, Mohammed decided to dedicate his life to the religion, and after he learned the Quran, he continued his Islamic studies and travelled widely mainly for that cause. For some ten years, between about 1880 and 1890, he travelled widely within the Somali Peninsula and abroad in search of Islamic learning. In addition to the regular meetings and travelling with the local sheikhs, the young Sayyid also visited the local Islamic centres of Harar and Mogadishu. At the age of eleven, he began to travel abroad and, on his first journey to the outside world, he accompanied an uncle to Berbera and from there travelled by dhow to Zeila and Aden. On the way back to Berbera, the dhow on which he travelled sailed up the Arabian coast to Mukalla, where goods from Aden were exchanged for dates brought down from Basra. The young Sayyid travelled four more times to Aden during his teens and on one of these journeys at the age of 17 he reached Jeddah, and in the following year, he made his first pilgrimage. It is also believed that he travelled as far afield as the Sudanese Mahdists' strongholds in Kordofan and also visited Nairobi.

In addition to Islamic learning, which was the main purpose of his journey and which he undoubtedly took to new heights, he learned a

---

[1] The date of birth of Sayyid Mohammed Adille Hassan is contested and both 1856 and 1864 are reported, but most historians state the latter date as the correct one. See for example I. M. Lewis, 2002, *A Modern History of the Somali*, James Currey, page 65; Ray Beachey, 1990, *The Warrior Mullah*, Bellew Publishing Company Ltd, page 32; and H. A. Ibrahim, 1985, *African Initiatives and Resistance in North Eastern Africa*, *General History of Africa*, UNESCO, Volume VII, page 84.

great deal about the outside world, both Muslim and non-Muslim. When he first arrived in Aden, he saw the great liners and naval vessels at anchor in the busy harbour, as well as the British military forces in the town, and that was his first glimpse of Britain's imperial might. In Aden, Mukalla, Jeddah and Mecca he met Muslims from all parts of the world and in those meetings, he learned generally about the world, and in particular about the Muslim countries. At that time most of the Muslim countries were administrated by Christian imperialists and the Muslims were held in subordination in many parts of the Muslim world. Although each visit brought him a new experience, the pilgrimage to Mecca was the most exciting and most beneficial to him in terms of worship, learning and happiness.

The young Sayyid gained enlightenment through learning and travelling, and at an early age became deeply conscious of the infidel's threat to Islam and to his people. Because of the knowledge and the experience, he gained, as well as the extreme intelligence he was bestowed by Allah, the Sayyid was now able to articulate his vision for the future of the Somalis.

The Sayyid made six more visits to Mecca to perform pilgrimage there in the following decade but the last one he made, in 1895, was not only longer than the other visits but had a more profound impact on him. He spent a year in Arabia and also visited Hejaz and Palestine after his last visit to Mecca, and during that time he joined the Salihia Order. While in Mecca he met with Mohammed Salah of Sudan. He studied under Sheikh Mohammed Salah and joined his sect, the Salihia Order. The profoundly influential Salah commissioned the Sayyid as khalifa (representative) of the Salihiya brotherhood in Somalia afterwards.

When he returned home from the pilgrimage, Sayyid Mohammed landed at Berbera. As Abdi Abdulqadir narrated in his book *Divine Madness*, the confrontation between the Sayyid and the British officials started at the harbour, when he returned home from Arabia: 'It is said that upon his return from Arabia to the Somali coast, the young Mullah was stopped and asked to pay customs duties on his personal effects by a British customs officer. The Mullah strongly objected to this new form of exploitation. He reportedly asked the Englishman "Did you pay customs duties when you landed here?"'[2] It was also reported that the Sayyid met a boy at the mission school in Berbera and asked him his name. The boy replied: 'John Adillahi.' In another story, the Sayyid met a group of boys from the mission and when he asked them what clan

---

[2] Abdi Abdulqadir Sheikh-Abdi, 1993, *Divine Madness*, Zed Books Ltd, page 202.

they belonged to they replied, "The clan of the Fathers."[3] Already aware of the danger the infidels posed on the Muslims, those incidents no doubt fuelled that sentiment and confirmed his belief that the Christian colonization sought to destroy the Muslim faith of his people. This fired his patriotism and from there the confrontation with the British started.

Soon after he settled in Berbera, the Sayyid began to teach Islam, preaching to his countrymen in the mosques and streets, urging them to return to the strict path of Muslim devotion, and persuading them to remove the English 'infidels' and their missionaries. Sayyid Mohamed urged the people to observe religious rules and in particular he advised them to join the Salihiya Order and tried to persuade the people to accept Mohammed Salah as the spiritual imam. He also condemned the lax practices of the Qadiriya Order, the main competitor of the Salihiya. The Qadiriya sect was more relaxed than the Salihiya in that it tolerated some of the Somali customs that were not in line with the Islamic teaching, such as the chewing of chat, women going outside without veils, and smoking. The Salihiya, on the other hand, were campaigning to put an end to all these practices and to ban alcohol drinking, which the foreigners had introduced. Furthermore, the Sayyid accused the Qadiriya of tolerating the planting of Christianity in the Somali territory through the Catholic mission at Berbera.

The British authority took the Sayyid's warning of the dangers of the infidels as a provocation, and his outspoken critics of the Qadiriya sect also angered that Order. The two felt threatened by the Sayyid and as a result formed an alliance against him. The Salihiya mosque in Berbera was closed down by the British administration as part of the campaign against the Salihiya in general, and in particular against the leader. The Sayyid then retired to Qoryawayne in the Nugal valley, the land of his maternal kinsmen, where he founded a settlement for his sect.

After finding a base, the Sayyid had turned his attention to the big issue of driving the imperialists from the Somali lands. He started this campaign by establishing a resistance army (the Dervish). He recruited the Dervish from within his Salihiya sect and in a short period he got enough soldiers. The second step he took was the mobilization of the public and the preparation for the jihad against the infidels. In fact, the Sayyid started this campaign while in Berbera. Using the twin banners of Islam and homeland, he tried to incite an uprising against the imperialists and, despite the clan division of the Somali society, he was successful in

---

[3] I. M. Lewis, 2002, A *Modern History of the Somali*, page 67.

so doing:

> One of the more serious factors hampering unity among the nomadic Somali was the traditional lineage system with its sectional loyalties. But through his personal charisma and brilliant leadership, al-Sayyid managed to command a heterogeneous following, consisting of various Somali clans, and create a standing army which was estimated at 12000 men. In this successful mobilization against alien colonial rule, al-Sayyid appealed to the religious sentiments of the Somali as Muslims irrespective of clan allegiance. He had, furthermore, composed a large number of poems, of which many are still well known throughout Somalia, by means of which he 'successfully' rallied a host of contentious clansmen behind the twin banners of Islam and homeland.[4]

The Sayyid repeatedly reminded the people of the dangers to their land and their religion and warned them of the Christianization of their children through the establishment of Christian schools in their homeland. 'Sayyid Muhammad was conscious that the Christian (European and Ethiopian) incursions had threatened the social and economic foundation of Somali society. As early as July 1899, he wrote to a Somali clan and gave them this warning: "Do you not see that the infidels have destroyed our religion and have made our children their own?" By this, he was apparently referring to the establishment of Christian schools in Somalia which he considered a threat to the kuranic schools.'[5]

Sayyid Mohammed aimed to rid the Somali peninsula of alien rule as his first famous letter of defiance, which he wrote to the British administration in August 1899 indicated. In the letter 'he accused the British of oppressing Islam without cause; and in effect claimed political sovereignty by his demand that they should choose between war and the payment of *Jizya*, the tax canonically due to a Muslim ruler from tolerated infidels. He was at once proclaimed a rebel.'[6] Having proclaimed the Sayyid a rebel, the British Consul-General at Berbera urged his government in London to prepare an expedition against the Sayyid. The government agreed to launch a war against the Sayyid in order to eliminate the Dervish force at an early stage, but the Dervish resistance movement was too strong to be destroyed and the ensuing war lasted for

---

[4] H. A. Ibrahim, 1985, African Initiatives and Resistance in North Eastern Africa, General History of Africa, UNESCO, page 85.

[5] H. A. Ibrahim, 1985, African Initiatives and Resistance in North Eastern Africa, General History of Africa, page 84.

[6] G.N. Sanderson, 1985, *The Nile Basin and the Eastern Horn, the Cambridge, History of Africa*, Cambridge University Press, Volume 6, page 672.

21 years.

3.2 The Armed Resistance of the Dervishes

The Dervish Resistance movement was engaged in armed conflicts with all the imperialist powers in the Somali lands except the French. Although their ultimate goal was to eject all the imperialist powers from the Somali lands, and their leader declared his defiance to the British, the place he wanted to start the Jihad was not the British Somaliland, but the Ogaden. Ethiopia proved the most brutal of the colonizers and early in 1899, the Ethiopian pressure reached a climax with a devastating raid into the Ogaden. The Sayyid offered his assistance in 1900 to the Western Somali people, who recently suffered crippling stock losses at the hands of the Ethiopians. In March 1900, a Dervish force of about 6000 stormed the Ethiopian garrison at the wells of Jigjiga, and the Dervish army recovered much of the looted stock in that action.

Although the Sayyid sent letters to the major Somali clans in the south, north and central regions, in which he urged them to take a common front against the entire colonial invaders, he wanted first to finish the war he started in the Ogaden against Ethiopia, before beginning the fight with the European imperialists. But the British did not wait for him and declared war on him. Because of the war declaration, he was forced to change his original plan of fighting the Ethiopians first. Instead, he turned against the British in self-defence. The war between the British Imperial forces and the Dervishes started in 1901 and continued until 1920. The details of that war are recorded elsewhere, and it will be presented here only in summary form.

The Ethiopian emperor Menelik requested a joint military action against the Dervishes and in response, an Anglo-Ethiopian force was prepared to deal with the Sayyid. The Italians also took part in the operation against the Sayyid by providing logistical support to Britain. Two British officers, Major Hanbury-Tracy and Captain Cobbold, who were assigned as advisers to the Ethiopian army acted also as coordinators of the two forces. According to the plan, Ethiopian forces were to advance into the western Ogaden and the imperial army of Britain, under Captain E.J. Swayne, was to attack the Dervishes in the Nugal valley.

On 22 May 1901 the imperial, expedition consisting of British, Somali and Indian armies under the command of Swayne, set out from Burao and headed for Nugal. The Dervish forces first attacked the expedition on its way to Nugal at Samala in June 1901. After the Samala battle, the Sayyid withdrew to the Mudugh Oasis, but returned to Nugal in July. The British continued their offensive against the Dervish army and attacked them at Fer-Diddin in July. Again, the Sayyid first retreated to the Mudugh Oasis after the attack, but by October 1901 the Dervish forces were back in the Nugal valley. An Ethiopian force 15 000 strong, which the British expected to attack the Sayyid from the Ogaden side, retired at Gerlogubi well before it reached its destination. In 1902 (June–August) the British forces again attacked the Sayyid's army in the Nugal valley in an attempt to drive the Sayyid and his forces out of the British protectorate but were defeated by the Dervish army.

Meanwhile, the Sayyid changed his base temporarily to the Mudugh valley and extended his territory eastward into the Indian Ocean. He acquired the port of Illig in the Italian claimed territory on the Indian Ocean by occupying it. He took over the port in order to secure the flow of arms and other supplies and reduce his dependency on the coastal clans that had supplied him in the past.

The plan for the second expedition was laid during the spring of 1902 and that expedition met the Sayyid's army at Erigo on 6 October 1902. The light-armed Dervish force faced a well-armed imperial force of 2 400 in that battle. It was a fierce fight with heavy casualties on both sides, but in the end, the imperial army was defeated and forced to retreat to Bohotle. Despite its huge number and arms superiority, the colonial force could not crash the brave and terrain expert Dervishes. The resistance movement became more powerful and the British realised that. At a Foreign Office conference in mid-October 1902 about the Somaliland crises, retirement from and even abandonment of the protectorate was debated, although, because of its importance to Aden, the conference eventually decided to defend the territory.

Despite the determination to hold the territory, the British authorities admitted that they could not defeat the Dervishes alone and hence formed an alliance with Ethiopia and Italy against the movement. The three imperialist powers agreed to undertake a common action against the Dervishes and the coordinated offences started in 1903. The 10 000-strong imperial army of Britain that took part in the campaign was the best of its seasoned army and consisted of Indian and African and its own troops. This multi-force was aided by 15 000 Ethiopian troops and Italian logistical support. The Dervish force which faced that strong allied army was '20 000 – of whom 8000 were cavalry. Although inferior in firepower and organization, the Somali resisters managed to hold their own by engaging in guerrilla tactics strongly suited to the terrain of the country. Breaking into small parties of 50–100 men, the Dervishes drew the British and the Ethiopians into the waterless shrublands of the Haud, lands that were well known to the Dervishes but pathless to the invaders, and in doing so, dictated both the time and place of subsequent battles.[7]

As reported by G.N. Sanderson: 'The third expedition attempted to destroy the Sayyid by pincer movements from Berbera and (by arrangement with the Italians) from Hobyo, combined with an Ethiopian advance into the Ogaden. The British columns met in the interior without encountering the Sayyid, who had withdrawn to the western Ogaden. Two detachments despatched in his pursuit were ambushed and roughly handled in April 1903.'[8] The first detachment under the command of Colonel Plunkett was destroyed at Gumburu. 'Nearly the whole British force, to the number of 200, including Colonel Plunkett and other British officers and a detachment of Sikhs, were killed.'[9] The second battle took place between Danot and Walwal in the Ogaden and, like Gumburu, the imperial army was badly defeated. In this battle too, several British officials, including Bruce and Godfrey as well as many Sikh soldiers, were among the causalities. In May, the Sayyid's forces met an Ethiopian force that was advancing northward from the Upper Webe Shebele River at Jayd, and because of the ensuing battle with Ethiopians, the Sayyid moved back to the Nugal valley across the British line of communication.

By the end of the third expedition, the allied forces had lost the war and the Sayyid's morale was higher as his second well-known letter of defiance, in which he demanded that they leave the Somaliland and return to their own country, showed. He warned them of the consequences if they reject his demand and added that they could expect nothing from him but war:

> I wish to rule my country and protect my religion. We have both suffered considerably in battle with one another. I have no forts, no houses. I have no cultivated fields, no silver or gold for you to take. You gained no benefit by killing my men and my country is no good to you. The country is jungle. If the country were cultivated or contained houses or property, it would be worth your while to fight. The country is all bushes and that is no use to you. If you want wood and stone, you can get them in plenty. There are also

---

[7] David D. Laitin & Said S. Samatar, 1987, *Somalia, a Nation in Search of a State*, page 58.
[8] G.N. Sanderson, 1985, *The Nile Basin and the Eastern Horn, the Cambridge, History of Africa*, page 676.
[9] Ray Beachey, 1990, *The Warrior Mullah*, page 52.

many anthills. The sun is very hot. All you can get from me is war nothing else. If you wish peace, go away from my country to your own.[10]

The British answer to the letter was one of defiance, and the fourth expedition went ahead and attacked the Dervish army at Jidbale in the Upper Nugal valley in January 1904. Lord Roberts, Commander-in-Chief at the War Office, instructed his army commanders to destroy or expel the Dervish forces from the protectorate. To lead the new drive against the Sayyid a new commander, General Sir C. Egerton, was appointed. The Dervish forces were at Jidbale at the time of the commencement of the fourth expedition. Before the attack, the British forces established posts in nearly all possible ways the Sayyid might use in the event of retreat. An Ethiopian force with seven British officers attached, together with a British force, occupied various positions within the Ogaden to prevent the Sayyid from retreating.

An army attachment was stationed at Halim east of Jidbale and another column, which landed at Hobyo (Italian protectorate), made its way to Nugal through Mudugh. Only the northern direction was left open to the Dervishes when the British forces attacked them from the west. The Dervish forces strongly resisted the allied colonial powers, but they were eventually defeated and forced to withdraw from the Nugal valley. The Dervish army retreated to Illig, from where they were ejected by a British naval landing in April 1904. By the end of 1904, the Sayyid's army had been greatly weakened and he, therefore, withdrew to the border between the Italian and British Somaliland protectorates near Gerrowei.

Despite the defeat, the Sayyid negotiated with Britain and Italy as if he were victorious, and dictated the terms of the Treaty of Illig, which he signed with Italians and which the British later accepted. In the treaty, he was allowed to return and settle at the port of Illig and territory from Ras Bowen down to Ras Aswad, a distance of nearly 200 miles on the seaward side, as well as much of the lower Nugal and Haud. The Dervish forces were weakened and almost destroyed but 'Muhammad Abdullah simply refused to admit defeat; and at Illig between 1905 and 1908 he recreated the Dervish movement almost entirely by his gifts as poet and propagandist. Previously, most Dervish poetry had been composed by the Sayyid's court poets. But from 1905 Muhammad Abdullah himself poured forth poems of defiance against the British, and of insult and

---

[10] Louis FitzGibbon, 1982, *The Betrayal of the Somalis*, Rex Collins, page 36: David D. Laitin & Said S. Samatar, 1987, *Somalia, A Nation in Search of a State*, Westview Press, page 58.

invective against the British-protected Somali, which have earned him his reputation as the greatest Somali poet; the power of these poems is discernible even in the dim reflection of translation.'[11]

At Illig, Sayyid Mohammed began to revive his movement and by 1908 he had mobilized the Dervish forces for a new round of fighting that forced the British to withdraw from the interior. Winston Churchill, the then under Secretary of State for the colonies, who visited the protectorate in October 1907, recommended the abandonment of the interior, but only after the failure of the Wingate mission to reach an accommodation with the Sayyid a decision was made in that regard. In November 1909, London ordered the withdrawal from the interior and decided to retain and concentrate only on the strategically important coast. The evacuation was complete by April 1910, but the Sayyid threatened to attack the coastal towns as well.

The Dervish forces returned from Illig to the Nugal valley after they drove the British from the interior. At Taleh, the new seat of the movement, the Sayyid built a massively fortified headquarters from which he led the Dervish resistance movement until 1920. The Dervishes became more emboldened and on 9 August 1913, they gained a major victory at Dul Madoba by annihilating the newly established camel constabulary. The British Imperial army was completely destroyed at Dul Madoba and the army commander, Richard Corfield, was killed there.

By 1914, Britain, however, reversed its defensive policy and decided to reoccupy the interior again, and defeat the Sayyid. The change in policy was caused partly by the threat the British felt after Dul Madoba and periodical raids on Berbera, and partly by the First World War and regime change in Ethiopia.

Prince Lij Iyasu, a grandson of Menelik (son of Menelik's daughter), succeeded to the throne in December 1913 after Menelik became incapacitated. Iyasu's father Ras Michael was originally Muslim, alias Mohamed Ali, but he converted to Christianity forcibly, and because of his father's background the Christian establishment in Ethiopia was always suspicious of him. As mentioned in chapter 2, his socialization with the Muslims and his frequent visits to the Ogaden further strengthened that sentiment against him. Iyasu's appointment of Abdalla Sadiq as governor of the Ogaden, his contacts with the Sayyid and the two leaders' support for the German-Turkish side of the First World War

---

[11] G.N. Sanderson, 1985, *The Nile Basin and the Eastern Horn, the Cambridge History of Africa,* page 677.

further angered his opponent and also prompted a reaction from the European powers in the region. The British, the French and the Italians all strongly objected to the nomination of Abdalla Sadiq as Governor of the Ogaden. However, Britain took the lead in the campaign to remove Sadiq from office. The British considered him not only as too close to the Sayyid, but they also accused him of sending arms shipments to the Sayyid and acting as his contact man to the outside world.

The British plan was to remove Sadiq and replace him with Tafari (Haile Selassie). In collaboration with the Ethiopian establishment, Britain eventually succeeded in removing both Sadiq and Lij Iyasu. The latter was overthrown on 27 September 1916 and subsequently began an Anglo-Ethiopian campaign against the Sayyid, which continued until he died in 1920.

As part of the new strategy to eliminate the Sayyid, the British reoccupied Buroa, Las Dureh and Shimber Berris without resistance in November 1914. Since the start of the new approach, the British became more aggressive while the Dervishes remained on the defensive for the most part. However, despite some minor defeats in Las Qorei in 1916 and Karumba in 1917, the Dervishes did not suffer major defeats until the battle of OK Pass in 1919, in which they were savagely beaten. In September 1919, the Dervishes moved their headquarters from Taleh, their stronghold since 1913, to Medishe and Jidali, leaving a small force at Taleh.

By 21 January 1920 Britain had launched the campaign that ended the 21-year war against the Dervishes. The final campaign against the Sayyid was different from the earlier expeditions against the Dervishes because of its intensity and because of the new warfare element, aerial bombing. The then Secretary for War and the Air Force, Winston Churchill, made available aircraft bombers that took part in the First World War to be used in the fight against the Dervishes, and on 8 October 1919, a full-scale expedition was approved by Downing Street. The force that was used in the final expedition campaign included a ground force that consisted of the camel corps, the Indian infantry, the scouts, and the navy and the air force. The scouts were first dispatched to the interior to gather information about the whereabouts of Dervish forces, and the navy patrolled the seaboard and the sea line to cut possible supply lines or prevent the Dervishes' escape by sea. The aerial attack was launched on Jidali and Medishe, the strongholds of Dervishes on 21 January and the ground forces moved slowly towards Jidali and Medishe. But the Dervishes left these places because of the aerial bombing before the ground forces reached them. The combined land and air forces were very effective, and the Dervishes had no other option but to flee, and most of what was left of Dervish forces escaped to the Ogaden. In one of his most-remembered poems, the Sayyid describes the awful situation after their defeat at the hands of that last British expedition. In particular, he described very eloquently the scene at the battlefield and the destructive effects of the aircraft bombers.

> Because of the furious thunder
> and lightning they had generated,
> the sky could not be told from the earth!
> They (the English) have brought with them
> Flying monsters from Aden!
> (Under these trying circumstances)
> what else was a person to do,
> but to make a run for his life?[12]

Although the Dervish army was defeated and driven from British Somaliland the Sayyid was determined to continue the Jihad. The Sayyid declined the offer from Archer, the British Commissioner, to refrain from political affairs and confine himself only to religious matters, and in return settle in the British Somaliland. Furthermore, his forces launched raids from the Ogaden into the British protectorate in May 1920 to confirm that determination. (Unfortunately, the death of the Sayyid of influenza on 23 November 1920 ended the struggle.) The Sayyid and a Dervish force of about 300–400 settled down on Guano Imi, a hill near Imi, overlooking the Webi Shebele, where they built a series of forts by October 1920. Some weeks later the settlement was struck down by smallpox and influenza. Fatalities were widespread and the Sayyid was among those who lost their lives. After the death of the Sayyid, the Dervishes disintegrated. Because of the epidemic, hunger, and loss of the leadership that once held them together, they dispersed.

3.3 The Legacy of Sayyid Mohammed

Under the able leadership of Sayyid Mohamed Abdille Hassan, the Somali people had resisted the European and Ethiopian imperialists for twenty-one years. The Dervish resistance movement did not achieve its goal of driving the imperialists out of the Somali peninsula, but it laid down the foundation for further action and aroused strong nationalist feelings. The Somali people had come to see themselves as single whole

---

[12] Abdi Abdulqadir Sheikh-Abdi, 1993, *Divine Madness*, page 167.

fighting against foreign incursions. Furthermore, the Dervish struggle under the leadership of Sayyid Mohammed left in the Somali lands a vivid memory of the heroic resistance and national history that has profoundly influenced successive generations up to now.

Sayyid Mohammed has been an inspiration to the Somali people since he stood against the imperialists, and in particular his leadership, nationalism and poetry are often cited and referred to with admiration. He lives with every generation and with nearly all sections of the Somali society because of his immense contribution to the culture, politics and identity of the Somali nation.

The Sayyid pioneered a new form of organization and leadership that surprised many. The organizational form of the Salihiya Order from which he built the Dervish movement was something new to the Somalis. The subordination-sensitive Somali people had no allegiance to any authority other than the loose clan affiliation and the sheikhs for religious matters. 'But his organization of the Salihiya as a militarised religious autocracy gave Somalia the unprecedented experience of a powerful centralised authority that transcended all traditional divisions of Somali society.'[13] By combining the function of spiritual and military leadership, the Sayyid built an unprecedented Somali institution, which made him the absolute ruler. Tribal loyalty was replaced by loyalty to the Dervish organization, and kinsman solidarity was abandoned and instead encouraged solidarity among the Dervish members. Their uniform (the white turban) gave them a distinctive look and they were easily identifiable.

Unorganized resistance was frequent throughout the Somali territories since the arrival of the colonizers there. For example, in 1896 the Somalis in the Benadir region rebelled against the Italian rule, killing the commissioner, ten other officers and seventy soldiers. In November 1900, the British Commissioner of Jubaland, Mr A.C. Jenner, was killed by Somali rebels in Jubbaland and sporadic resistance took place in nearly all the regions. The Dervish movement was, however, the first organized Somali nationalist movement. The two organized Somali resistance before the Dervish movement (Adal and Ajuran) were mainly motivated by religion. The Sayyid was, on the other hand, a nationalist and a jihadist who fought for the Somali cause against the Christian imperialists. Furthermore, he urged the Somali people to forget their divisions of clan lineage and become brothers united by jihad. 'His twenty years of defiant

---

[13] N. Sanderson, *The Nile Basin and the Eastern Horn, the Cambridge History of Africa*, page 679.

and successful resistance were undoubtedly an example and an inspiration for modern Somali nationalists. Retrospectively at least, he has been very widely accepted as a Somali national hero.'[14]

One of the reasons why the memory of the Dervish movements is kept by every generation is the great poetry that the Sayyid left for his people. Sayyid Mohammed, the greatest Somali poet, used his poems as a communication medium to mobilize the people for jihad and warn the enemy, as an entertainment for his people, and at the end of his life as a testament. The last words of his last poem reminded the Somali people of the tactics of the colonizers. The following is part of his last poem and is translated by Abdi Abdulqadir:

> O, You people! Listen to these words
> of wisdom – or again you may simply
> ignore them, as you are wont to.
> Or you can shriek, derisively,
> 'Oh, the windbag is holding forth again!'
> These are parting words of wisdom,
> and a warning to the wise—
> Let fools for ever remain in darkness!
> There is no prosperity or peace
> that can come from entering into treaties
> and agreements with the Infidel,
> for he cannot be trusted!
> He is merely laying traps for you,
> while you let your guard down.
> And the Dirhams he dispenses to you now
> will prove a poison in disguise!
> At first, he will disarm you and render you
> defenseless like women and children,
> Then, he will brand you,
> as though you were mere chattel.
> He will then press you to sell your lands
> to him for worthless trinkets;
> And, finally, having dispossessed you,
> he will turn you into braying donkeys,
> to bear his burdensome load.
> Ah, but what is the use of this warning
> to you now, for I, your only defender,
> have been driven past Harar and Iimey,

---

[14] N. Sanderson, *The Nile Basin and the Eastern Horn, the Cambridge History of Africa*, page 679.

beyond the proper confines of our common patrimony;
And, doubtless, he (the colonizer)
will be even here, before long,
with the speed of his diabolical telegraph![15]

3.4 The Somali Youth League (SYL)

The death of the Sayyid and the consequent disintegration of the Dervish resistance movement were very tragic. The Sayyid's death paved the way for the colonial consolidation of the Somali territories. Between 1920 and 1943 organized Somali resistance was absent from the scene and as a result, the colonial powers tried to pursue their imperial goals more aggressively in the Somali lands in that period. The renewed efforts by the occupiers to consolidate their rule and the competition among the imperialist powers after the disappearance of the Dervish resistance led eventually to conflicts among the colonizers themselves. Italy occupied the Ogaden and Ethiopia in 1935 and in 1940 took over British Somaliland. In 1941 Britain reoccupied British Somaliland and occupied the whole of the Italian colony in East Africa (the Ogaden, Italian Somaliland, Eritrea and Ethiopia) and thereby brought all the Somali territories (except Djibouti) under its flag.

The conflict among the colonial powers over the repartition of the Somali territories and consequent reunification of most of the Somali lands, first through the occupation of Italy and afterwards through the British occupation, to some extent undermined the consolidation of colonial rule on the Somali territories and encouraged the Somali reunification agitation. Britain had control of most of the Somali territories for about a decade (1941–50). During the British rule, national awareness and Somali nationalism grew and, in that period, the Somali movement that succeeded the Sayyid's Dervish resistance movement was established. The Somali Youth Club (SYC), which was formed on May 13, 1943, became the new flag-bearer of the Somali movements for freedom from colonial rule, the reunification of the Somali lands, and nation-building.

The Youth Club, which originated in the south, grew very rapidly and spread all over the Somali territories in a short period. The widespread acceptance of the youth organization was expected, because a measure of Somali consciousness and opposition to colonial rule had been present throughout the colonial period, most obviously in the campaigns of Sayyid Mohammed, and the twin banners of liberation and reunification,

---

[15] Abdi Abdulqadir Sheikh-Abdi, 1993, *Divine Madness*, pages 175–180.

which it made its political programme, were already the main national issues. The Somali youth organization emerged at a time when the issues of freedom and reunification were openly debated by all the Somalis living in the urban areas and the Somali intelligentsia was formulating ways of achieving those goals. Furthermore, the relatively more relaxed British administration during the period of temporary unification tolerated the debate about the issues involving the political future of the Somalis, and it was in that period that pan-Somalism as the most prominent component of Somali nationalistic ideology took root among the young intelligentsia. The Youth Club changed its name to the Somali Youth League (SYL) in 1947 and by then it was a national party with adherents throughout the Somali territories.

Like the Dervish resistance movement, which it succeeded, the prime goal of the youth organisation was to get rid of the alien rule of the Somali territories, but the means by which it wanted to achieve that goal were different from those of the Dervish movement. The SYL was a political party without a military wing, and it differed from the Dervish movement in the constitutionalist means through which it pursued its ends, and in its readiness to accept innovations such as Western education, which traditionalists had regarded with suspicion. As a national party, the youth organization attempted to repudiate the clan divisions on which the Somali society was based and was to some extent successful in that regard. However, unlike the Dervish resistance movement and most nationalist movements elsewhere in the African continent, the SYL had no single dominant leader and that was not a surprise given the egalitarian spirit of Somali nomadism.

The SYL campaigned for the liberation of all the Somali territories and aimed at establishing a united Somali state. The rejection by the big powers of the British Foreign Secretary's proposal for unified and eventually free Somalia, and the consequent handover of the Ogaden to Ethiopia and the association of NFD to the British colony of Kenya, however, disappointed the SYL and dashed the hopes and the aspirations of the Somali people. The youth organization continued the struggle for freedom and Somali unity, but after the repartition of the Somali lands concentrated on the liberation of Italian Somaliland and British Somaliland, although it never abandoned the notion of pan-Somalism and was active in the Ogaden.

The SYL and its supporters staged anti-Italian demonstrations when Italy sought to be given trusteeship over southern Somalia. 'In 1948–9 when the question was discussed in the UN, a wave of popular demonstrations in Mogadishu and elsewhere arose against the return of the Italians in any form. Women organized by the Somali Youth League (SYL) participated actively in the independence struggle and in January 1948 one of them, Hawa Ismen Ali was killed as the first woman martyr of the Somali national liberation movement. Although the anti-Italian feelings of the people were manifest even to various UN commissions, the three Western powers (USA, Britain and France) favoured the trusteeship under Italy while the Soviet Union supported a collective four-power control. On 21 November 1949, the General Assembly decided to entrust Somalia for ten years to Italian trusteeship under UN tutelage. The immediate independence hoped for by the people of Somalia was thus postponed for a whole decade"[16]

The Italian trusteeship over Southern Somalia and the consequent delay of independence for 10 years were setbacks to the Somali cause, which angered the Somali people; however, the UN intended to prepare the colony for independence. Meanwhile, although the SYL remained the leading political party, it lost its monopoly of Somali representation during the British administration as other parties were found in that period. Under the Italian Trusteeship Administration, many more parties, most of them clan-based and some with Italian support, emerged and the political system was fully polarized. Despite the difficult relationship in the first few years between the Italian Trusteeship Administration and the SYL, because of the latter's strong opposition to the Italian Trusteeship and the clashes between the two in 1950 and 1952, they eventually cooperated in preparing the trusteeship for independence. Ivan Hrbeck reported the development of political parties as well as the relationship between the Italian authorities and the SYL as follows:

> One major effect of Italy's return was the proliferation of political parties so that by March 1954, at the time of the first municipal election, there were 21 of them as against eight in 1950. This mirrored to a high degree the clan-based structure of the Somali society. Although the clan-based parties accepted officially nationalist and pan-Somali goals in their programmes, they nevertheless remained attached to the defence and promulgation of their own particular interests. The first three years of the decade were marked by Italian-SYL hostility as the party claimed more participation in administration and organized many anti-Italian demonstrations. Between the municipal election in 1954 in which the SYL confirmed its lead, and 1960, the former hostile attitude of the Italians towards the SYL changed as it became clear that after independence it would be the leading party and the

---

[16] Ivan Hrbeck, 1993, *The Horn and North Africa, General History of Africa*, UNESCO, Volume VIII. Page 152.

Italians did not wish to antagonize it unnecessarily. In the first general election to the legislative assembly in February 1956 the SYL again won the majority of votes. The new Assembly was given full statutory powers in the domestic affairs and the first Somali government under Abdillahi Ise was formed. Nevertheless, the head of the Italian Trust Administration retained the right of absolute veto and jurisdiction over military and foreign affairs and the Italian councillors were attached to the Somali ministers.'[17]

As Laitin and Samatar described, political and social development in the British Somaliland lagged behind that of Italian Somaliland: 'Political parties were illegal until 1959. The British administration insisted on clan representation in governing councils, and this prohibited the development of national or supra-clan parties. Also the British refused civil servants the right to engage in politics, thereby emasculating the potential size of an educated political class. However, there were two de facto political parties from the 1950s that existed on the edge of legality. First, the SYL was a branch of the pan-Somali party of the south. British administrators saw SYL members as communists and encouraged the development of a countermovement among the merchants, traditional leaders, and religious sheikhs. This group was the seed of the second party, the Somali National League.'[18] Two other parties were later formed, namely the United Somali Party (USP) and the National United Front (NUF).

The SNL – the dominant party in the territory – boycotted the first general election, which took place in March 1959. In February 1960, another election was held. In this election, the SNL gained twenty of the thirty-three seats, the USP won twelve seats, the NUF got one seat. The SYL failed to win a single seat. The leader of the SNL, Mohamed Haji Ibrahim Igal, became the leader of government business. Despite the elimination of the pan-Somali party, the SYL, in the 1960 election, there was a consensus among the political parties in the territory on the issue of Somali unification. All the parties favoured and advocated reunification with the south and there was considerable grass-roots pressure for this to take place as soon as possible.

Soon after its formation, the SYL sent a delegation consisting of two officials to the Ogaden to open a branch for the organization there. The officials were Mohamoud Malinguur and Ahmed Alore. When they

---

[17] Ivan Hrbeck, 1993, *The Horn and North Africa, General History of Africa*, page 153.
[18] David D. Laitin & Said S. Samatar, 1987, *Somalia, A Nation in Search of a State*, page 66.

arrived in Dagahbour, their first station, they were welcomed by Garad Makhtal Dahir, who was preparing to launch a new resistance movement and had been active for more than four years by then. The delegation opened the branch office of the league in Dagahbour with the help of Garad Makhtal who also joined the organization. Despite the early establishment of the SYL in the Ogaden and the widespread support for its ideals among the population, it did not make big headway there, because of the Ethiopian suppression. To silence the popular public outcry against the Ethiopian reoccupation of the Ogaden and eliminate the resistance to its rule, the Ethiopians made the SYL adherents and sympathizers a prime target.

In 1948, twenty-five SYL members were killed in Jigjiga for protesting against the handover of their land to Ethiopia and for refusing to remove the SYL flag from the headquarters of the organization in Jigjiga. In 1957, seven SYL members were hanged, and their bodies were displayed in the same town. In 1960, hundreds of innocent people were massacred in and around Aysha for allegedly supporting the SYL and its greater Somalia vision.

4

The Independence of Somalia and the Greater Somalia Dream

Nation-building and the search for the Greater Somalia

British Somaliland became independent on 26 June 1960 and four days later Italian Somaliland took independence. The two independent parts joined together and formed the Republic of Somalia on 1 July 1960. On that day, the people celebrated wildly, singing with joy for the freedom and dignity they regained, and expressing their gratitude to Allah for the victory. However, both the blue flag they waved and the song they sang indicated an incomplete victory. The five-pointed star on the flag stands for the five parts of the Somali lands (Former British Somaliland, former Italian Somaliland, Djibouti, Ogaden and NFD) and in the song they referred to the unification of all five parts. The crowds that came out on the streets all over Somalia for the independence and the unification celebrations of the south and north also confirmed their determination for the liberation of the three other parts. The liberation of the Somali lands still living under occupation and their unification with Somalia became Somalia's biggest issue since independence. A similar celebration took place in the other Somali territories and the message was the same.

The Somali leaders shared with the public the aspiration to unite the lands populated by the Somali people in a single state. Thus, the Somali government that was formed in 1960 under the leadership of Adan Abdulle Osman made commitments to liberate the three remaining parts and incorporate them into Somalia, and from there the dream of Greater Somalia was launched. The colonial boundaries were not to be recognized and the Somalis were given equal rights within Somalia, irrespective of where each person was born. In other words, the Somali lands belong to all, and both those living inside and outside Somalia agreed to build the new state and fight for the liberation of the territories still under colonial rule collectively.

After the honeymoon was over, the new government found itself under pressure from three often conflicting sides. First, there was a need to develop the institutions, the economy, and to improve the living standard of the people inside Somalia. Second, there was domestic pressure to further the cause of unification of all Somalis, and the Somalis still living under colonial rule sought its help in driving out the imperialists from the Somali territories. Third, the Ethiopian and Kenyan governments demanded that Somalia give up its territorial claims on these countries and stop the sheltering and the backing of the Somali liberation movements in the Ogaden and NFD. To find a balance on these pressures was difficult, if not impossible; however, Somalia had no other choice and had to confront the reality. In so doing, the civilian government (1960–69) first listened to her heart, ignored the unjust demand of her neighbours, and concentrated on both state-building and 'Greater Somalia' designs. However, it softened her position regarding the Greater Somalia issue and tried to improve relations with her neighbours since 1967.

Somalia has seen two different systems of government since independence. During the period 1960–69 Somalia was ruled by democratic governments and from 1969-91 by a military government. The two systems of government differed not only in style and ideology but also in their approach to national issues. In the next sections, we briefly review the civilian government's achievements and failures on the domestic front, as well as on the issue of Greater Somalia designs, during the period of its reign.

4.1 State-Building (1960–69)

Somalia faced many problems at the dawn of independence, which the new government was to tackle. Among these were social and economic problems, writing language script, integrating the two different systems of the two territories that formed the republic, etc. However, the new state had to establish a system of government before it had to deal with those pressing domestic issues head-on.

The new government that was formed after independence was a coalition made up of the members of the two assemblies in the south and the north. In both the south and the north there were political parties before independence, and the members of the two assemblies in both parties were elected and thus democratic representation came with independence and unity. Soon after independence, the legislators of the two parts met in a joint session and with near unanimity elected Adan Abdulle Osman as provisional president. The president nominated Abdirashid Ali Shermarke as prime minister, and this was approved by the joint assembly. The first cabinet reflected the clan and party strength within the assembly.

The 1961 constitution was a step forward in the democratization processes and it laid down government foundations. The constitution gave Somalia a parliamentary system of government in which parties could organize and compete for political office. Regular elections were held and the citizens would vote for members of the parliament. The members of parliament would elect the president, who in turn would nominate the prime minister. The constitution also provided an independent judiciary and a free press, and opponents to government policies were free to criticize the government. The constitution provided a framework for a parliamentary system of government; however, the rule of the game was not straightforward to some extent and there was room for political manoeuvres. During the civilian period, Somalia was governed by a system founded on consent and participation, in which the competing political parties made their ambitions relevant to the mass of the people through their close reflection of clan interests and alliance. In short, the political framework provided by the constitution and the political behaviour of which clan politics was a major component produced a fragile democracy.

The parliamentary system was put to the test in March 1964, when the first election after independence took place. In that election the SYL won a clear majority with 69 seats, followed by 22 and 15 for its two main rivals, the Somali National Congress and the Somali Democratic Union, and 17 for independents. After the election, the president nominated a new prime minister, Abdirizaq Haji Hussein, but because of splits within the SYL over the replacement of Shermarke and the nomination of the new prime minister, the government of Abdirizaq Haji Hussein was not confirmed in office until September. Abdirizaq introduced some tough anti-corruption measures and was determined to create an effective central government. However, his single-minded reform measures further widened the division within the SYL, paralysed the party, and fuelled the confrontation. Abdirashid Ali Shermarke was elected president by the National Assembly in June 1967 and one month later the new president nominated a new prime minister, Mohamed Haji Ibrahim Igal, who was part of the alliance that defeated President Osman. Igal tried to impose party discipline but was not successful in that regard. The elections of March 1969, fought by 64 parties and over 2000 candidates, saw a further step towards breakdown and led to some 25 deaths. The SYL won 73 seats and its opponents 51, all but two of whom immediately crossed to the governing party in a search for posts.'[1]

Economic development was top of the 1960s government's agenda; however, the task was enormous. As is the case today, livestock and subsistence crops dominated the Somali economy as well as the livelihood of the Somalis. At independence, the economy was near the subsistence level and the new state lacked the administrative capacity to collect taxes from the subsistence herders and farmers. Taxes on other areas such as customs duties did not bring in enough income to finance the development projects of the government and thus the government was not able to balance the budget. Help, however, came from the former colonial powers of Italy and Britain, who filled the gap and provided about 31 per cent of the budget. The country also got support in the form of grants and loans from other countries in the West and East, and these transfers from abroad made possible the articulation of an ambitious five-year plan by 1963.

The budget of the plan was more than US$100 million in grants and loans, and it focused on investment in infrastructure. The government tried to improve, among other things, the ports, the roads, transport facilities and irrigation works. To increase the output and thereby exports, the production of livestock and crops were given priority, since those were the two main items of the output.

The development projects that the Somali government undertook during the 1960s had some successes. For example, livestock production and banana exports increased, investment in roads and irrigation facilities resulted in some genuine improvements, and the country became nearly self-sufficient in sugar.

Despite some improvements in the infrastructure and increased production, the country remained dependent on foreign aid, in order to balance the budget. The agricultural sector failed to produce enough to meet the demand for food, and as a result, food imports rose. Besides that, the corruption that became a major problem had adversely affected the management and the resources of the economy.

Although the two administration systems in the north and south of the country that were inherited from the colonial governments of Britain and Italy were different, the government succeeded in merging and integrating the two parts. The main reason for this success lies in the homogeneity of Somali society. The Somalis are united by religion, language, and culture, and, above all, they shared a common national

---

[1] Christopher Clapham, 1984, *The Horn of Africa, the Cambridge History of Africa*, Cambridge University Press, Volume 8, page 475.

consciousness. Those common bonds outweighed the differences in administration and other technical problems.

On the question of choosing an official script for the Somali language, the parliamentary regime failed. There were three alternatives from which to choose a script for the Somali language and those were Roman, Arabic and an indigenous Somali script called Osmaniya. Each script was promoted and advocated by a particular section of the society and the pressure to get a national script was enormous because both the bureaucracy and the educational system were operating in three different languages. The successive civilian governments, however, failed to make any decision on that issue.

4.2 The Search for Greater Somalia

The foreign and defence policies of the new Somali state were based and determined to a great extent by the dream of Greater Somalia. The Somali people did not accept the colonial partition of the Somali nation, and from day one the government of Somalia tried to liberate the three other missing parts of the nation and incorporate them into Somalia. But the issue of Somali unification was not an easy one because, on the one hand, the colonial powers that partitioned the Somali lands had no sympathy for the Somali cause, let alone for reversing the unlawful occupation of the Somali lands and their injustice policies toward the Somalis. On the other hand, Somalia was not able to take back the Somali territories by force. Despite the difficulties, the Somalis could not swallow the status quo and the Somali government had no choice but to act on the issue of Greater Somalia designs.

In pursuing the goal of unification, the government of Somalia encouraged the freedom movements in the Ogaden, the NFD and the French Somaliland of Djibouti, and on the diplomatic front, it stepped up the pressure on the colonial powers and demanded that Britain, and later, after independence, Kenya, Ethiopia and France end their occupation of the Somali territories. The determination of the Somali republic to liberate the Somali-occupied territories and unite all the Somali people under a single flag automatically brought her into conflict with Britain/Kenya, France and Ethiopia.

4.2.1 The Northern Frontier District (NFD)

The first confrontation with the colonial powers took place in the NFD. In 1961, the British Secretary of State for Colonial Affairs, Reginald Maudling, visited Kenya in preparation for the constitutional conference that was due to begin in London in 1962. Maudling met with a delegation of chiefs and political leaders including Mr Ali Adan Lord, the leader of the Northern Province People's Progressive Party (NPPPP). The delegation presented their case for secession and the NFD politicians were invited to attend the conference. Mr Abdirashid Khalif, who took over the leadership of the NPPPP after Lord's death, attended the plenary session of the constitutional conference, which was held at Lancaster House in February 1962. Mr Khalif told the conference that he was not a member of Kenyan political parties, but a secessionist.

The official delegation that attended the conference in London consisted of leading figures from each of the five districts of the NFD and was accompanied by representatives of three secessionist political parties, namely the NPPPP, the Northern Frontier Democratic Party (NFDP) and the People's National League (PNL). The NFDP and PNL were represented by their leaders, Mr Yusuf Haji Abdi and Mr Guyo Dube, respectively. The NFD delegation demanded secession and union with Somalia on the principle of the right to self-determination. 'The Delegation asked that, before any further constitutional changes affecting Kenya were made, autonomy should be granted to the area which they represented (namely the districts of Isiolo, Garissa, Manderea, Marsabit, Moyale and Wajir) as a territory wholly independent of Kenya, in order that it might join in an act of Union with the Somali Republic when Kenya became fully independent.'[2]

After its consultation with both Kenyan and NFD delegates, the British government announced that it would send a fact-finding commission to the NFD to ascertain public opinion regarding its political future. Mr G.M. Onyiuke from Nigeria and Major General M.P. Bogert from Canada were appointed as members of the commission. The Secretary promised that his government would act on the findings of the commission.

The commission submitted its report in December 1962 and in that report, it documented that the majority of people living in the NFD supported secession from Kenya and unification with Somalia. Both the Somali government and the movements for self-determination in the NFD pressured the British government into making a decision on the future of the territory based on the commission's report before Kenyan independence. Furthermore, the Somali government invited the most prominent Kenyan leaders (Jomo Kenyatta and Ronald Ngala) to persuade them to accept the inhabitants' demand for unification with

---

[2] John Drysdale, 1964, *The Somali Dispute*, Pall Mall Press Ltd, page 111.

Somalia. But the British government failed to act on the findings and the recommendation of the commission, and the Kenyan leaders refused to let the territory decide its future. Britain wanted to make peace with the Kenyan nationalists to maintain its interests in Kenya and the handover of the NFD to the Kenyans was the price it paid for that friendship. In March 1963, the Somali government broke off diplomatic relations with Britain over her refusal to allow the NFD to join the Somali Republic.

After it gained independence in 1963, the Kenyan government refused to give self- determination to the Somali people in the NFD and that denial led to the formation of a resistance movement that was in operation by 1963. The resistance army waged hit-and-run attacks against Kenyan forces and planted land mines along trails used by Kenyan forces. Although the Somali government openly supported the movement, it denied the Kenyan claim that the rebels had been armed and trained by Somalia with the help of the Soviet Union. The NFD resistance movement battled with the Kenyan police and army for four years. The armed resistance came to an end in 1967 after Somalia reversed its policies toward the region and made border agreements with Kenya.

4.2.2 French Somaliland (Djibouti)

In 1957 an elected legislature with responsibility for internal affairs was established in the French Somaliland territory. The *Union Republicaine*, led by Mohamud Harbi, won the first election. A council of ministers was formed under the presidency of the French governor and Mohamud Harbi, a Somali leader, became the vice-president. Hassan Guled, who also came from the Somali community, became the opposition leader. Both men led an electoral coalition representing sections of both the Somali and Afar communities and the Arab population. A referendum manipulated by the French was held in 1958 in which, according to the colonial authority, the population voted against independence. The assembly was dissolved following the referendum and a new election was held in November 1958. Guled, who campaigned for continued French rule and was supported by colonial authority, won the election that followed the referendum and succeeded Harbi as the vice-president in the council. Hassan Guled was replaced in April 1959 by Ahmed Diini, an Afar member when Guled was elected to the French National Assembly, and Diini was succeeded by Ali Arif, another Afar member, the following year. After a brief visit to the territory in 1959, General de Gaulle announced that France had no intention of relinquishing control of the territory. Mohamud Harbi's party disintegrated, and the leader fled to Somalia where he continued the pan-Somali struggle until his death in a plane crash in 1960.

Pro-independence movements continued the pressure for self-determination after Harbi's death and the confrontation with the French government reached a climax in 1966 when de Gaulle visited the territory again and reiterated the French government's determination to hold on to the protectorate. De Gaulle met a massive demonstration instigated by the Somalis during his visit. The parliamentary regime in Somalia supported the movements for freedom, like *Front de la liberation de la Cote des Somalis* (FLCS), which had its headquarters in Mogadishu. As a countermove to the pan-Somali campaigns undertaken by the Somalis, in 1967 the French government changed the name of the French Somaliland territory to the French Territory of the Afars and the Issas and deported many Somalis from the territory.

4.2.3 The Ogaden

Somalia was concerned with the fate of the Somalis in all three missing parts (the NFD, the Ogaden and Djibouti), but it was the liberation of the Ogaden that became the prime focus for successive Somali regimes. As it did in the NFD, the Somali regime supported the resistance movement in the Ogaden politically, morally and militarily, and besides that, Ethiopia and Somalia fought over the Ogaden cause twice.

In addition to the support of the Ogaden liberation movement, the Somali regime led the diplomatic front on behalf of the Somalis in the Ogaden. It denounced the Ethiopian government for its occupation of the Ogaden and on its designs to colonize fellow Africans. In May 1963 President Adan Abdulle Osman attacked Ethiopia at the inaugural conference of the Organization of African Unity (OAU) in Addis Ababa and tried to unveil the ugly face of the Ethiopian Empire. However, Somalia did not have much success on the diplomatic front, because of Haile Selassie's pre-emptive diplomatic offensive. Haile Selassie seized the right moment for his diplomatic offences against Somalia. Because of the long experience in government and international affairs and several other favourable factors, such as the African understanding to recognise the colonial boundaries and the wrong image of associating colonization only with white people, he achieved his goal of getting support for the occupation of the Ogaden:

> Ethiopian involvement in African diplomacy, of which the 1963 Addis Ababa conference was the outstanding achievement, was indeed partly a response to the threat presented to Ethiopia by a permanently hostile state

on her south-east frontier. Although the democratic and anti-colonial Somali Republic might seem to have had more in common with other new states in the continent than did his own anachronistic empire, Haile Selassie soon appreciated that almost every African state shared Ethiopia's interest in retaining the existing international frontiers, and that this could be used to isolate the Somalis. In addition, his own prestige as the senior African statesman and defender of Ethiopia against Italian fascism could be used to promote a common continental organization which other African leaders could not at that time achieve. For some ten years after 1963, through Haile Selassie's tireless travels around the continent, his mediation of disputes between African states, the location of the OAU headquarters in Addis Ababa, and the championing of African causes in the UN and elsewhere, Ethiopia could claim to be the diplomatic leader of Africa.[3]

The Ethiopian diplomatic success isolated the Somali state in the African continent and disappointed the Somali people. Ethiopia not only gained the support of the African leaders but was also getting substantial military assistance from the United States. Somalia complained that the United States was helping Ethiopia to maintain its grip on the Ogaden and expressed concern over the US-supplied military build-up of Ethiopia. The United States responded that the US aid to Ethiopia predated Somalia's independence and told Somalia to respect the territorial integrity of Ethiopia and Kenya. The United States also turned down a Somali request for military assistance, because of its alliance with Ethiopia.

In response to the position of weakness in which the Ethiopian diplomatic initiatives and western military support for Kenya and Ethiopia left her, the Somali government did two things: it upgraded its military capabilities and improved relations with its neighbours.

First it turned to the Communist bloc for military assistance. The Somali leaders recognized that their hopes for a unified Somalia might one day bring them into armed conflict and therefore wanted to increase the country's military strength. They knew also that the Western powers were committed to the defence of the territories Somalia sought to acquire in Kenya, Ethiopia and Djibouti. Thus, in the longer term, Somalia needed to build a military capability and she took the first step in that regard when she announced in November 1963 her acceptance of Soviet military aid worth nearly £11 million, and began to form a large modern army.

---

[3] Christopher Clapham, 1984, *The Horn of Africa, the Cambridge History of Africa*, page 482.

The brief but intense fighting between Ethiopia and Somalia in 1964 put further pressure on Somalia to soften her stance on the territorial dispute and because of her relatively small army and diplomatic isolation she could not resist that, at least in the short term. She tried to improve relations with her neighbours, Kenya and Ethiopia, especially after Mohamed Haji Ibrahim Igal became prime minister in 1967. We will deal with the détente policy in the next chapter.

5

Modern Ogaden Resistance

The birth of the Ogaden Liberation Front; the 1964 Ogaden war; the aftermath of the 1964 Ogaden war: the détente policy; the Ogaden cause; arms race and superpower rivalry

5.1 The Birth of the Ogaden Liberation Front/Nasrullah

The Ogaden Liberation Front, which is also known locally as 'Nasrullah', was formally established in 1963 but its origins go back to the political activities of its leader Garad Makhtal Dahir in the 1940s and the underground movements in the 1950s and early 1960s, as well as to the general uprising in the period 1960–63. Thus, the organization was in action long before its official organizational establishment.

In 1940, Garad Makhtal Dahir became determined to liberate the Somali lands from the colonial powers and began to think of ways of achieving that goal. Eventually, he realized the importance of forming a movement, but by then the young man had no idea of how to form an organization. He began to discuss the idea with those whom he could trust and even took their oath that they would not reveal the matter under discussion to anyone else before the start of the conversation. He continued the discussion about the formation of a liberation movement and the recruitment for its future members until 1943 when the Somali Youth Club (SYC) which later changed its name to Somali Youth League (SYL) was formed in southern Somalia.

After its establishment in 1943, the SYC/ SYL sent a two-man mission to the Ogaden to found branches for the organization in the region. When the two officials, Mohamoud Malingur and Ahmed Alore, arrived in Dagahbour they were welcomed by Garad Makhtal Dahir, who immediately joined the organization and helped them open the first branch office in Dagahbour. The SYL's twin banners of liberation and unity attracted the Garad and because of his belief in pan-Somalism and his membership of the SYL, he felt that there was no need for a separate organization for the Ogaden at that point. The Garad worked for the Somali cause through the SYL until 1948, when the UN delegation came to Mogadishu. Garad Makhtal was among the Somali delegates that met the UN delegation in Mogadishu on 12 January 1948, and in that meeting, he learned that the mandate of the UN mission was to discuss with Somalis only the future of the former Italian Somaliland. He came back from that meeting disappointed because that announcement confirmed the news of the handover of the Ogaden to Ethiopia that was already circulating.

In 1949 he left Aware, which was at the time under British rule, and headed for Jigjiga. His mission was to attack the town and start an uprising against the Ethiopian occupation. He was alone when he left Aware, but he was expecting to recruit other men on the way. When he reached the outskirts of Jigjiga, he found that two of the clans he was expecting to get a helping hand from were fighting against each other. He put off his mission for some days in order to mediate the two clans. In the meantime, the Ethiopian occupation force in Jigjiga learned of his whereabouts and became suspicious. They thought he had come to cause trouble and, as a result, they mobilized their forces in Jigjiga and requested reinforcements from Harar.

Garad Makhtal was still alone and had only one rifle when the news reached him about the mobilization and the reinforcement of the Ethiopian army, but he put on a brave face and played his cards well. He told the people that he was not alone and claimed that he had the support of the British forces in Aware. Both the Amhara regime forces and the Somalis believed him because it was known at that time that some British officials, including the commissioner in Aware, were not happy with the handover of the region to Ethiopia. He made clear that he would attack the town and requested the evacuation of the civilian population from the town. At that stage, his aim was not to defeat the enemy militarily but to instigate an uprising and start the armed struggle. At dawn, he and five other men attacked the town.

A few days later Garad Makhtal and his followers attacked the town of Dagahbour. After the attack of Dagahbour he increased the number of his small fighting force and, as he had expected, the uprising took place in many areas of the region. After the Dagahbour attack, the small guerrilla fighters under Garad Makhtal headed for Qabridahare to attack the Ethiopian force there. However, before they reached their destination a letter came from the SYL head office in Mogadishu, in which the SYL demanded to put an end to the Garad's armed resistance. The SYL believed only in peaceful resistance and the Garad's military activities contradicted the League's political programme. In addition, the League wanted to have a normal relationship with Ethiopia to use it as a base in the event of a confrontation with Italy. Although Garad Makhtal was a prominent member of the League, he never agreed with it on the issue of opting out of armed resistance, because he did not think that peaceful resistance was a realistic way of achieving the common goal. To explain his position and persuade the League to change its programme, he left for Mogadishu in 1949. The Garad was very firm on his stand regarding the armed resistance issue and was ready to break off with the SYL if it refused to change its position on that issue.

When the Garad arrived in Mogadishu, the British governor there arrested him. A few days later the British authority took him to Harar and handed him over to the Ethiopian authority there. He was sentenced to death and spent 12 years in Ethiopian jails, 8 of them on death row in jail in Addis Ababa. After he had been imprisoned for about 12 years, the Ethiopian emperor pardoned him and released him in1962. At the time of his release, there was uncoordinated underground resistance in the Ogaden. There were resistance activists throughout the Ogaden region, but because of the security situation, they were unable to coordinate their work inside the region. As a result, many of the young intelligentsia that led the movements fled to Somalia and from there began to coordinate the resistance movements. From their centre in Mogadishu, they continued the mobilization of the resistance and made contacts with the outside world until the formation of a national front. Garad Makhtal joined the underground resistance movement soon after his release and became its leader after its formal establishment.

The underground resistance movement organized a general conference in 1963 at Hodayo (a village near Warder), at which the clan leaders, the intellectuals, the religious leaders and the public attended. The liberation of the territory was the issue in focus. In the conference, the formation of the Ogaden Liberation Front (OLF) was announced on 16 June 1963 and Garad Makhtal Dahir was elected as the new leader of the liberation front, making the several-years-old Nasrullah movement a formal organisation but one with many names, such as the OLF, Nasrullah, and Gaysh. The OLF was the name used abroad because of its use of 'Ogaden'; the others were local names. Since the organization had a foothold within the entire region before its official formation, it did not need a long preparation to start its work. In a short period, the organization was active and began to conduct military operations.

5.2 The 1964 Ogaden War

The inhabitants of the region were already at war with the Ethiopian occupation army before the formation of the OLF (Nasrullah). Ethiopia never stopped the terror campaign it began when it occupied the region, and the Western Somali inhabitants continued the resistance. In the early 1960s, Haile Selassie tried to legitimise the Ethiopian occupation by establishing clan chiefs, intended to mediate between the Ethiopian administrators and the Somali inhabitants. He also attempted to institutionalise the tribute paid by the Somalis to the Ethiopian occupants by introducing, in February 1963, a head tax. In practice, the chiefs were responsible mainly for the collection of the tribute, which the Ethiopians called "tax", and since the chiefs did not exercise any real power, the system was not beneficial to the Somali people.

Despite the use of the chiefs, the people rejected Haile Selassie's plan and the issue of tribute/tax collection remained the biggest clash point. Although it was not organized, the armed resistance intensified, especially after Somalia's independence. Six months after the independence of Somalia, the armed Somali resistance in the Ogaden clashed with Ethiopian troops. The clashes were initially about tax collection but spread as nationalistic sentiment grew. The mass killings in Jigjiga and Aysha mentioned earlier were intended to suppress the general uprising. In 1961 another massacre took place in Dagahbour and the town was burned after some youths hoisted the Somali flag and lowered the Ethiopian flag. Following similar uprisings, Qalafe, Danot, Shilabo and other places were also destroyed. In 1963 the Ethiopian army killed two resistance leaders, Abdi Barqab and Ibrahim Amey, at Tuuk Kalalkal village, then cut off their heads and paraded them in Qabridahare. Thousands of people were killed during the period of unrest from 1948-1964.

There was consensus among the public on the question of the liberation of the homeland. Furthermore, the grass roots were already prepared by the underground movement. As a result, the Ogaden Liberation Front/Nasrullah was able to organize a guerrilla fighting force within days and to undertake armed engagement all over the Ogaden region in few weeks.

The resistance movement started its offences with the attacks on Elkere in June 1963 and took offensive campaigns against the occupation forces in all the main towns and restricted the movements of the Ethiopian forces between the towns. The resistance movement intensified the fighting in early 1964 and inflicted heavy casualties on the occupation forces of Ethiopia.

In response to the defeat of its forces by the liberation forces, the Ethiopian government accused the new Somali state of being responsible for the fighting and invaded Somalia, by land and air, in January 1964. The second clash took place between the Ethiopian and Somali forces at the border town of Tug Wajale during the period February 6–8. The Ethiopian invading army was repulsed and despite some heavy casualties on both sides, the Ethiopian forces were eventually defeated by the Somali army. In addition to the land invasion, the Ethiopian aircraft raided targets far into Somalia, including Hargeisa, Somalia's second-largest city.

The Organization of African Unity (OAU) finally tried to mediate the conflict and held a preliminary discussion about the problem at Dar-es-Salaam, Tanzania, in February 1964. The OAU foreign ministers discussed the problem in depth afterwards in Lagos, Nigeria, but further referred it to the OAU Heads of State meeting in Cairo in July 1964. Meanwhile, with the help of Sudan, the two countries had agreed in March 1964, in Khartoum, to a ceasefire and a demilitarized zone. The Cairo meeting was not fruitful because at that summit the African leaders adopted the so-called Cairo Declaration, which reaffirmed Article III, Paragraph 3, which demands that the OAU members accept the colonial boundaries. As a result of the OAU summit failure to support the Ogaden cause and the March ceasefire agreement between Ethiopia and Somalia, the liberation movement in the Ogaden could not continue the armed struggle, and the fighting ceased completely in 1965. The struggle, however, continued on the political and diplomatic fronts and both the Ethiopian and the Somali sides began to prepare for the next challenge.

5.3 The Aftermath of the 1964 Ogaden War

5.31 The Détente Policy of Somalia

The détente policy pursued by Somalia in the period 1967–69 was in sharp contrast to the Somali unification efforts made by previous Somali governments. The policy was single-handedly initiated by the then prime minister, Mohamed Ibrahim Igal, who had long held strong private convictions about what he considered to be suicidal policies that the government of the Somali Republic had followed during the time of his predecessors. Those policies had, in his view, neither gained international support for the government of Somalia nor contributed to the internal economic and social development of Somalia. Furthermore, he was a critic of the Somali government's diplomatic break-up with Britain in 1963 and he wanted to improve ties with the West.

The prime minister questioned the viability of the Somali unification dream in the face of regional and international opposition to the Somali cause. The détente policy, which the new prime minister promptly embarked upon, however, brought a great dilemma to the Somali government. On the one hand, abandoning the Somali cause was not imaginable to any Somali leader, given the popular support for it; and whatever the cost the prime minister could not of course repudiate – at least publicly – the self-determination rights for the Somalis in the Ogaden, the NFD and Djibouti. On the other hand, the governments of Kenya and Ethiopia demanded categorical renunciation by the government of Somalia of its territorial claims as a condition for normalization of relations. Despite the difficulties, premier Igal was determined to trade between those two thin threads and decided to see what might be achieved by more conciliatory diplomacy.

The dilemma was exacerbated by the US government's response to Igal's détente policies. Although the US government welcomed the Somali move to normalize relations with Kenya and Ethiopia, it refused to mediate between Somalia and its neighbours. The US government argued that the parties directly concerned in the conflict should work out enduring solutions to their problems. Further, it urged all the parties to contribute to a solution by concessions to and modification of positions that had led to the disputes and related tensions. The US government believed that Somalia's territorial claims were the chief cause of the conflict and thus considered the concessions of Somalia as the key to the solution. For the détente policies to succeed, the US government demanded specifically that Somalia demonstrate that it was prepared to live in peace and cooperation with its neighbours, indicate its willingness to stop giving material and training to the Somali dissidents who operate within Kenya and Ethiopia and cease inflammatory exhortations in the press and on the radio.

Premier Igal, who was long known in Somalia for his pro-West politics, was very keen to improve Somalia's relations with the West and to win American support for his plan. He also realized that the Somali government had to take the initiative, in order to get the support he needed, and thus positively responded to the US demands. He promised the US government that he would make a serious effort to halt 'violent' actions by Somali dissidents in Kenya and Ethiopia; and that though the Somali government could not control fully Somalis outside the republic, his government would make a maximum effort in that regard. He also requested to meet US president Johnson to personally explain to him his new policies in the region. The US government, however, wanted more progress in relations with the neighbours before such a meeting could take place.

Following encouraging exchanges with the Ethiopian emperor Haile Selassie at the OAU Heads of State meeting at Kinshasa, Congo, in September 1967, Premier Igal met President Kenyatta at Arusha, Tanzania, in October of that year. After the meetings, diplomatic relations with Kenya and Ethiopia, as well as Britain, were resumed. Furthermore, Igal completely reversed Somalia's policies towards the resistance movements in the missing territories. Putting his chips on a turnaround from belligerence to détente with Ethiopia and Kenya, he not only stopped assistance to the Somali resistance in the Ogaden and NFD, but he also made every effort to silence them.

By the beginning of 1968, the US government was so pleased with the progress the Somali government made regarding détente policy that it invited Igal to the White House on March 14, 1968. However, despite the warm welcome, the US government's responses to the Somali requests for political and economic assistance were not encouraging. The Somali government asked the US government to mediate between Somalia and its neighbours (Ethiopia and Kenya) and persuade them to be more responsive to its effort to improve relations with them. On the economic side, it wanted more assistance in general and the designation of Somalia as an aid-emphasis country in particular. On the latter, Igal returned with an economic assistance agreement of $1.1 million and a promise for further assistance through the East African common market, if Somalia joined that market. On the détente policies, he was urged to take further steps to normalize relations with Somalia's neighbours and to apply for the membership of the East African market.

The détente policy had neither the support of the Somali public nor the full backing of the president in the first place. The public viewed the détente policy as a 'sell-out' to Ethiopia and Kenya and President Shermarke, who was a strong supporter of the idea of Greater Somalia, was not prepared to abandon the idea under any circumstance. Igal wished to renounce Somalia's territorial goals in exchange for Western economic support. However, he did not achieve substantial economic assistance from the West. The lack of concession from the neighbours on the Somali cause and the US government's refusal to put Somalia on the preferred list for US economic assistance further confirmed the public's view about the policy, and the disagreement between the president and the prime minister over the issue eventually paralyzed the working of the government. In the end, the détente policy contributed to the downfall of civilian rule.

5.3.2 The Ogaden Cause

The war between Somalia and Ethiopia over the Ogaden region in 1964 on the one hand publicised the conflict and brought that cause to the regional and international arenas. After the war, the OAU and some individual member-states like Sudan tried to mediate the conflict and the US government encouraged those mediation efforts. On the other hand, the war contributed to the misconception of the Ogaden cause. The conflict was originally between the occupied Somalis in the Ogaden and the Ethiopian occupiers, and the liberation of those oppressed Somalis in the Ogaden was the goal of that just cause. Because of the Ethiopian manipulation, the conflict was portrayed afterwards as a border dispute between Ethiopia and Somalia.

Ethiopia skilfully manipulated the OAU during the establishment of the organization and later after it succeeded in making Addis Ababa its permanent seat. Haile Selassie used the experience advantage he possessed over his counterparts to promote Ethiopia's territorial goals. By the time most African countries were gaining their independence, Haile Selassie was a well-known figure on the international stage. The defeat of Italy by Ethiopia at Adowa in 1896 and the Italian occupation of Ethiopia forty years later made Ethiopia and Haile Selassie famous. The first one (the defeat of the European state) gave Ethiopia a prestigious image, whereas the latter made Ethiopia a victim. Ethiopia benefited immensely from both images. The victor image enabled her to participate in the scramble for the Horn of Africa and to occupy territories three times larger than she originally possessed, and the victim image allowed her to get away with the land she occupied.

Ethiopia was instrumental in forming the OAU and because of Haile Selassie's prestige as an elderly African statesman, his long experience in international diplomacy and his hospitality to the African leaders when they gathered in Addis Ababa in 1963, he was able to persuade the new leaders to accept the kind of organization he wanted to create. Before the announcement of the establishment of the organization, Haile Selassie secured backing from the African leaders on the boundary issue. His motive was to legitimize the occupation of the Ogaden and other occupied territories, but the emperor presented the issue as an African one and he successfully convinced the heads of state that the stability of the continent lay with the preservation of the colonial borders. Because of the arbitrary colonial borders that divided communities and tribes in many African countries and the lack of visionary leaders determined to face the real problem and ignorance on the part of the leaders about the true nature of the Ethiopian empire, the leaders approved Haile Selassie's proposal of recognizing the colonial boundaries. The adoption of this principle was a big diplomatic breakthrough for the Ethiopian emperor.

The Charter of the OAU was adopted by a conference of heads of state and government in Addis Ababa on 25 May 1963, and at that very first meeting Article III of the Charter was adopted as a result of Ethiopian efforts. The article demands respect for the sovereignty and territorial integrity of each member state and its inalienable right to independent existence. After securing that diplomatic victory, Haile Selassie provoked Somalia, by attacking the Somali state instead of the Ogaden Liberation Front. He used the principle of accepting the colonially set borders and the principle of non-interference in internal affairs of another African country to isolate Somalia.

The inexperienced Somali leaders themselves contributed to the isolation of their country by refusing to accept the colonially set borders and thus breaching the rule of the game outlined in Article III Paragraph 3 of the OAU charter, and reaffirmed by the declaration at the Cairo Assembly of Heads of State and Government of the OAU, 17–21 July 1964. The Somalis had every right to liberate the three missing parts of their nation, and the Somali-Ethiopian border was provisional because Italy and Ethiopia never agreed on a permanent boundary (see Appendix 4). However, the method by which Somalia wanted to achieve that goal was in direct conflict with the charter of the OAU, and played into the hands of the Ethiopian leaders. As Ethiopia wanted, the Ogaden cause became a border dispute in which Somalia is seen as the aggressor and Ethiopia as the victim. As a result of this wrong image of the Ogaden cause, Ethiopia succeeded in misleading world opinion. Because of the incorrect interpretation of the conflict, those who tried to mediate took the wrong approach and, as a result, it was not possible to find a solution to the problem.

The détente policy pursued by Igal in the period 1967–69 further undermined the liberation efforts in both the Ogaden and NFD. That government not only cut the supply lines of the resistance movements in the Ogaden and NFD, but also agreed to a joint military commission to monitor the boundaries. Furthermore, she stopped some programmes from Radio Mogadishu, which used to encourage resistance. In exchange for promised economic assistance and participation in the East African common market, the government of Somalia took those policies, which reversed the liberation policies and damaged the Somali cause. In the end, the economic assistance that was promised did not materialize and

Somalia failed to achieve any of its objectives.

Despite this unfortunate situation of presenting the Ogaden conflict as a dispute between Somalia and Ethiopia and the subsequent presentation of the occupier as a victim, and the retreat of Somalia from the cause, after the introduction of the détente policies, the people the conflict was concerned with continued their resistance under the leadership of the Ogaden Liberation Front, which led the struggle and represented the people of the region. Its army was, however, dispersed in 1965 following the Khartoum Agreement of March 1964 between Ethiopia and Somalia. But despite the restrictions imposed on it by Somalia, after the agreement, it continued not only to exist but made its own preparation for inevitable future conflicts with Ethiopia.

Although Somalia froze the military activities of the resistance movement and restricted the diplomatic movements of the Liberation Front, the resistance movement's office in Mogadishu continued to operate informally under the leadership of Sheikh Ibrahim Hashi who led the Nasrallah movement before the Hodayo conference and Mohamed Diriye Urdoh. The movement opened offices in some of the progressive Arab countries such as Syria and Iraq, and behind the scenes, it was in preparation throughout the period 1965–1975. By 1976 the reorganization of the movement was complete. Among the issues discussed during the preparation period was the name of the new organization. The members of the movement were sharply divided over the name. Some of them preferred the use of the name 'Western Somali', while the majority was in favour of the name 'Ogaden'. Eventually, the Somali government intervened and recommended the use of the name Western Somali and its position on the issue prevailed: a new organization by the name of the Western Somali Liberation Front (WSLF) was established. The WSLF led the Ogaden struggle for freedom from 1976 and Abdullahi Hassan Mohamoud became its first leader.

5.3.3 Arms Race and Superpower Rivalry: The General Picture

The arms race between Ethiopia and Somalia and the subsequent superpower rivalry in the region were the most obvious results of the Ogaden conflict. Ethiopia and Somalia agreed to a ceasefire and Somalia even pursued a policy of détente when Igal came to power in 1967, but the differences over the central issue of the Ogaden grew wider and thus both Ethiopia and Somalia saw the inevitability of future conflicts. As a result, each country pursued diplomatic campaigns both within the African context and within the wider world to promote its case and isolate its opponent. Somalia denounced Ethiopia for its colonial ambitions and the subjugation of the Somalis in the Ogaden, whereas Ethiopia accused Somalia of aggression and invasion of its territory. Military build-up and an arms race went hand in hand with the diplomatic offensive. Both countries saw the necessity of increasing their military capabilities and both turned to the superpowers to realize that goal. Ethiopia went to its old ally the US to upgrade the military assistance she had been getting since 1953 and Somalia sought the help of the Soviet Union. For their part, both the superpowers wanted to have maximum influence in the region without taking part in the conflict, but reluctantly they were dragged into it.

The US government wanted to maintain its Kagenew base as well as its friendly relationship with Ethiopia, while at the same time keeping the Soviets out of Somalia. While supporting Ethiopia's territorial integrity the US also wanted economic development and an easing of the harsh Ethiopian policies in the Ogaden. Further, it encouraged and economically supported the so-called moderate elements within the Somali government, to help them gain power, and promised them increased economic assistance and improvement of the lives of the Somalis in the Ogaden and NFD if they agreed to the US plan of regional economic integration. On the question of the territorial dispute, the US avoided direct involvement and referred the matter to the OAU. It argued that it was an African issue and encouraged the OAU and individual African countries such as Sudan to mediate.

The Soviet Union's motive was similar to that of the US. It wanted to dominate the region and reduce the American influence as much as possible. The Soviet Union strongly opposed the Bevin plan for the reunification of the Somali territories, and it did not change its mind on that issue, despite its friendly relationship with Somalia. Like the US, however, it favoured some kind of settlement for the Ogaden region within the Ethiopian context. Although it would not allow Somalia to attack Ethiopia, especially with Soviet-supplied weapons, it wanted to strengthen the capability of the Somali army to put pressure on Ethiopia to accept a negotiated settlement over the issue. The Communist bloc countries also promised substantial economic and military assistance to Ethiopia – provided that it switched to their side – and hoped that she would eventually abandon the West and could find a solution to the Ogaden problem after she joined their club.

In the end, neither could the Soviet persuade the Ethiopian emperor to switch sides nor was the US able to persuade the Somalis to abandon their cause, whatever the cost. Thus, the hostility between Ethiopia and Somalia continued, and the superpowers were dragged reluctantly into the conflict and the consequent arms race between Somalia and Ethiopia. In the following, we will go through the background of superpower involvement in the region, the effect of the Ogaden conflict on superpower rivalry and the arms race in the Horn of Africa.

5.3.4 Arms Race and Superpower Rivalry: The Ethio-US Alliance

American and Ethiopian diplomatic relations began in 1903 with the Skinner Mission, named after the American envoy, Robert P. Skinner, who was commissioned by President Theodore Roosevelt to go to Ethiopia and negotiate a commercial treaty. Skinner signed a treaty of friendship and commerce with Menelik on 27 December 1903. A rapid expansion of trade between the two countries by the end of the nineteenth century was the main reason for the mission, and after the treaty, trade increased further. Ethiopia exported to the US coffee, hides and skins and imported from the US cotton cloth termed *merikani*. 'In 1902, the US bought $820,443 worth of Ethiopian coffee. The total Ethiopian foreign trade (imports and exports) amounted to $2, 316 000 in 1902 and the American share was $1, 389 000 – 59 per cent. Of this, $579,000 was accounted for *merikani* exports to Ethiopia, $675,000 by imports to the US of Ethiopian hides and skins and $135,000 by coffee imports. In 1905/6 *merikani* accounted for half of all Ethiopia's recorded cotton imports.'[1]

Despite the great trade with Ethiopia, the American diplomatic involvement in the Horn was minimal until the end of the Second World War, mainly because of the European powers' engagement there. Haile Selassie met President Franklin D. Roosevelt in 1945 in Egypt and this meeting was the starting point of American engagement in the region. In that meeting, Haile Selassie offered the American president concession rights for American oil companies to prospect for oil in the Ogaden, which at that time was under British rule. The emperor intended the concession primarily to insert sovereign rights over the Ogaden and get American backing for that claim. Haile Selassie's attempt to acquire the Ogaden by granting a concession to the Americans to exploit its natural resources was not only illegal but absurd. However, in terms of the real politics of the day, it was a clever move. Although America had great sympathy for Ethiopia because of the victim image she acquired after the

---

[1] Paul B. Henze, 2000, *Layers of Time, A History of Ethiopia*, Hurst & Co Ltd, page176.

fascist occupation of Ethiopia, still the Ethio-US diplomatic relationship was based on trade, and thus Haile Selassie thought that the concession for the exploitation of Ogaden resources would encourage the business-minded Americans to back his claim to the Ogaden. But as stated by Bahru Zewde, the US government hesitated to support Ethiopia's claim to the Ogaden at that stage:

> In 1945, the emperor met President Franklin D. Roosevelt in Egypt, and discussed issues of vital concern to Ethiopia at the time – Eritrea, the Ogaden and the railway. The granting of concession to the American Sinclair Company to prospect for oil in the Ogaden was designed as much to reassert Ethiopia's rights in the region as out of eagerness to exploit a lucrative natural resource. But the Americans were not particularly keen about giving diplomatic support to Ethiopia's territorial claims, or about offering the military assistance that the Ethiopian government so persistently and ardently requested.[2]

The Ethio-US relationship reached a turning point in 1953. Because of the British withdrawal of the program known as the British Military Mission to Ethiopia (BMME), and the Egyptian revolution in 1952, the US government changed its regional strategy and became more involved in Ethiopia. Britain assisted the Ethiopian government with the organization, training and administration of its army through the BMME until late 1950 when the programme was withdrawn. The vacuum left by Britain was filled by the US in 1953. 'The withdrawal of the BMME in late 1950 leant weight to the Ethiopian request for military assistance. The Egyptian revolution of 1952 forced on Washington a rethinking of its alignments in the Middle East and the Red Sea. These developments formed the background for the Ethio-US Treaty of 1953, which defined the relationship between the two countries in the following decades.'[3]

As part of the treaty, the US was given a communication base in Asmara, which became known as Kagenew base. In return for continued use of the communication base in Asmara, the US government committed to upgrading Ethiopia's military capabilities. 'The United States undertook to launch a military aid programme. A Unit called the Military Assistance Advisory Group (MAAG) was set up to train three divisions, each of 6,000 men at 5 million US dollars. The USA made further commitments to military assistance in subsequent years. By 1970,

---

[2] Bahru Zewde, 1991, *A History of Modern Ethiopia (1855–1974)*, James Currey, pages 184–185.
[3] Bahru Zewde, 1991, *A History of Modern Ethiopia (1855–1974)*, page 185.

Ethiopia had come to absorb some 60% of US military aid to the whole of Africa.'[4]

As we explained in earlier sections, the American heavy involvement helped the Ethiopians a great deal in reoccupying the Ogaden in 1948 and 1955. In the war over the Ogaden in 1964 between Somalia and Ethiopia, the USA backed the Ethiopian occupation of the territory and, as a result, the Ethio-US relationship was further strengthened. In addition to diplomatic support, the US gave Ethiopia the lion's share of its military assistance to Africa, but the Ethiopians wanted more. Although Ethiopia was getting more than half of the US military assistance to the whole of Africa, it continued to press for more military assistance using the Ogaden conflict as a pretext. Although the US government was willing to give more help to Ethiopia, the American diplomats became concerned during the 1960s about the unending press for more military assistance. Expressing their concern, some US diplomats predicted that the situation would get worse instead of better and that even if they continued to raise the ante every time the Ethiopians pressed them, there would eventually come a time when that type of haggling would break down. They further argued that US relations with Ethiopia would inevitably deteriorate unless the US government took the initiative. To find a mechanism for controlling the ever-increasing Ethiopian demand for more military assistance and at the same time meet the Ethiopian desire, the diplomats recommended basing the programme on the development of effective Ethiopian military forces.

Because of those concerns and its commitment to assist in improving the capability and efficiency of the Ethiopian military forces, in 1964 the US government accepted the recommendation of its diplomats and based its military assistance programme on the development of an effective Ethiopian Military force. Under the new approach, the US government was to assist the Ethiopian government in building an efficient army and air force capable of maintaining internal security and legitimate self-defence which would permit Ethiopia to participate as appropriate in defence of the area or in UN collective security arrangements and measures. Priority was given to organize, equip, train and support an effective Ethiopian army of 40 000, and air force and naval forces, as rapidly as Ethiopian capabilities would permit. The package also included an additional jet squadron of 12 F-5 aircraft over several years and the continued support of the F-86 and T-28D squadrons. Under the new approach military assistance rose sharply.

---

[4] Bahru Zewde, 1991, *A History of Modern Ethiopia (1855–1974)*, page 186.

All in all, American military assistance was enormous during the rule of Haile Selassie and especially after the Ogaden war. 'American military influence was most evident in the fields of training and equipment. US military aid in the period between 1946 and1972 came to over $US180 million. Over 2,500 Ethiopians underwent diverse forms of military training in the United States between 1953 and 1968. The jet aircraft, anti-tank and anti-aircraft weapons, naval craft, infantry weapons and sometimes even the uniforms were of American origin. In both equipment and training, the air force remained the most prestigious showpiece of American military aid in Ethiopia. It was also reputedly the most modern and efficient unit of the armed forces.'[5]

American assistance to Ethiopia was not confined to military aid. In almost all aspects of Ethiopian life, the Americans left their mark. The American assistance was particularly valuable in the areas of civil aviation, education, the road network, communications and banking.

5.3.5 Arms Race and Superpower Rivalry: The Somali-Soviet Alliance

The Somali-Soviet diplomatic relationship started with the birth of Somalia in 1960, and that relationship warmed up after the Western countries ignored Somalia's security needs and the Soviet Union filled the vacuum. To maintain its internal and external security needs, Somalia tried to build an army after independence. Like any other nation Somalia needed a defence force and besides the search for the lost territories (the Ogaden, the NFD and Djibouti) to which Somalia was committed necessitated the need to organize a defence force with at least equal capabilities to that of its main opponent, namely Ethiopia. In 1960 at the time of Somalia's independence, Ethiopia created a security problem for Somalia because by then it already had three army divisions and the bodyguard. To realize its goal, Somalia first went to the US and sought military assistance, but because of its alliance with Ethiopia, US assistance was not forthcoming. The US and its allies provided some assistance to the Somali police, but they were not prepared to support the army Somalia wanted to build. The Soviet Union was, however, willing to meet Somalia's military needs. In November 1963 it was officially announced that the Republic had refused an offer of Western military assistance valued at almost £6.5m in favour of Russian military aid to the tune of nearly £11 million. By 1962 the Soviet Union had agreed to grant loans

---

[5] 5 Bahru Zewde, 1991, A History of Modern Ethiopia (1855–1974), page 186.

that eventually reached $52million and to help build a 14 000-troop army. The Soviet Union provided the Somali army with T-34 tanks, armoured personnel carriers, and MiG-15 and MiG-17 aircraft. Some 300 Soviet advisers worked in Somalia and more than 500 Somali personnel were trained in the Soviet Union during the 1960s.

The clashes between Ethiopia and Somalia in 1964 over the Ogaden, in which the US supported the Ethiopian territorial claim, and the resistance activities in the NFD during the 1960s further widened the gap between the US and Somalia and pushed Somalia to the Eastern bloc countries. A military agreement was signed between Somalia and the Soviet Union in 1962 and, as a result, Somalia's parliamentary regime became more dependent on the Soviet Union. Despite the détente policy pursued by the Igal government in the period 1967–69, Somalia not only relied on the Soviet Union for military and economic assistance but moved further to that bloc after the military regime took over the power in Somalia in 1969.

Soon after the takeover, the military government of Mohamed Siyad Barre indicated its willingness to strengthen Somali-Soviet ties and took several steps in that direction. On the foreign policy, the military regime denounced the US as imperialist, anti-Muslim and against Somali unification efforts. The Somali public shared that view with the new government, and they cheered the government when, in December 1969, it gave the US Peace Corps volunteers notice to leave the country in two weeks. Other signals included changing the name of the Somali Republic to the Democratic Republic of Somalia, proclaiming the state as a scientific socialist with more state control of the economy and social life. The alliance was strengthened further by the treaty of friendship and cooperation, which Somalia and the Soviet Union signed in 1974. The military government under Mohamed Siyad Bare had already built one of the strongest armies in black Africa by that time. After the treaty, Somalia further upgraded its military capabilities.

During the 1960s the Soviet Union provided Somalia with a substantial number of T-34 tanks, armoured personnel carriers, MiG 15 and MiG 17 aircraft, small arms and ammunition. After the signing of the 1974 Treaty of Friendship, the Soviet Union increased its military assistance to Somalia. The military hardware Somalia received from the Soviet Union during the 1970s included 50 MiG 21 jet fighters, a squadron of 11–28 bombers, 150 T-35 and 100 T-54 tanks, a SAMA-2 and a modern torpedo and missile-armed fast attack and landing craft for the navy. By the time the Soviets were expelled from Somalia in 1977, about 2 400 Somali military personnel had undergone training in the

Soviet Union and another 150 in Eastern Europe. About 3 600 Soviet advisers were stationed in Somalia to train the Somali army and other government workers.

6

Prelude to the 1977/78 Ogaden War

The Revival of the Ogaden Resistance Movement; the emboldening of the Somali state; Somalia's diplomatic efforts' failures; Ethiopia's preference for a military resolution

The strength of the Somali state, the independence of Djibouti, pressure from the Somali inhabitants in the Ogaden and the regime change in Ethiopia were among the factors that contributed to the intensification of the national unification efforts, the reactivation of the armed struggle in the Ogaden and the ensuing confrontation between Somalia and Ethiopia. How much these factors contributed to the war and whether all diplomatic channels were exhausted before the war are the focus of our investigation here.

6.1 The Revival of the Ogaden Resistance Movement

During the period 1965–75, Somalia did not allow the Somali resistance movements in the NFD and Ogaden to fully operate in Somalia, and all armed engagements from within its territory were terminated after the introduction of the détente policy in 1967, although she was active on the diplomatic front for the Somali cause to some extent. The military government, which took power in 1969, denounced the détente policy pursued by its predecessor while at the same time keeping the restriction on the activities of the Somali resistance in the Ogaden and the NFD. Several factors led to the policy changes towards the resistance. The regime change in Ethiopia and pressure from the Somalis in the Ogaden were the main reasons. The Western Somalis in the Somali government, the veteran liberation fighters and the young intelligentsia were the main pressure groups that lobbied for the resumption of the armed struggle in the Ogaden. The Ogaden Liberation Front, which was established in Hodayo in 1963, gradually disintegrated. By 1975 the Western Somali people decided to revitalize the liberation movement and Somalia reluctantly agreed the following year.

Having secured the backing of the Somali government, the grassroots began to reorganize the liberation front. In January 1976, a general conference was held at a place called Yaqbadhiweyn near Balidogle, about 100 km from Mogadishu. All sections of Western Somali society, especially those living in Somalia, as well as important people from the Somali government attended the conference. There were differences of opinion among delegates about the future name of the organization as well as about the leadership direction. The people disagreed on whether to revive the OLF or form a new organization, namely the Western Somali Liberation Front.

On the recommendation of the Somali government, the Western Somali Liberation Front (WSLF) was formed. The organizational structure of the WSLF, as well as the strategy of the struggle, was adopted in that conference and new leadership was elected. Abdullahi Hassan Mohamoud became the new leader of the WSLF. The WSLF took the leadership role of the struggle for the liberation of the Ogaden region soon after its establishment and became the political representative of the inhabitants of the region.

A 25-member committee was elected to lead the WSLF, and the Liberation Front began to reorganize itself and make the necessary preparation for the armed struggle in 1976 after it got the green light from the Somali government to do so. The leader, Abdullahi Hassan Mohamoud, was a well-educated man with both administrative experience and great communication skills. He previously worked at the Department of Education in Somalia, both as a teacher and an administrator. However, he had limited experience in the struggle and that was his main weakness. In an extraordinary meeting, which was held in November 1978 as the term of the central committee was coming to an end, the number of Central Committee members was increased to over 150 and Abdullahi Hassan retained his position as leader.

With assistance from the government of Somalia, the leadership of the organization opened training camps in 1976; first inside Somalia and later in the Ogaden. Freedom fighters were recruited from all over the Ogaden region and trained in those camps which the WSLF set up. The first training camp was opened in Qoriley inside Somalia, and throughout the year the resistance fighters were preparing themselves in that camp. Later, when the armed resistance began its operations in the Ogaden, the training camp was closed and, instead, mobile training camps were set up inside the Ogaden region. The training included military, medical, and communications. Having completed their training, they went ahead with their liberation mission.

6.2 The Emboldening of the Somali State: Building the

State and Broadening the Anti-Colonial Front

The problems that the post-independence governments faced were also pressing the revolutionary government of Mohamed Siyad Barre. State-building and the unification of the Somali nation were the prime focus of both regimes. Both the civilian governments and the military regime attempted to build the independent state and at the same time liberate the missing parts of the Somali nation and incorporate them into Somalia. We are not investigating here all the factors that contributed to the success or failure of the government regarding these two related issues, but simply how internal progress and the search for the missing parts affected one another during that period.

The main internal problems for which the military government was to find immediate solutions were the language script, which the civilian government could not solve, and the economy. In dealing with these issues the government's ideological approach was scientific socialism and its practical tool was the crush programmes. On the first anniversary of the revolution (21 October 1970), the president proclaimed that Somalia would henceforth be a socialist state and declared that what he called 'scientific socialism' would be the guideline for state policies. 'Scientific socialism (in Somali literally, "wealth-sharing based on wisdom" – *hanti-wadaaga ilmi ku dhisan*), was now the cornerstone of official policy, closely linked with the ideals of unity or 'togetherness' (*waddajir*), 'self-reliance' (*is ku kalsonnaan*) and 'self-help' (*iskaa wah u qabso*).'[1] However, as is evident from his economic policies, scientific socialism did not mean for Siyad Barre sharing the wealth of private individuals. It was merely a framework for a set of policies that the government wanted to carry out collectively, and scientific socialism provided the collective consciousness required to carry them forward. Using the twin banners of self-help and self-reliance, the government successfully carried out many national policies in the areas of economic development, literacy public institutions, etc.

Although the government carried out many socialist policies such as the nationalization of some private industries, for the Somali leader scientific socialism was no more than rhetoric, and nationalization was more showmanship than a radical change in the economy. Siyad Barre relied on the Soviet Union for advice and assistance, but unlike the Somali leftist intellectuals, he was not a committed socialist, and in fact

---

[1] I.M. Lewis, 2002, *A Modern History of the Somali*, James Currey, page 209.

the Somali economy during the socialist period was a mixed one. For example, animal herds were not nationalised, and Siyad Barre assured the pastoralists that socialism would not affect their animals. Furthermore, to encourage international investment, in 1972 he announced a liberal investment code.

The government relied on crush programmes for the most direct implementation of its revolutionary ideals, especially in the economic sector. The creation of the cooperatives was one of the main elements of the socialist programmes. The authorities had set up many agricultural cooperatives in many parts of the country. In 1973 the government decreed the law on cooperative fund development, with most funding going into the agricultural sector. During the period before the revolution, agricultural programmes had received less than 10 per cent of total spending, but by 1974 the figure was 29.1 per cent. Cooperatives also aimed at the nomads, although on a smaller scale. The 1974–78 development plan allocated 4.2 per cent of the budget funds to livestock. Government officials argued that the scientific management of the rangeland, the regeneration of grazing land and the drilling of new water holes, would be possible only under socialist cooperation. In the 14 government-established cooperatives, each family received an exclusive area of 200 to 300 hectares of grazing land; in times of drought, common land under reserve was to become available. The government committed itself to provide educational and health services as well as serving as a market outlet for excess stock. Despite the major drought that devastated the pastoral economy during 1974/75, the rural economy had shown encouraging signs. Siyad's government also established fishing cooperatives in several districts, and in 1973 such cooperatives were established at Eyl, Gudale and Barawe.

The revolutionary government was keen to promote industrialization and the investment of the industrial sector increased sharply. It had established many factories and among those were a tomato-canning factory, a wheat flour factory, a pasta factory and a milk factory. It also opened a plant that manufactured cardboard boxes, established several grain mills and a petroleum refinery and put into operation a meat processing plant as well as a fish-processing factory. The overall picture of the economy in the first half of the 1970s was good and the government was praised for its handling of the drought disaster.

The writing of the Somali language and the literacy campaign that followed were, however, the most spectacular achievements of the government. In 1973, the government decided to adopt the Roman alphabet as the official script for the national language, Somali. The successful urban literacy campaign of 1973 was followed by a second literacy campaign, which concentrated on the rural districts and which also achieved its aim. 'Although the government's initial emphasis was on urban literacy, in March 1974 a major effort was made to promote rural literacy. Previous rural literacy campaigns had failed because of the nomadic resistance, the lack of a script for the indigenous language, and the necessity to teach a foreign language as well. But this time secondary schools were closed for a year so that student teachers could teach the nomads in their common language. Vast strides were made in the development of rural literacy. The Ministry of Information and National Guidance estimated a countrywide literacy rate of 55 per cent in 1975, as opposed to a 5 per cent literacy rate before the adoption of a national script.'[2]

Increased literacy, cross-sector economic investment, and uniform education contributed to the reduction in inequality that the government was pushing for. As the Somali language became the official language, knowledge of foreign languages ceased as a requirement for most jobs and thus the Western-educated privileged group, which was the backbone of the civil service, lost much of its power as a result of the adoption of the Somali script. Furthermore, the agricultural and pastoral sectors, which had been neglected by the civilian governments, got their share of economic investment and that led to more redistribution of wealth. In addition, as the state became more active it became more powerful. State control was evident in both the urban and rural sectors, and the government was able to mobilize both the urban and rural populations easily. All in all, Somalia became a more organised state under the effective control of the government.

The success story of the military government boosted its confidence and, as a result, it became more outward-looking and more active in foreign policy. Of course, Somalia's foreign policy preoccupation with the missing parts of its nation remained the same, but it combined its pan-Somalism banner with a pan-Africanism slogan partly to change the 'bad boy' image it got in its earlier confrontation with Ethiopia and Kenya. Somalia was ready to widen the liberation struggle by supporting liberation movements elsewhere in Africa and to contribute to the stability of the continent by mediating inter-African conflicts, while at the same time continuing the struggle for the unification of the Somali

---

[2] David D. Laitin & Said S. Samatar, 1987, *Somalia, A Nation in Search of a State*, Westview Press, page 83.

nation.

Having built one of the strongest armies in sub-Saharan Africa, dealt with most of the pressing internal issues and consolidated the authority of the regime, Siyad Barre turned to the big issue of Somali unification. The dramatic progress which had been achieved on these fronts encouraged in the second phase of Siyad's government a more extrovert policy with greater involvement in external affairs, both locally and internationally. Tentative steps had already been taken in this direction on several occasions—for instance, in 1972 when Somalia successfully mediated in the confrontation between Uganda and Tanzania. But this forward external policy assumed much greater prominence in 1974 when, having joined the Arab League as the only non-Arabic-speaking member state, Somalia also acted as host for the Organization of African Unity.[3]

Somalia returned to the struggle of pan-Somalism after nearly a decade of détente or restraint policy. However, the military government's diplomatic approach was different from that of the previous civilian governments. The military regime presented itself as the champion of freedom and wanted to lead the anti-imperialist movements throughout the continent. It supported the liberation efforts in Mozambique, South Africa, Eritrea and Angola and presented the liberation of the Somali territories as part of the wider anti-imperialism struggle. Despite the extension of the anti-colonial struggle to the other parts of the continent, Somalia did not support the resumption of the struggle in all the three missing parts of the Somali lands. To lighten the burden, it concentrated on the Ogaden and supported the wind of change that began to blow in favour of the Somalis and independence fighters in Djibouti.

6.3 The Emboldening of the Somali State: The Independence of Djibouti

Using the divide-and-rule tactic, the French empowered the Afar politicians headed by Ali Arif Bourhan, who had favoured continued French rule of the territory since the independence of Somalia. It regarded pan-Somalism as a threat to be resisted and the Somali politicians had been marginalized since 1959, because of their demand for independence and, as a result, Somali-French relations deteriorated. Furthermore, France and Ethiopia cooperated and closely coordinated their policies in containing pan-Somalism. By the mid-1970s, however, the wind of freedom has reached Djibouti and the French realized that

---

[3] I. M. Lewis, 2002, *A Modern History of the Somali*, page 226.

they could not hold the territory any longer.

In December 1975, following a meeting between the premier Ali Arif Bourhan and the French president Giscard d' Estaing, it was announced that the territory would be granted independence, with France retaining a local military base. The background for the announcement was a division within the Afar and a stepped campaign by the Somalis. The Afars in Ethiopia formed a liberation front and clashed with Ethiopian forces. The anti-Ethiopian sentiment that followed divided the Afar community in both Djibouti and Ethiopia and the anti-Ethiopian and French voices became louder than those of their supporters. As a result, the Afars and the Somalis were able to form a united front against the French occupation and Ali Arif Bourhan lost the support of the Afars and was forced to resign in 1976. He was succeeded by Abdallah Muhammed Kamil, an Afar married to a Somali. The new premier headed an interim coalition government including all the main parties and was instructed to prepare the territory for independence. In November 1976 it was announced that the territory would gain independence the following summer and talks on the preparation for independence were held in Paris in March 1977. The main parties attended the meeting and the participants agreed to hold a referendum in May on the issue of independence as well as elections for an enlarged assembly. With a turnout of 77 per cent, 99 per cent of the voters voted for independence. At midnight on 27 June, under the name of the Republic of Djibouti, the territory became independent and Hassan Guled became its first president.

6.4 Somalia's Diplomatic Efforts' Failures

Siyad Barre was encouraged by the 1976 independence plan announcement of Djibouti and the instability in Ethiopia following the overthrow of Haile Selassie in 1974, and at the same time was pressured by the Somalis in the Ogaden, especially the Western Somali Liberation Front (WSLF) and the Somali Ogaden members in the government and armed forces, to support the liberation efforts in the Ogaden. President Barre eventually agreed to lift the restriction imposed on the resistance and to support the WSLF in its preparation for the armed struggle. The president, however, wished to start the struggle with diplomacy to see if Somali goals could be realized by peaceful means.

The government tried to find diplomatic support in the OAU and the Arab League for the Somali cause. In past Somalia failed to win the support of the African states, largely because of Haile Selassie's successful diplomatic campaign against the Somali cause and the consequent adoption of Article III by the OAU. But Somalia's standing in the continent had improved since then because of its anti-imperialist campaigns elsewhere in the continent, its successful presidency of the OAU in 1974 and its relative progress domestically. In return for the support Somalia gave to the liberation efforts in other parts of the continent, Siyad Barre expected his counterparts in the continent to be more sympathetic and supportive to the Somali cause. Somalia got some sympathy for the Somali dilemma from some African leaders and, in response to the Somali diplomatic initiatives, the OAU set up a mediation committee headed by president Ja'far Nimeiry of Sudan and General Yakubu Gowon of Nigeria. The committee recommended a joint development of the Ogaden within the context of Ethiopian sovereignty. The committee's declared intention to find a solution to the Ogaden problem within an Ethiopian context was appreciated, but it fell short of the Somali aspiration for a unified nation and thus the position of the OAU remained the same in the Somali view.

Somalia's diplomacy was also unsuccessful in the Arab League for several reasons. The members of the Arab League were divided in terms of alignment and the majority were either on the Soviet or the American side, and both the superpowers worked against the Somali unification efforts and expected their allies to follow suit. To the disbelief of the Somalis, some Arab countries even supported the Ethiopians during the 1977/78 war and sent troops to fight alongside the Ethiopians and against the Somalis.

The third group that Somalia hoped to get support from was the socialist world. On 16 March 1977 two countries of that group, namely South Yemen and Cuba, brought together the Ethiopian and Somali leaders in Yemen in an attempt to mediate the two parties. The plan was to form a loose socialist confederation consisting of Somalia, Ethiopia and South Yemen and to make the Ogaden an autonomous region within Ethiopia. The proposed autonomy by the mediators did not go far enough to satisfy Somali aspirations, while it went too far in the view of the Ethiopian government.

After the fiasco of the peace mission, the Somali and Ethiopian leaders blamed each other for the failures, but the chief mediator, Fidel Castro of Cuba, was more impressed by Mengistu and appeared convinced by the latter's accusation that Siyad Barre was not a committed socialist. Mengistu projected himself as a pro-Soviet, revolutionary leader and a comrade who was committed to the socialist ideals and appealed for the defence of what he called the socialist state under construction in Ethiopia, whereas Siyad Barre concentrated more on the Somali cause and how to end Ethiopian imperialism. Fidel Castro went to East Berlin on 3 April 1977 to report on his African mission and consult with the East German leader Erich Honecker. The transcript of that meeting records Castro's vivid first impression about Mengistu, revealing the latter's apparent success in winning over both the heart and the support of the Cuban leader after the successive meeting with him during Castro's visit to Ethiopia (14–15) March and during the mediation in Aden. Castro described Mengistu as a quiet, honest, intellectual and revolutionary leader, while Siyad Barre is described in the same report as a chauvinist whose principal idea was nationalism, not socialism. Castro presumably presented the two men to the Soviet leader, as described to Honecker, when he flew later to the Soviet Union. Although Castro made known his preferences regarding the two leaders, he talked about the dilemma facing the Soviet bloc. He said that if the socialist countries did not help Ethiopia the revolution there would be lost and if Ethiopia is to be saved Somalia would be lost.

Another round of talks at 'the expert level' was arranged in Moscow to avert an all-out war between Somalia and Ethiopia between the last week of July and the third week of August 1977. The Somali delegation of experts arrived in Moscow on 24 July and was headed by Hussein Abdulkadir Kasim, Minister of Mineral and Water Resources. A similar delegation from Ethiopia was also in Moscow at the time and the Russian intention was to mediate and bring the two sides together in order to reach a negotiated settlement. The two delegations from Somalia and Ethiopia, however, never met because after Moscow listened to their views it felt the two parts did not leave room for manoeuvre. Instead, it negotiated the two parts separately and at the end of the talks gave them recommendations. The Deputy Foreign Minister of the Soviet Union, Leonid F. Ilichev, who headed the Soviet team, had recorded the conversation between the Somali delegation and the Soviet officials. Meetings took place at the residence of the Somali Delegation in Moscow, and the following is L. F. Ilichev's record of negotiations between the Somali and Soviet officials in the period 25–29 July 1977.

25 July
In a one-on-one conversation which took place on the initiative of H. A. Kasim, before the beginning of the first meeting the Minister announced that the Somali delegation had arrived in Moscow with a feeling of good will and with absolute faith in the efforts of the Soviet Union to offer its good

services toward the resolution of disputed issues between Somalia and Ethiopia. The Somali delegation, in the words of Kasim, experiences doubt, however, as to the candor and good intentions of the Ethiopian side, taking into account that Somalia had repeatedly proposed to Ethiopia to resolve the disputed issues within the framework of creating a federation of the two governments, to which Ethiopia reacted by publishing the protocols of secret negotiations between the two sides and by carrying out a campaign attacking Somalia in the press.

As is well known, other African and non-African countries attempted to play the role of mediator in the settlement of the disputed questions between the two countries, but these efforts were not crowned with success.

The Somali delegation considers that the object of discussion at the forthcoming meeting of experts, in addition to the substance of the disputed issues between the two countries, should include neither the tension in relations between the two countries, nor the questions of demarcation or of changing the borders, but rather the colonial situation which currently characterizes a part of the Somali territory and the population living there, which is under the colonial government of Ethiopia. The Somali delegation considers that no country should call itself a socialist country, or a country which adheres to a socialist orientation, if this country continues the colonial oppression of a people and a part of the territory of another country. This colonial situation arose in the time of the existence of the Ethiopian Empire and up to Somali independence. In the opinion of the Somali side, the changing of the name Abyssinia to Ethiopia and the Ethiopian Empire to Socialist Ethiopia did not change in the slightest degree the state of affairs. This is why the Somali delegation considers that the central question for discussion at the forthcoming meetings of the delegations of experts from the two countries is the question of granting self-determination and independence to the oppressed Somali minority, which lives within the borders of Ethiopia.

At the forthcoming negotiations, continued the Minister, there are two alternatives: either [his aforementioned proposed topic, or] to limit the discussion to a range of secondary problems, which would be tantamount to simply beating about the bush. Somalia considers that the military actions currently being conducted are the actions of Somali patriots in the colonial territory who are struggling for their right to self-determination and independence, therefore the first question on the agenda of the forthcoming meeting of experts should be the question of decolonialization, and, only having resolved that question, will it be possible to move on to the discussion of other secondary questions, such as the lessening of tension in relations between the two countries.

H.A. Kasim noted that the currently existing situation is a result of the fact that Ethiopia, over the course of many years, violated the territorial integrity of Somalia, [and] oppressed and annihilated Somalis, living in the colonized territory.

In conclusion, H.A. Kasim underscored the readiness of the Somali delegation to assist the Soviet side in fulfilling its mission of offering its good services at the meeting of the delegations of experts from Somalia and Ethiopia.

For my part, I declared that the tension which has been created in the relations between two countries, with both of whom we are friendly, is the cause of great alarm and anxiety. I underscored the impossibility of resolving the disputed questions by means of the application of force, particularly given the contemporary global situation. I took note of the real danger that such tension might be used by enemies of Africa, enemies of progressive transformations in Somalia as well as in Ethiopia. I remarked that there are no questions in the interrelations of socialist countries or countries of socialist orientation, which could not be resolved without the application of force, by peaceful means. The Soviet side, offering its good services, sees its task at the forthcoming meeting of the delegations of experts in the following:

1) to create an atmosphere of goodwill between the two countries;

2) to ensure an understanding of the fact that it is impossible to resolve disputed questions through force;

3) to undertake efforts to ensure that as a result of the meetings of experts there would be recommendations elaborated to the governments of both of these countries with the goal of creating a situation of friendship and good relations as a basis for resolving the disputed questions which exist between Somalia and Ethiopia.

I indicated that the Soviet side did not intend to impose any particular resolution of the disputed questions between the two countries.

After the conclusion of the one-on-one conversation a meeting of the Soviet representatives and the Somali delegation of experts took place.

I greeted the delegation of Somali experts and expressed satisfaction with the fact that the Somali and Ethiopian parties had decided to begin a dialogue toward the normalization of their relations in Moscow.

I announced that, having concurred with the request of President Siad that we offer our good services in organizing and leading the meetings between representatives of Somalia and Ethiopia in Moscow, the Soviet side was guided exclusively by its international obligations to offer assistance to countries with whom we are on friendly terms, by its interests in the development and strengthening of all-around cooperation with them.

I noted that we treat the parties without biases of any sort, in a friendly and candid manner.

I expressed the hope that the forthcoming Somali-Ethiopian meeting would lead to positive results. I said that it would not be candid for us not to say that the current situation in the region had grown complicated and that decisive and immediate measures were necessary. We would hope that the two delegations would strive from the very beginning to create a businesslike atmosphere, to show their good will, [to take a] constructive approach and not to take categorical positions, which have the nature of ultimatums, and would rule out even the slightest possibility of conducting negotiations.

We are convinced that the normalization of the situation in the Horn of Africa and the establishment of friendly relations with Ethiopia is in the interest of Somalia. It is clear that a peaceful situation, and friendly ties with Ethiopia would create more favorable conditions for the successful resolution of complicated problems pertaining to the national economy, which confront this country, in its attempts to raise the well-being of the Somali workers.

I said that we would like hear the full opinion of the Somali delegation concerning the range of questions, which the delegation considers necessary to submit to a joint discussion, and likewise concerning the procedure for the meeting, in particular, with regard to its general duration, and other procedural questions. From our side, we have no intention of imposing any temporal limit on the meeting and are prepared to take into account, insofar as it is possible, the wishes of the two parties in this regard.

I noted further that, as we know, the Somali side proposes to discuss the issue of the Ethiopian government's concession of the right to self-determination of national groups. We are unable to predict beforehand what might be the position of the Ethiopian government, but we can surmise, that such a formulation of the question will most likely be interpreted by the Ethiopian government as interference in the internal affairs of a sovereign state.

We know, as you do, that the Ethiopian leadership in its programmatic documents announced its intention to resolve the nationalities question on a democratic basis. It goes without saying that the realization of such a program requires the appropriate conditions.

To our mind, the examination of the issue of normalizing relations between the two countries at the meeting of experts, and precisely this, as we understand, is their first and foremost task, should not be made conditional upon the preliminary resolution of fundamentally disputed questions. This is a point of view which we have expressed more than once to the Somali leadership and it was not met with objections by their side.

The meeting of the delegation with the good services of our side would be genuinely successful if it was concluded by the elaboration by the experts of recommendations to their governments concerning the steps which would lead to the normalization of Somali-Ethiopian relations.

The Soviet side is prepared to cooperate and to offer all possible assistance to the experts of both sides in their elaboration of recommendations for their governments, but does not plan to insist on any particular position. We are prepared to assist actively in the search for a mutually acceptable resolution. If the desire should be expressed, the Somali and the Ethiopian delegations may meet without the participation of the Soviet representatives.

We would be prepared after the meeting with the Ethiopian delegation, if it should be deemed necessary, to engage in further discussion with the Somali experts with the objective of working out a unified approach, of identifying a range of questions, which would be appropriate to discuss, and likewise of identifying procedural questions.

The views which might be expressed in this connection by our delegation, may be reduced, in summary, to the following;

1) the acknowledgment that the continuation of tensions between the two countries is not consistent with the interest of the Ethiopian and Somali nations;

2) the renunciation by the two sides of the use of force in the resolution of disputed questions; the attempt to apply every effort to their settlement by peaceful means, by means of negotiations;

3) the obligation of the two sides to maintain peace and security on their borders, to abstain from every sort of hostile activity, from engaging in hostile propaganda against one another by means of the mass media and to foster, in every possible way, those efforts which will lead to the development of friendly relations;

4) the efforts of the two countries to take measures which are directed at developing economic, trade, and cultural relations, at developing connections between voluntary organizations in the two countries, the exchange of experience, etc., and, in particular, the readiness of the two sides to conduct regular mutual consultations at all levels.

It goes without saying that first and foremost it is necessary to cease military activities on both sides.

The principled efforts of the Soviet Union toward the development of all-around cooperation with the Somali Democratic Republic are well known. Our country has never been guided in its policy by opportunistic considerations. The Soviet Union will continue in the future to strengthen its friendship and revolutionary solidarity with the nation of Somalia, to offer assistance and support in full accordance with the Treaty of Friendship and Cooperation between our countries.

July 26

[...] [I] Remarked for my part, that the interlocutor repeated all of those factors, which had been expressed by him during the previous discussion. Meanwhile, the situation in the Horn of Africa continues to become more complicated and explosive. We think that this situation dictates the necessity of introducing certain amendments to the considerations of the two parties.

From the declaration of the Somali delegation it follows that the delegation possesses the authority to discuss only territorial problems. We were told that the efforts of the Somali leadership, the efforts of the leaders of certain African countries, and likewise the efforts of Comrade F. Castro in the settlement of the disputed problems of Somali and Ethiopia did not meet with success. From this [fact] should the conclusion be drawn that, insofar as the efforts of third countries have not been successful, the disputed questions must be resolved with the assistance of arms, by means of open military actions? Our point of view is that all disputed questions should be resolved by peaceful means, by means of negotiations. For the sake of this objective no efforts of any sort should be begrudged.

The Soviet side regarded with satisfaction the declaration of President Siad that Somalia would never, not under any circumstances, attempt to resolve disputed questions with the assistance of arms. This was discussed in the message to L.I. Brezhnev, and the same declaration was made by the Somali party-state delegation which visited the USSR in the previous year. In a word, we have been assured of this more than once and on various levels. We have treated this declaration with complete faith.

However, certain information we possess bears witness to the fact that open military actions have currently commenced. Regular military units in Somalia, using tanks and aviation, have crossed the Somali-Ethiopian border. I want to stress, that we are discussing concrete facts, not conjecture.

From our point of view, in order to resolve any sort of problem which has arisen between states, first and foremost it is necessary to have a favorable atmosphere. We, as the party which is offering its good services, consider that the central task should now comprise the cessation of military actions. This is the appeal we make to both the Somali and the Ethiopian sides.

It is our opinion that the issue currently stands as follows: either the Horn of African will become an arena where imperialist and reactionary intrigues are carried out, or by our common efforts we will succeed in turning the Horn of Africa into a region of friendly relations and peace.

We appeal to both delegations to take a seat at the negotiating table, to speak forth their own views and, correspondingly, to listen fully to each other's point of view, having devoted their full attention to the search for a path to the normalization of the relations between the two countries.

This is our point of view.

[...] Returning to the bilateral Somali-Ethiopian meeting, H.A. Kasim said, that if the question should be raised concerning the military actions of Somalia against Ethiopia, that the Somali delegation would have nothing further to discuss at the negotiating table. A war is going on between Ethiopia and the liberation movement of the Somali people who live in occupied territory. The struggle is being conducted precisely by this movement, and not by the Somali Democratic Republic.

What military actions should be ceased? After all we are discussing a struggle for liberation, and, as is well known, from the moment of the Great October socialist revolution the Soviet Union has invariably supported liberation movements in all corners of the globe. The very activities of the Soviet Union in the United Nations are a testimony to this fact.

I would like to repeat once more that we are prepared to sit down at the negotiating table, if the Ethiopian side will discuss the territorial dispute as a fundamental issue, but if the Ethiopian side will only put forward the issue of the alleged Somali military actions, then there will not be any progress either in the work of this meeting, or in our bilateral relations.

I do not know, H.A. Kasim said in conclusion, whether the Soviet Union will be able to do anything under these circumstances. Unfortunately, we have the dismal example of the mediation of F. Castro, when Mengistu Haile Mariam declared the inexpedience of raising the territorial question, but was prepared to discuss any other questions of secondary importance.

Trust in our candor, we will regret it if the good services of the USSR do not lead to a positive result.

July 29

[...] Taking into account the separate exchanges of opinion taking place with the main Somali and Ethiopian delegations, the Soviet representative, by way of offering his good services, will introduce for consideration in the course of the work an idea of the first steps, which would lead toward the normalization of relations between Somalia and Ethiopia:

1) The renunciation of the application of force in the resolution of disputed questions. The assumption of immediate measures in the cessation of military and other hostile activities.

2) The assumption by both parties of the obligation to maintain peace and security on the borders.

3) To abstain from conducting hostile propaganda against one another by means of the mass media, to encourage efforts which would lead to the development of friendly relations.

4) The acknowledgment by both parties of the fact that maintaining tensions between Somalia and Ethiopia is not consistent with the interests of their peoples and impedes the unification of their efforts in the struggle against the common enemy, imperialism.

5) The two parties express their agreement to establish and maintain contacts with each other at a variety of levels in the interests of reaching the above-mentioned goals.

[I] underscored the fact that we regard this as a working document which contains the recommendations of the Soviet side, which is fulfilling its mission to offer good services. It goes without saying that we are proceeding from the assumption that it will be brought to the attention of the Somali government.

H.A. Kasim declared that the Somali delegation had nothing to add to the considerations which the delegation had expressed earlier, and offered his assurance that the recommendations which were expressed by the Soviet side, would be brought to the attention of the Somali leadership.

[...] [I] thanked H.A. Kasim for his communication and said that I would like to make note again of certain elements, which were contained in the message of response from L.I. Brezhnev to Siad Barre's appeal to him in May of this year. "In agreeing to offer our good services," announced L.I. Brezhnev, "we approach this matter with seriousness and a sense of responsibility. We think that it should be possible to begin a dialogue on a broad basis with the goal of establishing good relations between Somalia and Ethiopia. We consider that the key which might open the road to cooperation in the search for a settlement to difficult disputed problems lies in neighborly relations in the Horn of Africa."

It is hardly necessary for me to comment on this text; it speaks for itself.

The Soviet Union offered its good services even before the exacerbation of relations between Somalia and Ethiopia. But even after this exacerbation we consider it necessary to continue our mission, in order to achieve the improvement of relations between the two countries, to create a favorable atmosphere for the successful discussion of all disputed issues.

Meanwhile, while our consultations are going on, the Soviet leaders have appealed twice with a personal message to President Siad. As recently as yesterday, L.I. Brezhnev sent President Siad a personal message, the substance of which, in brief, consisted of his desire that the Somali side should take the appropriate steps and should stop the escalation of tension.[4]

The record of negotiations speaks for itself, and there is hardly a need for comments; nevertheless, there are some points that require emphasis. The minister made the position of the Somali government regarding the issue of self-determination for the Somalis in the Ogaden very clear from day one and the position of the Somali delegation remained unaffected on that issue by the negotiations that followed, whereas the Soviet Union officials, who did not hide their frustration with the inflexibility of the Somali position, prioritised ending the hostility between Somalia and Ethiopia. The talks were the last chance to find a negotiated settlement for the crises within a socialist framework. However, the concluding remarks as well as the huge Soviet supply of weapons to Ethiopia and the arrival of Cuban troops there all indicated that the talks reached a dead end. Since the talks led nowhere, continued friendship with both countries was not sustainable, and after the failure of the peace mission,

---

[4] Leonid F. Ilichev, 1977, Record of Negotiations between Somali and Soviet Officials in Moscow, 25–29 July 1977, from the Journal of L.F. Ilichev. The document was part of a collection of declassified documents from the former Eastern bloc on the Horn of Africa crises 1977–78.

Moscow began serious deliberations about its strategic options in the Horn and its future relations with the states and liberation organizations in the Horn of Africa.

6.5 Ethiopia's Preference for a Military Resolution

Ethiopia was an empire formed under the barrel of the gun, which still owes its existence to the military might of its armed forces. When Emperor Haile Selassie was overthrown in 1974, the oppressed ethnic groups like the Somalis, Eritreans, the Oromos and Afars looked forward to the outcome of the regime change in Ethiopia in the hope of finding alleviation for their suffering. To their dismay, the military regime that came to power was more totalitarian and oppressive than the monarch as the bloodbath that took place within the ruling military junta exposed. The provisional Military Administrative Council (PMAC), or Derg, engaged in three major successive rounds of bloody power struggle before Mengistu emerged as the uncontested leader:

The first round of weeding out opponents was carried out in November 1974 when Gen. Aman Andom, the first PMAC chairman, along with a few other members of the Council and more than 50 former high-ranking officials, were summarily executed, shocking both Ethiopians and the international community. The second round of executions occurred in July 1976. This time the victims were active educated officers within the PMAC, like Major Sisay Habte and Lieutenants Bewiketu Kassa and Sileshi Beyene, who maintained connections with radical elements among university students, teachers, and labor organizers and who were instrumental in initially steering the Council to the Left from its original nationalist orientation. A major restructuring of the PMAC in December 1976, when its members voted to strip Mengistu of power and institute "collective leadership," served as the prelude to the third and decisive round of killings. The architects of the restructuring included respected PMAC members like the nominal chairman who succeeded Aman Andom: Gen. Teferi Banti, Maj. Alemayehu Haile and Capt. Mogus Wolde Michael. Again, especially the last two, like those mentioned earlier, were important figures in introducing socialism to the Council. However, on 3 February 1977 Mengistu embarked on a sudden and swift retaliation. With the help of the chief of the palace security force command, he essentially carried out a mafia-style coup by simply ambushing and executing the ringleaders of the restructuring who were unsuspectingly preparing for a regular Council meeting in the palace grounds. The following day he was "unanimously voted" chairman by the remaining PMAC members.[5]

Before the Ethiopian revolution, Ethiopia's main opponents, the Somalis and the Eritreans had an Eastern bloc orientation, whereas Ethiopia was primarily oriented towards the Western countries, first and foremost toward the US and countries of the 'European common market'. After having consolidated his authority, Mengistu turned to the east to get support for both his military and political policies instead of strengthening the ties with the West. He capitalized on the Soviet bloc alliance for several reasons, which included the ongoing internal wars, the deterioration of Ethio-US relations and the arms race in the Horn of Africa.

In early 1977 the liberation movements in Bale, Eritrea, the Ogaden and Afar were waging war against the Mengistu regime and some of them were making headway in their armed struggle. After the bloody coup, Mengistu made clear that he had no solutions to the Ethiopian problems other than a military one. By then relations between the new Carter administration in America and the totalitarian regime in Addis Ababa had also gravely deteriorated. The Carter administration was at the time withholding some military supplies and urging a negotiated settlement with Eritreans, who were much in control of their territory, and the US administration was also demanding improvement in the human rights situation in the country.

It is not clear whether the Soviet bloc had helped Mengistu in seizing power, but the Soviet Ambassador to Ethiopia, Anatolii P. Ratanov, was reliably reported at the time to have been the first to congratulate Mengistu after the spectacular bloodbath in the Derg, and Mengistu also visited Moscow secretly in December 1976. The Cuban leader, Fidel Castro, was no doubt instrumental in bringing Ethiopia aboard the Soviet boat a few weeks after Mengistu seized power. The first head of state from the Communist bloc to meet with Mengistu after his coup was Fidel Castro. He visited Addis Ababa on March 14-15, 1977 and the next day he chaired the unsuccessful mediation attempt in South Yemen between Mohamed Siyad Barre and Mengistu Haile Mariam. After that failed peace mission, Castro reported to the Soviet bloc about his trip and in that report, he provided an excellent report card for Mengistu by describing him as a committed socialist and revolutionary potential.

---

[5] Ermias Abebe, 1995, *The Horn, the Cold War and New Documents from the former Eastern bloc: An Ethiopian View*, CWIHP Bulletin, Ethiopian Review Com, pages 1–3. The document was part of a collection of declassified documents from the former Eastern bloc on the Horn of Africa crises 1977–78.

After he successfully presented himself as a loyal revolutionary dedicated to the socialist cause, Mengistu's regime took a campaign of discrediting the revolutionary potentials of the Somali regime. The following abstract from the archives of the former Eastern bloc on the Horn of Africa crises 1977–78, mentioned a conversation between the Ethiopian head of foreign affairs, Maj. B. Bayeh, and S. Sinistin, a Soviet diplomat based in Ethiopia, in which the former gives some examples of that propaganda campaign:

Mengistu also indulges in a diplomatic contribution to widen the emerging rift between Somalia and the socialist states by discrediting the revolutionary potential of its leadership. In one record of conversation held on March 18, his head of foreign affairs, Maj. Berhanu Bayeh, quotes the Egyptian newspaper *Al-Ahram* to point out to Sinitsin the possibility of Somalia joining Sudan, Egypt and Syria in a unified political command. He adds that Barre had been on record declaring that Somalia achieved its revolution independently and can acquire help from other countries besides the Soviet Union and its allies. Given the recent Soviet loss of Egypt and Sudan, this information was probably intended to arouse Moscow's apprehension.[6]

During his secret visit to Moscow, Mengistu signed a military aid agreement with the Soviet leadership on 14 December 1976. Full implementation of the agreement was, however, conditional on the Derg's severing its US military link. To get military support from the Soviet Union, undermine the Somali-Soviet relations and ultimately defeat his enemies, Mengistu gambled on alliance with the Soviet bloc and turned his back on the West. Mengistu decided to sever ties with the West as demanded by Moscow by abrogating Ethiopia's friendship treaty with the US and closing the latter's military base in Ethiopia:

Supporting his own professed commitment to Marxism-Leninism and the Soviet Union with practical deeds, at the end of the following April Mengistu ordered the closure of the U.S. communications station in Asmara, the U.S. Information Service (USIS) centre, and the American military assistance advisory offices, and abrogated the Ethio-U.S. Mutual Defense Assistance Agreement – the official treaty of alliance with the United States

---

[6] Ermias Abebe, 1995, *The Horn, the Cold War and New Documents from the former Eastern bloc: An Ethiopian View*, CWIHP Bulletin, Ethiopian Review Com, pages 1–3. The document was part of a collection of declassified documents from the former Eastern bloc on the Horn of Africa crises 1977–78.

dating from 1953.[7]

In May 1977, Mengistu flew again to Moscow and during that visit, he was warmly received and treated as a respected member of the Soviet club. The visit was a turning point in the Ethio-Soviet relations in that it started the process that led to the shift of Soviet patronage from Somalia to Ethiopia a few months later. Although the Kremlin was still apparently hoping to limit its commitment, the Soviet Union agreed during the visit to provide a substantial package of military hardware to Ethiopia. In response to Mengistu's urgent pleading, the Soviet Union also agreed, during July 1977, to send in urgently needed transport equipment to enable the Ethiopians to utilize some of the tanks and guns the Soviets had already provided as a result of agreements reached during Mengistu's December 1976 and May 1977 visits to Moscow.

The Soviet Union had already concluded a treaty of friendship and cooperation with Somalia and the Ethiopian revolution opened new possibilities for the Soviet Union to expand its influence. The Soviet bloc attempted persistently to keep both Somalia and Ethiopia within the socialist camp and until August 1977 the Soviet Union was trying to bring the Ethiopians and Somalis together in negotiations at 'the expert level'. Despite the lack of progress in the talks, Moscow appeared reluctant to choose between Somalia and Ethiopia and tried to delay hard decisions for as long as possible, but as the war between the Somalia-supported WSLF and Ethiopia progressed, the mission reached a dead end and Moscow had to make a choice. By the beginning of September 1977, Moscow's stand on the crises as well as its preferred ally in the region was very clear. Ethiopia was chosen as the Soviet's partner in the Horn and with that choice, a military resolution remained the only option to the crisis in the Ethiopian view. In September 1977 Ethiopia broke off diplomatic relations with Somalia and rejected a mediation attempt by the OAU.

---

[7] Ermias Abebe, 1995, *The Horn, the Cold War and New Documents from the former Eastern bloc: An Ethiopian View*, CWIHP Bulletin, Ethiopian Review Com, pages 1–3. The document was part of a collection of declassified documents from the former Eastern bloc on the Horn of Africa crises 1977–78.

7

The 1977/78 Ogaden War

The war began first between the WSLF and Ethiopia at the end of 1976. Somalia directly took part in the war during the period 23 July 1977– March 1978, but then left the battlefield to the WSLF forces who continued the liberation war until 1988. Historians often put emphasis on the middle part of the so-called 1977/78 Ogaden war without mentioning the first and third stages of the war. All the three phases of the war will be emphasised in this book. This chapter deals with the first two phases of the war and the last phase will be discussed later, in chapter 8.

By the end of October 1976, the first part of the new WSLF forces had completed its training and was ready at Qoriley, the main training centre. A few weeks later they were sent to various locations inside the Ogaden region to start the liberation campaign. The liberation army of the WSLF was divided into several divisions and each one of them was given a particular name and sent to a particular part of the region. For example, Gulweynne was to operate in Afdheer and Godey zones, Ahmed Gurey division was given responsibility for the Jigjiga zone, and Duufan operated in the Jarer and Nogob regions, Iltire in Shinille zone and Yasin in the Qorahay and Wardher areas.

The operations began simultaneously in all parts of the region and in a short period the WSLF militants defeated the colonial forces and began to liberate the small towns. The southern districts of the region, such as Hamaro, Barey and Elkare were the first to be liberated. The Afdher zone and most of the Nogob zone were liberated in the first six months of the liberation war. In addition to the liberation of these zones, the liberation forces had by then succeeded in cutting the land supply lines of the enemy. The inter-town roads were blocked by the WSLF forces, the air link was the only means of transport that connected the towns and was the only safe supply line in most parts of the region.

As the fighting came closer to the big towns, it became more intensified and the Ethiopian side launched a counter-offensive, using both ground and air forces. The Ethiopian counter-offensive, however, provoked a reaction from Somalia. On 23 July 1977 divisions of the Somali regular forces were ordered to resign and join the WSLF.

Somalia's regular force under the guise of the Western Somali Liberation Front, together with the militant forces of the WSLF who were already on the battlefield, coordinated their operations. The liberation movement concentrated more on intelligence, ground attacks and nearly all stages that did not require heavy equipment, whereas the regular army led the classical warfare operations, which required the use of heavy weapons, such as artillery, tanks, air defence, etc.

The result of the combined operations was a very quick victory. The victorious Somali forces began the capture of the main towns in July 1977 with the liberation of Godey in July 1977, followed by Shilabo, Qalafe Qabridahare, Wardher, Aware, Dagahbour, Dagahmadow, and Fiiq. Jigjiga, which was liberated on 12 September 1977, was the last major town to be taken by the liberation forces. With the fall of Jigjiga the Ethiopians lost new American-supplied battle-management radar that had only recently gone into operation at the Karamardha Pass.

The scene of jubilation and celebration that followed the liberation of the various towns across the region was almost indescribable. 'Thanks to Allah freedom has reached us at last', the people chanted. They had also shown their joy in action but in different ways. Some of them laughed and danced wildly on the streets, while others prostrated more to Allah, thanking Allah for the mercy of freedom. Whatever the form of gratitude giving, many happy, smiling faces were to be seen everywhere. Despite the celebration, the jubilant always looked forward to the news of the front with apprehension. Furthermore, they were active participants in the war, and it was rare to see someone who was not involved in the liberation war in one way or another. Each freed town got something to be proud of, but two things were common to all the people in the liberated part of the region – national pride and a dream of self-realization. The word 'Somali' was the symbol of the new pride in that it brought a new identity to the people as everything was 'Somalized': Somali government, Somali schools, Somali literacy campaign, Somali army, etc. Likewise, the word 'freedom' became the catchword for the new opportunities of life after liberation. People began to talk about freedom of movement, freedom to decide one's destiny … and freedom to do whatever they wanted in life. The mood and sentiment of the people in Somalia were remarkably similar to those of the people of the Western Somali region. Describing the war efforts and the mood of the people in Somalia, I.M. Lewis wrote:

> Nationalist sentiments in the Republic, stimulated to an unforeseen degree by Somali literacy, had reached a climax. The fighting in the Ogaden,

in which many were directly and all indirectly involved, had become a national obsession. All interest focused on the progress of the war and the unofficial contribution to the war effort had unquestioned priority over all the other activities. All aspects of life in the Republic were affected. In every government department and ministry there were conspicuous absentees away 'on leave'; while in the armed forces those from the Ogaden had similarly gone to join their brothers and clansmen in the fight against the Ethiopian usurper. Mother-and-child care centres were hastily converted into cottage factories for making uniforms. Radio reports of the progress of the war were followed throughout the state with rapt attention; such was the demand for news that it became impossible to find transistor radios and batteries in the shops. This consuming preoccupation with the Ogaden left little time or need for the official cult of the Glorious Leader, President Siyad, which was quietly allowed to subside – at least for the time being.[1]

By the summer of 1977, the Somali victory on the ground was unquestionable but, at the same time, the Ethiopians were making headway on the diplomatic front. The Derg regime was successfully presenting Ethiopia as a victim of Somali aggression and managed to get military supplies from both superpowers. Although the Ethiopian regime opted for the Soviet bloc and the Ethio-US relations were deteriorating, US military supplies were still reaching Ethiopia in 1977, even after the abrogation of the friendship treaty of 1953. 'The US military aid program continued into 1977 and elite Ethiopian air force pilots were sent to the United States to learn to fly the Northrop F5-E fighter-bombers promised to Haile Selassie in 1973. Despite misgivings about Derg offensives in Eritrea, US military assistance was increased, and Ethiopia was permitted to buy an additional $100 million worth of military supplies from the well-supplied treasury the Derg inherited from Haile Selassie.'[2] The F5-E fighters promised to Haile Selassie were delivered in July 1977.[3]

In the first week of May 1977, Mengistu visited Moscow after he closed down the American military mission and the Kagenew station in April. The visit was successful in that Mengistu signed an agreement with Moscow to supply Ethiopia's military needs. At the end of August, Siyad Barre flew to Moscow to persuade the Soviet Union to refrain from supporting Ethiopia, but by then the Soviets had already decided to rescue the Mengistu regime and they were clear on their stand. The

[1] I.M. Lewis, 2002, *A Modern History of the Somali*, James Currey, pages 236
[2] Paul B. Henze, 2000, *Layers of Time, A History of Ethiopia*, Hurst & Co Ltd, page 297.
[3] Paul B. Henze, 2000, *Layers of Time, A History of Ethiopia*, page 298.

Soviets told the Somali leader to back off or face the consequences. The Somali leader was not only warned in words but in practical terms too. The Soviet Union began to cut its military assistance to Somalia, and at the same time undertook massive shipment of military hardware to Ethiopia. 'By August 1977 the Soviets halted all military aid to Somalia and began to supply arms to Ethiopia. Many Soviet military advisers went straight from Somalia to Ethiopia, even taking with them virtually all the Somali maps of the region. From May 1977 through March 1978, by land and by sea, the Soviet Union supplied about $1.5 billion in military equipment to Ethiopia. This represented more than seven times the military aid that the Soviets had supplied to Somalia during the previous three years.'[4]

On 13 November 1977 Somalia unilaterally abrogated the 1974 Treaty of Friendship and Cooperation with the USSR. The breach was predicted as Russia rallied to Ethiopia's defence and began to airlift South Yemeni and Cuban combat troops as well as Russian and East German advisers. The shift of Soviet patronage put Somalia in a difficult position. President Siyad was unable to entice the US into resupplying his troops, despite previous tacit promises that it would replace the Soviet Union as Somalia's patron power. The US government and its Western allies were neither willing to support Somalia diplomatically nor to supply it with the military equipment that it desperately needed. The Western countries claimed that they accepted the OAU doctrine of preserving the colonial borders and that the Ogaden conflict was an African problem, which should be resolved within an African context. The OAU supported Ethiopia always on the Ogaden issue and the Western powers did not want to provoke the OAU for the sake of Somalia, despite the desire to contain the Soviets. In the words of Harold G. Marcus: 'Try as it might, the Somali government could not gain international support for its position, since every other country in Africa and the major powers supported the notion of the inviolability of Africa's frontiers as negotiated by the colonialists.'[5]

The Eastern bloc countries, the West and the OAU all demanded that Somalia refrain from supporting the WSLF and abandon the issue of self-determination for the Somalis in neighbouring countries. Somalia refused to accept their demands and, as a result, became friendless in both the West and the East. A few Arab countries (Saudi Arabia, Iraq, Egypt) and

[4] David D. Laitin & Said S. Samatar, 1987, *Somalia, A Nation in Search of a State*, Westview Press, Page 142.
[5] Harold G. Marcus, 1994, *A History of Ethiopia*, University of California Press, page 199.

Iran offered limited support to Somalia. These Muslim countries were ready to support Somalia to defend its independent territory from a possible attack from Ethiopia, but they were not backing the liberation efforts in the Ogaden. 'With only this limited support from a handful of Arab States, with no battle-hardened foreign auxiliaries to set against the Yemenis and Cubans, and with Russian equipment smaller in quantity and inferior in quality to that now so abundantly available to Ethiopia, the Somali position was increasingly precarious.'[6]

The Somali forces were near to the liberation of Harar and Dire Dawa when the Soviet Union began a massive air- and sealift of military equipment (worth about one billion dollars), 12 000 Cuban combat troops, about 1 500 Soviet military advisers and a South Yemeni regiment with artillery to Ethiopia in November–December 1977. Moscow's apparent objective in this spectacular military show was to guarantee the swift and decisive end of the Ethio-Somali war with a quick and unconditional withdrawal of Somali forces from the Ogaden. The Soviet Union wanted to avert at all costs the internationalisation of the conflict and the possible involvement of the UN Security Council which it believed would be in the interest of Western powers. Such an outcome, Moscow argued, would be possible if an armistice were reached without the withdrawal of Somali troops from occupied Ethiopian territory while Western powers simultaneously pushed for Security Council involvement. A takeover by the Security Council, moreover, would delay a resolution of the conflict in a similar fashion as in the Middle East, possibly increasing the danger for superpower confrontation as the West and other unfriendly states demanded Soviet exit from the region as a precondition and blame it for causing the conflict.

In mid-January 1978, Somalia launched its last offensive, but the Somali army was no match for the huge numbers of Russian, East German, Yemeni and Cuban troops, and the completely re-equipped and enlarged Ethiopian army. By the end of November 1977, the total number of Cuban combat troops reached 18 000 and the south Yemeni troops were about 4 000. The Yemenis helped to train the Ethiopians in the use of tanks and the Cubans helped to contain and finally to expel the Somali army. Furthermore, several divisions of the newly recruited militia swelled Ethiopia's forces, while Somalia's manpower was stretched to its limits. Somalia officially entered the war in February 1978 and announced a general mobilization. At that time, the battle lines had

---

[6] I.M. Lewis, 2002, *A Modern History of the Somali*, page 238.

hardened around Dire Dawa and Harar and the Somali army lost momentum and began exhausting its supplies and all hope of remaining victorious. By late February, after weeks of artillery shelling, a combined Ethiopian and Cuban force broke through softened Somali lines on the road to Jigjiga. I.M. Lewis reported on that offensive as follows:

> The long-awaited Russian and Cuban counter-offensive was now properly underway and already claiming some successes. The final putsch occurred at the beginning of March when, after subjecting the 8,000 strong Somali force between Jigjiga and Harar to heavy aerial bombardment, the 10th Ethiopian division supported by an entire Cuban armoured brigade of sixty to seventy tanks bypassed the Marda Pass and attacked Jigjiga from the unexpected direction of the north. Cuban-crewed tanks were also air-lifted behind the Somali lines and Cuban-piloted M.I.G.s supported the attack in which a number of sophisticated new Russian weapons seem to have been deployed. Having evacuated the local civilian population to Somalia, the Somali defence abandoned Jigjiga to the invaders. A relief brigade thrown into the battle from Somalia, strafed by M.I.G.s was unable to stem the Ethiopian advance.[7]

Jigjiga fell on 5 March 1978 and on 9 March Siyad Barre announced that, in response to American requests, Somali regular forces were being withdrawn from the Ogaden and he demanded the withdrawal of Russian Yemeni and Cuban forces from the region. Siyad Barre did not demand the withdrawal of the Ethiopian forces, but that did not mean the abandonment of the Ogaden cause as the continued support for WSLF after the withdrawal was confirmed. On 23 March 1978, Radio Addis Ababa announced that the Ethiopian government had regained control over all Ogaden military posts and administrative centres. But despite the reoccupation of the towns the war did not end there.

By the end of March, the mood of the Somali people sharply contrasted to that when they were marching forward and expelling the hated enemy from their towns one after the other. Everything was now going in reverse. The Somali force that chased the enemy westward and northward began to retreat in the reverse direction leaving the liberated towns to the enemy. Silence replaced the laughter and there were no happy faces to be seen among the Somali population, and there was hardly any exchange of news of the front as nearly everyone in the region became an eyewitness to the gloomy picture that appeared before them. Similarly, the crowds in the busy cafes of Mogadishu Hargeisa, Kismayo and other cities that used to gather for tuning to Radio Mogadishu for

---

[7] I.M. Lewis, 2002, *A Modern History of the Somali*, page 238.

the news of the front were not to be seen anymore.

The Soviet Union led alliance that denied the Western Somali people their basic right of self-determination and brought back the colonial rule to their homeland inflicted widespread suffering on the Somalis. But the alliance, too, returned with a big loss. The Ogaden war had adverse effects on Russia's aggressive foreign policy and its economy. The Ogaden war put an end to the expansionist policies of the Soviets in the region and they were forced to change their original plan of forming a confederation of communist countries in the region. The huge cost of the war, which was estimated at over $3 billion, no doubt enlarged the Russian budget deficit. The economic and power decline of the Soviet Union that came to light after the Afghan war began with the Ogaden war. Unlike the Yemenis and the Cubans, the Soviets had strategic interest, which they thought was worth the fighting. But the South Yemenis and the Cubans entered the war for no obvious national interest at stake or related to the conflict, and it was hard to imagine what these countries achieved in return for their heavy loss of lives.

Despite the reoccupation of the Ogaden, Ethiopia was also a loser, not only because of the loss of human lives and materials but also because of the damage to its national pride. The image of the lion of Africa with which Ethiopia proudly presented itself after the Adowa war was no longer acceptable after the swift defeat of its huge army by the relatively small Somali force. The Somali army, estimated at 35 000, was less than one-third of the Ethiopian army that took part in the war. Furthermore, the resistance war did not end with the reoccupation, and it is unlikely that it will cease as long as the occupation continues. Thus, the short-term Ethiopian victory postponed the independence of the region, but it by no means ended the resistance war.

The reoccupation of the Ogaden by the allied forces was no doubt a big setback to the Somali cause, and the reaction of the Somali people to the reoccupation was one of sadness and anger. It was an incredibly sad thing to lose the freedom they recently regained and tasted, and the occupation of their home by an alliance of foreign aggressors was something they neither comprehend nor could swallow. They sacrificed a lot in terms of human life and materials to regain their freedom, but there were no regrets, on the contrary, they are always ready to sacrifice more for that cause. Thus, the casualties, the suffering, the destruction and the displacement of people that the war left behind were not their main concerns. Their main preoccupation was the cause of self-determination, and what worried them most was the fact that their land, their nation and their freedom were at stake. They were very angry with the alliance of aggressors that came to reoccupy their land to subjugate them, rob their resources and deny them the basic human rights that people normally take for granted elsewhere.

The alliance of invaders also reminded them of the major Christian powers that helped Ethiopia in occupying the Ogaden in the first place, although this alliance was different from earlier ones because of the Muslim element in it. South Yemen was the Muslim country that entered the war on behalf of Ethiopia and contributed both combat troops as well as advisers. It is very strange that countries as far away as Portugal, Britain, Cuba and the Soviet Union always come to the Horn of Africa to support Ethiopia's aggression against its powerless neighbours. The Somali people, however, became used to the foreign intervention, because of the long history of the Christian powers' support to Ethiopia and its aggressive policies in the Somali region. Because of the common faith of Christianity between Ethiopia and the Christian powers that always backed it they used to interpret it as a Christian crusade against the Muslims. The Muslim element in the new alliance, however, did not fit that picture and the Somalis could not find an answer as to why South Yemen joined that aggressive and oppressive alliance of Christian nations.

Despite the defeat, the Somali people were not demoralized and were proud of the early victories over Ethiopia because they knew that they were not defeated by Ethiopians, but by a big alliance from four continents, headed by a superpower, and in that sense, they did not lose their pride because of the defeat. In fact, the liberation of most parts of the region, which was achieved within months, was proof that the Somali people are capable of throwing the colonial yoke from their land if foreigners do not intervene on behalf of Ethiopia. Ethiopia's occupation of the Ogaden was neither possible without the help of Britain, Italy, France and Russia nor could it maintain its rule over that region without the help of foreign powers, particularly the superpowers of the world.

In addition to that, the liberation war did not end with the withdrawal of the Somali regular forces from the region. The armed struggle of the WSLF continued almost unaffected by the withdrawal of the regular army of the republic, and the continuation of that liberation war confirmed the determination of the Somali people to liberate their missing territories and unify the nation. Soon after the reoccupation of the region, the WSLF militants regrouped and quickly set up defensive positions. The armed struggle continued for nearly a decade after the withdrawal of the army of Somalia in 1978.

President Siyad Barre also quickly assured the liberation movements of his government's support for the freedom fighters. By this time, it was clear to the Somali officials that the US had double-crossed Somalia and thus Siyad Barre was not counting on US support for his backing of the liberation movements. The move was dictated by the Somalis, who thought that was the least they could do for their cause. Siyad knew both the internal public pressure as well as the position of the West on the Ogaden issue and for that reason he tried to find alternative sources for the supply of military needs. The president's visit to China a few weeks after the Somali army's withdrawal from the Ogaden was prompted by that need.

Encouraged by Somalia's commitment to the struggle, the WSLF redeployed its forces. Divisions of the liberation front such as Ahmed Gurey, Dufan, Iltire and Guulweyne, began operations in their respective areas, employing the guerrilla tactics of hit and run. The enemy had control of the main towns, but their movements were soon restricted by the operations of the WSLF militants. From Dire Dawa to Luq the estimated 15 000-strong force of the Western Somali Liberation Front was in operation, paralyzing the function of the occupation and making the region effectively ungovernable. The huge army of the alliance, which drove the Somali army, lost the initiative and became less effective in the guerrilla warfare that the WSLF waged in the occupied Ogaden region.

As a result of the pressure of the WSLF forces, Ethiopia continuously attacked Somalia by air and land during the following years. Ethiopia's aircraft frequently bombarded many towns in Somalia, and in 1982 it occupied two towns of its territory and pursued a campaign of destabilization. In the next chapter, we will go through this destabilization campaign and its impact on the stability of the Somali government as well as its effect on the liberation struggle in the Ogaden.

8

The Implications of the 1977/78 Ogaden War

The refugees; the liberation struggle; the decline of the Somali State

8.1 The Refugees

The most immediate effect of the war was the displacement of the people, which followed the re-conquest of the Ogaden by the Russian-led alliance. The conquering forces bombed the towns indiscriminately during the reoccupation campaign and, as a result, the towns were emptied by the inhabitants before the enemy reached them. The displaced people began to move in their tens of thousands eastward, northward and southward toward Somalia and Djibouti respectively, some of them in vehicles, but most of them on foot in the search for a safe haven. The Soviet-led alliance, however, was strafing the refugees from the air as they were making their way to the border areas. The alliance claimed that they continued the aerial bombing to destroy the capabilities of the fleeing Somali army, but in reality, they did not differentiate between the civilians and the army, and most of those killed were civilians. Other atrocities that followed the reoccupation included the bombing of villages, the massacre of nomads, the poisoning of water wells and the killing of livestock.

Unfortunately, there was no international outcry against the inhuman treatment of the inhabitants by the conquering alliance, and none of the so-called champions of human rights organizations was to be seen on the ground to document the atrocities that took place. Ironically, the Ethiopian regime sought help on behalf of the very people who were fleeing from its bombardment and repression. It appealed for help to the UNHCR in March 1978. The new commander in the Ogaden, Lemma Gutema, stated that 70 per cent of the region had been affected by the war and that most of its smaller towns were razed. He estimated the number of displaced persons in the region at one million. Despite the appeal for help, Ethiopia refused to allow international observers to enter the Ogaden region to assess the situation of the people it claimed was appealing for their help. Whatever the Ethiopian motive, it became clear from the huge influx of refugees in Somalia that the situation was much worse than the Ethiopian authorities reported.

According to the Somali government, some 500 000 refugees had arrived within Somalia by May 1978. A further 10 000 refugees were reported to have gone to Djibouti in the same period. During 1978–79, the number of refugees arriving in Somalia continued to grow and by February 1980 had increased to 600 000. Somalia set up thirty-five refugee camps in four areas of the country. The registered refugees in the camps in Somalia were estimated in 1982 at about 700 000 by the UN, but that figure did not include the estimated 600 000 unregistered refugees in the country at large, who mingled with the local population. By 1981 the number of refugees in Djibouti had reached 45 000. The number of displaced people within the Ogaden was greater than those who fled to the neighbouring countries, and more than 80 per cent of the population was affected by the displacement tragedy. Because of the repression that followed the reoccupation, most of the displaced people within the region did not return to their homes for years after the re-conquest. The refugees in Somalia found a safe haven there and were well treated by their Somali brethren until 1991 when the Somali state collapsed, and some refugees were attacked by armed militia. Unlike the refugees in Somalia, the refugees in Djibouti did not get full protection, as we will see shortly.

The huge number of refugees in Somalia, which the UNHCR described 'as the most serious refugee problem in the world especially when taken with the total population of only four million'[1] posed big challenges to the Somali government. The Somali government appealed to the international community for help, which positively and generously responded to the appeal. The Somali government also promptly set up a National Refugee Commission (NRC) to administer the refugees and it quickly established a number of refugee camps around the country. Much of the initial cost of the refugee programme was met by the Somali government. 'The immediate programme for refugees in Somalia consisted of the supply of food, shelter material, water tanks, insecticides and transport. The arriving refugees had mostly travelled long distances and suffered from malnutrition and disease, and they lacked every basic necessity of life; over 75 per cent of them were women and children.'[2] The UNHCR, donor governments and non-governmental organizations

---

[1] Louis FitzGibbon, 1982, *The Betrayal of the Somalis*, Rex Collins Ltd, page 62.
[2] Louis FitzGibbon, 1982, *The Betrayal of the Somalis*, Rex Collins Ltd, page 62.

provided long-term help, and the UNHCR, in collaboration with the NRC, coordinated an aid programme that cost over $100 million annually.

The government gave the refugees a safe haven and the international community generously provided basic necessities to refugees in Somalia, but that was only a temporary solution that could not be sustained in the long run. Therefore, a permanent solution was needed to deal with the problem effectively. The huge presence of refugees was a burden to the host country as well as to the donor countries. Further, refugee camps could never be a substitute for their homeland to the refugees. Thus, the sensible thing to do was to find the causes of the refugee problem and remove them, to ensure the safe return of the refugees to their homeland. The removal of the causes would have alleviated the suffering of the refugees, taking the heavy burden of caring for them off the shoulders of the host as well as donor countries, thus making everyone involved better-off, and that part of the world a better place to live in.

The government of Somalia, while grateful to the international community for the generous response in assisting the refugees, always reminded the world body of the need to solve the refugee problem by removing the root causes. In a paper prepared by the Somali government and presented by General Jama Mohamed Qalib, the Minister for Rural and Local Governments, at the First International Conference of Assistances to Refugees in Africa, which took place in Geneva in April 1981, the government stressed the need to deal with root causes of the refugees' problem. The paper was entitled: 'Short- and Long-term Programme for Refugees' and included the following text:

> Today short- and long-term assistance is vital, as is the development of an overall strategy aimed at the resolution of the chronic refugee crises which so greatly hamper the development of some of the least endowed nations of Africa. In this context my Government endorses the recent decision of the General Assembly of the United Nations to table an item entitled "International cooperation to avert new flows of refugees" on its agenda. Let us trust that this step will prove a milestone for it must involve the impartial examination of the root causes of these phenomena. Those causes must be tackled, sooner rather than later. As we concentrate, here in Geneva, as is our undoubted humanitarian duty, on the alleviation of the problem of today's refugees, we must never forget that those problems are a symptom of most serious underlying issues – persistent colonialism, racism, genocide and drought. It is they that are the real problems: refugees flee from persecution and oppressive policies, which a just world should

declare unacceptable, and from a deteriorating environmental conditions which are not beyond the possibility of amelioration.[3]

The refugees' hopes around the world were raised when the UN appointed a special rapporteur to examine the relationship between massive exoduses of refugees and human rights, and the Somalis thought that their calls to deal with the root causes of the refugees' problem were headed. However, by the time the report was delivered, it became clear that nothing fundamental was to change. Because of pressure from Ethiopia and Russia part of the report including the section about Ethiopian refugees, was deleted and the main issue of the root cause of refugees was ignored. FitzGibbon, who witnessed the event when the report was delivered and saw both the original and modified versions, described the report and what happened afterwards as follows:

> On 9 April 1981 the UN commission on Human Rights appointed Prince Sadruddin Aga Khan as "Special Rapporteur to study the question of human rights and massive exoduses". No better choice of rapporteur could have been found in that the Prince Sadruddin had himself been the UN High Commissioner for Refugees and thus would be able to draw upon a deep well of information and experience. He duly got to his task with both energy and determination and produced a heavy report for presentation at the Thirty-Eighth Session of the Commission on Human Rights which is part of the UN economic and social council; it was numbered E/CN.4/1503 and dated 31 December 1981. It consisted of a letter of transmission, three chapters on conceptual framework; the relationship between Mass Exodus and violations of Human Rights, and a Synopsis as well as Conclusions and Recommendations. It also contained three long annexes and an extensive bibliography, and it should be noted that whereas the first part (the introduction, three chapters, conclusions and recommendations) ran to 140 pages, the total of the annexes and the bibliography ran to a further 305 pages so that they formed over seventy-five percent of the whole, in fact they took up more than twice the total number of pages. Annex 2 contained four "Case Studies" on Afghanistan, Ethiopia, Indo-China (Kampuchea, Lao People's Republic, Vietnam) and Mexico. They were all brutally honest and immediately a flurry ensued within the corridors of the United Nations. Under great pressure from the Ethiopian junta and the Soviet Union, the original report was withdrawn "for technical reasons", and later appeared again shorn of all the annexes and the bibliography which contained no less than 414 valuable sources of information. It bore the same reference numbers and date but with a note attached indicating "re-issued for technical reasons". There was no mention at all of the deleted material which, as has

---

[3] Louis FitzGibbon, 1982, *The Betrayal of the Somalis*, page 69.

been shown, formed a far larger part of the whole report. Thus were the official records of the United Nations mutilated to cover-up the horrendous deeds committed by some of its own members. When I heard this I queried the reason for the deletions and was informed that it had been agreed in order to produce unanimous approval of the main part of the document. ... It should be added that when the Somali Permanent Representative at the UN protested there were immediate and angry protests from Ethiopians and, in the event, a key part of a formal report from the Secretary General's own Special Rapporteur was kept away from the public eye.'[4]

The deleted document highlighted, among other things, the plight of refugees in the Horn and pointed out the causes of the flow of these refugees. The bulk of the refugees in the Horn were from Ethiopia, and armed conflict and repression were found to be the chief causes of this. In the case of the Ogaden, the colonial borders, the consequent conflict between Ethiopia and freedom fighters as well as the gross violations of human rights and the repression committed by the Ethiopian regime, were the main causes of the refugee's crises. According to the rapporteur, the aim was to seek speedy and effective ways of preventing disastrous effects of large-scale population movements, since the cost of inaction might soon become unbearable. Although some of the representatives called for the examination of the causes and their removal, the prince admitted that the causes had not received due attention. The removal of over half of the document beforehand and the ensuing debate that failed to address the causes of the exodus were clear examples of the failures of the UN to live up to its responsibilities. Commenting on this UN failure FitzGibbon wrote:

> Here, then, is an example of the United Nations at work; an example of a debate on a document of which well over half had been removed beforehand, and a debate which paid only lip-service to both root causes of refugee flows and the right to self-determination. At the time of writing in Sudan and Somalia there were no less than 2 million refugees from Ethiopia, yet Ethiopia duly stood up to talk about a report partly decapitated by its mission and in full knowledge that the refugees of the Horn come from nowhere else than from its country. As an exercise in hypocrisy it would be hard to beat; even worse is to come.[5]

The UN failures were even more evident in its handling of refugees in Djibouti. Forced repatriation of refugees from Djibouti to Ethiopia

---

[4] Louis FitzGibbon, 1985, *The Evaded Duty*, Rex Collins Ltd, page 11-12.
[5] Louis FitzGibbon, 1985, *The Evaded Duty*, page 13.

took place in 1983, and the UNHCR was a willing partner and implementer of policies that run directly counter to the long-proclaimed principles of refugee relief and of every humanitarian tenet. Most of the refugees in Djibouti used to live in two main refugee camps, namely Ali Sabeh and Dikil. Despite the resettlement, the refugees in Djibouti did not get the protection they sought and that became clear to them when the host country, Djibouti, and the UNHCR agreed with Ethiopia on a forced repatriation plan. In February 1983, the implementation of a forced repatriation scheme prepared by Ethiopia, Djibouti and the UNCHR began and most of the Somali and Oromo refugees were returned forcibly to Ethiopia. In 1979 an Ethiopian official had visited Dikil one of the refugee camps in Djibouti, bearing an amnesty for the refugees and promising them compensation for goods and properties lost. The refugees rejected his overtures, but the tripartite commission (Ethiopia, Djibouti and the UNHCR) went ahead with its plan. The refugees were told that they would all be repatriated and threatened if they did not sign on. This was followed by a gradual reduction of rations in Ali Sabeh camp and again people were told that there would be no food for those who did not agree to go back. Having lost faith in the UNHCR and the government of Djibouti, they tried to flee from Djibouti. Some managed to flee to other countries, but most of the refugees, especially those at Ali Sabeh, were rounded up and eventually forcibly sent back to Ethiopia. The UNHCR did not follow up the situation of the forced returnees and thus their fate remained unknown, perhaps, to the UN. But from local sources, it was reported that the lives of many of those forced returnees ended brutally as was expected.

Ethiopia not only successfully fooled the international community on the repatriation scheme, but another sinister programme, partly financed by the International Community was also going on in the Ogaden. The programme, which the Derg regime began to carry out right after its re-conquest of the Ogaden, aimed at changing the make-up of the population. The plan was first to depopulate the Ogaden by displacing the indigenous people and then to resettle people there from other regions of Ethiopia. Mengistu requested aid for what he called the displaced people within the Ogaden, but the aid obtained was used for military purposes and the resettlement of Amharas in the valleys of Godey. The scandal was brought to the attention of the world by Somalia and independent sources including the international media in 1980. Leaked documents from Ethiopia in 1983 showed the use of donated food for military ends and the German magazine *Der Spiegel* published an article in which it highlighted the evil motives of the Derg. On 6

December 1982 Somalia's Permanent Representative at the UN, Ambassador Ahmed Mohamed Adan, delivered a speech at the Third Committee on Assistance to Refugees in which he commented about that sinister plan of Ethiopia. In his remarks, the ambassador referred to articles from *Der Spiegel* describing the aims behind Ethiopia's resettlement programme in the Ogaden. In its issues of 17 March 1980 and of 16 June 1980 the magazine stated:

> Ethiopia's governing Military Council was attempting to solve minority problems with a massive resettlement programme. Provinces not inhabited by the Amhara were rapidly being colonized by farmers from the central province of Shoa... The Ogaden region in which primarily Somalis live was being systematically depopulated. Ethiopian and Cuban troops go from village to village burning down the huts, poisoning wells and watering holes and shooting down the livestock with machine guns. What the Amhara and Cubans leave falls victim to the drought.
>
> The tribal transfer is supposed to help break resistance in the long run. No less than three million people are to be resettled.... For the benefit of the outside world, Mengistu has masked the action as a humanitarian one.... Using the generally favourable cover of resettlement the Government has succeeded in getting the United Nations and the European Community to subsidize the paramilitary operation.[6]

Having presented the evidence produced by *Der Spiegel* the ambassador continued his comment and said: 'The ability of the Ethiopian government to use humanitarian assistance for sinister ends was pointed out by the Somali delegation two years ago in the debate on the same items before us now. We expressed then our deep concern over the request for 11 million dollars for the upgrading of the airstrip at Gode in occupied Ogaden, ostensibly so that the relief aid could be freighted there for distribution to camps for displaced and drought-stricken people in the Ogaden. The airstrip at Gode, improved through international assistance, has been used this year as a base for the large-scale and sustained military aggressions launched by land and air against my country. The concern we expressed two years ago was indeed justified.'[7]

The Somali efforts to turn the world's attention to the root causes of the refugees' plight and gross violation of human rights in the Ogaden were fruitless. Ethiopia and its superpower patron, the Soviet Union, got away with their atrocities in the Ogaden, and after having carried out its

---

[6] Louis FitzGibbon, 1985, *The Evaded Duty*, page 75.
[7] Louis FitzGibbon, 1985, *The Evaded Duty*, page 77.

sinister demographical policies, it falsely presented itself with a new human image. She claimed the hosting of 70 000 refugees and 150 000 returnees and requested for them help from the international community.

The Somali government questioned the number of returnees reported by Ethiopia and asked the world body to check the Ethiopian claim and supervise the proper use of humanitarian aid. Furthermore, Somalia alleged that the new Ethiopian programme was part and parcel of its wider programme of depopulating the Ogaden of its indigenous Somali people and replacing them with other nationalities like the Amharas. The people presented as returnees were, in the Somali view, people from other parts of Ethiopia that the Derg regime wanted to resettle in the Oromo and Somali regions, and for that reason, Somalia urged the world body not to subsidise the inhuman policies of the Derg in the Ogaden and elsewhere. Despite these warnings by Somalia and others, and the confirmation of independent sources on the exaggeration of the figure of refugees and returnees in Ethiopia, the international community did not supervise the aid it extended to the brutal Derg regime, which used it mainly for sinister ends. The international community also failed to address the root causes of the refugees' crises.

8.2 The Liberation Struggle: The Diplomatic Front

The Ogaden conflict was internationalised in 1977 because of the superpower involvement. As the war progressed, so was the diplomatic confrontation between Somalia and Ethiopia intensified and fought in international arenas. The Somalis went to these arenas to advocate and promote self-determination rights for the Somalis in the Ogaden, and condemn Ethiopia for the colonization of the Ogaden and its repression policies there. Ethiopia for its part accused Somalia of interference in its internal affairs and aggression. Although the Somalis had every right to restore the freedom in their occupied territory, they lost the diplomatic war to Ethiopia both during and after the war. History repeated itself and the diplomatic situation was remarkably similar to the aftermath of the 1964 Ogaden war. The unjust system of the world was the main reason for the diplomatic failures of the Somalis. Governments follow their own interests and power is the main parameter that determines how much of those interests a country can acquire.

As we saw above, the humanitarian departments of the UN failed to make a link between refugees and human rights and to a large extent ignored the findings of its own commission. Similarly, the political organ of the UN, the Security Council, did not intervene in the Ogaden crises.

In the days of the scramble for the Somali lands, as we saw in earlier chapters, it evaded its duty by simply ignoring the violations of the UN principles and the protectorate treaties. The Russians, as we saw, were not prepared under any circumstances to bring the Ogaden issue to the UN Security Council and the Western countries were not only unprepared to confront the Soviet Union on the Ogaden issue but were also unsympathetic to the suffering of the Somalis in the Ogaden. Both the east and the west urged Somalia to improve relations with its neighbours, abandon Somali rights for self-determination in the Ogaden and NFD, and refrain from backing the liberation movements of the Somalis in the missing territories. Russia even went further, by supporting Somalia's dissidents and by calling for the overthrow of the Somali regime.

In Arab and Islamic organizations, member countries were of three categories regarding the Ogaden conflict. Some of them supported the WSLF and its liberation struggle by giving the liberation movement representative offices; these were Algeria, Iraq, Syria and Kuwait. The positions of these countries regarding the Ogaden issue were relatively stable and the offices were opened in their countries during the 1960s and 1970s. Some other countries such as the Gulf States, Egypt, Iran and Pakistan supported Somalia in one way or another before and after the war, but their support did not go as far as backing the liberation efforts in the Ogaden. Neither the Arab League nor the Organization of Islamic Conference officially endorsed fully the position of Somalia towards the Ogaden conflict or gave the WSLF a representative seat. Despite some condemnation of the Ethiopian policies in the Ogaden and calls for human rights improvements there, the Ogaden cause is yet to become an official Islamic and Arab issue. The majority of member states in these two organizations sympathized with the suffering of the Somali people in the Ogaden but did not support the Somali government or the Somalis in the Ogaden, except for some humanitarian assistance to the refugees. Three countries deserve special attention. South Yemen, as we saw, was part of the Soviet alliance that defeated the Somalis in the 1977/78 Ogaden war and it stayed in the Russian camp after the war. Libya's position was unstable and changed frequently sometimes supporting the liberation efforts in the region, but most of the time – and especially during the 1977/78 war – she was on the Ethiopian side. Sudan also proved to be unreliable regarding the Ogaden issue. Her initial position in the conflict was often neutral or sympathetic, but after the 1977/78 war she openly supported the Ethiopian position on the Ogaden issue.

In Africa, Ethiopia always enjoyed the backing of the OAU, for reasons mentioned in the preceding chapters. In August 1977, the OAU attempted to mediate the parties in the conflict, but the talks collapsed because Ethiopia refused to discuss the issue of self-determination for the Somalis in the Ogaden or to negotiate with the WSLF. The OAU also called for the withdrawal of non-African forces from the region; however, Russia ignored the call. After the war, and especially after Sudan changed its mind about the liberation efforts in the Ogaden, the OAU adopted the Ethiopian position and began to prepare a resolution confirming that position. The 1969 OAU summit set up a committee consisting of several countries including Tanzania, Sudan, Algeria, and Nigeria, but because of disagreements on the issue its chairman, Nyerere, delayed the decision and the first partial report was presented in Lagos in 1980 when Sudan changed its stand on the Ogaden issue. The full report was presented at the OAU summit in Nairobi in 1981. In that summit, the organization approved the committee's findings, which stated that the Ogaden belonged to Ethiopia. The decision of the committee was based on Article III of the OAU which stated that colonial boundaries should be left unchanged.

Despite the lack of diplomatic support for the Ogaden cause in the regional and international bodies, as well as in most countries of the world, the determination of Somalis in the Ogaden for the liberation of their country remained unaffected by these diplomatic setbacks. Of course, they had to reflect on the problems and had to ask themselves what went wrong and caused the failures, but they always looked forward to the next challenge in their struggle. As mentioned earlier, they blamed the powers of the world for the suffering and the ill-treatment, and that blame is justified because since the fourteenth century they were invaded and occupied and remained victims of foreign aggression. But this time they were mature enough to take self-criticism and examine the tactical mistakes they made pursuing their liberation goal. In the subsequent debates and reviews that were conducted, they identified their contributions to the failures. In their pursuit for the just cause of self-determination for the Somalis in the missing territories and the unification of the Somali Nation, the Somalis ignored an important rule of the game in diplomatic engagement, namely the emphasis on what is possible under the circumstances rather than what is right. The critics argued that the representation of the Somalis in the Ogaden by Somalia in diplomatic circles and in sending its armed forces there made the conflict look like a dispute between Somalia and Ethiopia, and made the latter easier to project itself as the victim and to persuade the world that

Somalia was an aggressor seeking to conquer parts of Ethiopia.

8.3 The Liberation Struggle: The WSLF and the Armed Struggle

The WSLF forces continued the armed struggle after Somalia withdrew from the region and were to some extent successful in their armed engagements. They operated from Dire Dawa to Luq, destroying the capability of the enemy forces and paralyzing the occupation administration. The militants were in control of the countryside and contained the Ethiopian and Cuban troops in the towns. 'The Western Somali Liberation Forces continued their guerrilla tactics against the Ethiopian military regime, and with considerable success; on 7 June it was claimed that more than 500 Ethiopians had been killed and 12 Russian-built tanks had been knocked out, but it was also reported that the Ethiopians were carrying out massacres in the Ogaden as reprisals for WSLF activity.'[8]

The armed clashes between the liberation army and Ethiopian and Cuban forces were too many to be counted especially in the period 1978–80. The Sasabane battle, which was witnessed by independent sources, was a typical one. In early April 1978 fierce fighting took place at Sasabane, a village near Dagahbour, between the Ethiopian forces and a WSLF division, Dufan. The result was a total defeat for the Ethiopian and Cuban forces. In a reprisal move, Ethiopian airplanes bombed Garbo, a town not far from Sasabane, with napalm. On 8 April 1979, a reporter from the British newspaper the *Sunday Telegraph* visited both places. The correspondent reported 72 army carriers or vehicles destroyed at Sasabane. The same reporter also visited Garbo and took some pictures of the destruction of the aerial bombing there, which he later displayed.

Although the military side of the resistance was going forward with great success, the diplomatic front was not making headway, and thus the overall progress of the struggle was not going as well as the freedom fighters expected. Questions were being asked as to why the struggle was not gaining the support of the international community. The close relationship between Somalia and the WSLF leadership, as well as the competence of the leadership of the WSLF, became a subject of debate and there was a new determination by the public to change the status

---

[8] Louis FitzGibbon, 1982, *The Betrayal of the Somalis*, page 59.

quo.

In November 1978, an extraordinary central committee meeting was held in response to the growing demands for change. The term for the central committee was coming to an end, and the critics used this as a pretext to launch a campaign to remove the leadership of the organization. They wanted to replace the leading members of the committee with people less connected to the Somali regime, with capabilities to launch different strategies for the struggle. The extraordinary conference ended with a compromise, in which the number of the central committee members was increased from 25 to 150 and the top leadership retained its position.

The compromise, however, did not put an end to the debate about the future of the WSLF as there were no fundamental changes either in the structure of the organization or in the strategy of the struggle. On the contrary, the voices against the policies of the WSLF and the government of Somalia towards the Ogaden struggle were getting louder, and the call for the removal of the central committee was taken by all sections of Western Somali society. The young intelligentsia, the veteran leaders and the armed forces all added their voices to the call for separation between Somalia and the WSLF, as well as to the dismissal of the central committee.

The debate, however, heated up as the other side put its objection to the demand for independence. The leadership of the WSLF and the government of Somalia denied that the WSLF was controlled by Somalia, and they argued that the struggle was a common cause for all the Somalis in both Somalia and Ogaden and that the two were not in conflict. Furthermore, Somalia had sacrificed a lot for the Ogaden cause and suffered economically and politically as a result, and that Ethiopian aggression against Somalia was a reprisal for that support. Without denying all this, the opposition claimed that the separation was best for both. Ethiopia was able to turn the conflict into a border dispute and portrayed Somalia as an aggressor in the eyes of the international community because of the fusion between the WSLF and Somalia. Somalia was punished because it was seen as an aggressor, and that policy also undermined the struggle a great deal because its image was changed from its true colonial question and turned into a dispute between two sovereign states. Eventually, the opposition won the argument, and a general conference was called to discuss the situation.

In 1981, a third general conference was held to which all sections of the society were invited. The armed forces, the intellectuals, the elders, and the women and the youth organization all sent representatives to the conference. In that conference, both the central committee and the WSLF leader, Abdullahi Hassan Mohamoud, were replaced by a central committee consisting of 51 members and headed by Mohamed Diriye Urdoh. The newly elected leader was at the forefront of the campaign for change, and he was twice imprisoned for his critical views regarding the unequal relationship between the WSLF and the government of Somalia. For that reason, he was the favourite for the position and, as expected, he beat his main contester, Abdirizaq Makhtal Dahir.

The conference also approved a constitution for the WSLF, which defined among other things the objectives of the liberation movement, the borders of the territory it represented and the symbols of the people and the territory, as well as the internal organization of the liberation front. As the political representative of the people in the Ogaden, the WSLF was given the role of a shadow government in both the internal and external affairs of the country it was struggling to liberate.

The movements for change emerged the winners from the conference in that they got the leadership of their choice and a constitution that gave the WSLF the political representation of the people. However, in practice, things were not that easy. The idea of complete independence and full freedom from Somali government interference was unrealistic. Among other things, Somalia gave the WSLF offices, bases and financial and political support. Furthermore, because it backed the WSLF, Somalia came under attack from Ethiopia, and that support also led to adverse effects on the Somali economy and its foreign policy, as detailed in the next section. Because of Somalia's backing for the liberation front and the ensuing difficulties the country faced, some kind of policy coordination was unavoidable, but the independent-minded Urdoh refused to compromise on that issue. As a result of the standoff, Somalia halted financial assistance to the liberation front. Because of the confrontation between the WSLF leadership and the Somali government, and the consequent paralysis of the working of the WSLF, the leadership of the organization again became a subject of heated debate, only months after the election.

Urdoh's opponents accused him of incompetence and demanded his resignation. The government of Somalia backed that demand and promised that it would resume the financial support to the organization if Urdoh left office. The chairman and his supporters dismissed the opponents' claim as cheap propaganda intended by the Somali government to use as a pretext to oust Chairman Urdoh. They further argued that the new administration was not given sufficient time to prove its competence and that Somalia was never willing to let the WSLF lead the struggle and represent the people it was fighting for. No doubt the latter's arguments were the ones the public believed, nevertheless the chairman decided to leave his post to ease the situation and not cause further deterioration of the relationship between the WSLF and Somalia. Despite protest from many members of the central committee and the public at large, Mohamed Diriye Urdoh gave up and resigned in 1982.

In 1982 Sheikh Abdinasir Sheikh Adan, the former vice-chairman during the chairmanship of Abdullahi Hassan Mohamoud, was elected to replace Mohamed Diriye Urdoh, but only to finish the remaining time of Urdoh's chairmanship. No other election took place after Sheikh Abdinasir took office and he became the last leader of the WSLF.

8.4 The Liberation Struggle: The Support Organizations

Two support organizations appeared on the struggle platform in the 1970s. The Western Somali Youth Liberation Organization (WSYLO) and the Western Somali Women Liberation Organization (WSWLO) joined the struggle to support the WSLF. These were support organizations in the sense that their prime aim was not to take the leadership role, but they were also politicised organizations. In fact, they were the main forces behind the strategic and political changes towards the struggle after their establishment. On the whole, both organizations were supportive in assisting the WSLF leadership and in correcting it, although politically the contribution of the youth organization was greater than that of the women group.

The WSYLO began as an underground organization in 1978/9 and worked in that manner for some time. Among the main aims of the organization was to take the administration of the struggle from the hands of the government of Somalia. Because of the government's opposition to the idea, and the lack of free expression there, the organization began its operations secretly. But as the demand became a public demand by the end of 1979, the organisation declared its goals publicly and became part of the visible struggle. The organization was formed in Mogadishu, but in a short period, it established branches in all the main towns and refugee camps in Somalia. It organized and mobilized the grassroots of the WSLF and at the same time scrutinized the activities of the leadership by demanding accountability and pointing out the right direction that, in their view, the struggle should take.

Despite the difficult relationship between the WSLF and WSYLO, especially in the early years, gradually the WSLF leadership recognized the importance of the contributions of the WSYLO and gave it an office at the headquarters of the WSLF, and recruited some of its leaders from the ranks of the WSYLO. The WSYLO sent candidates to the third general conference, who were elected and became members of the central committee as well as the executive committee of the WSLF. After the disintegration of the WSLF, the WSYLO became the backbone of the revival of the liberation movement and dominated the political organizations that replaced the WSLF as well as the political scene of the Ogaden region during the 1990s.

The Western Somali Women Liberation Organization (WSWLO) was less political than the youth organization, but more humanitarian. It began its work before its formal establishment as nurses of the wounded and victims of the war. The women used to collect whatever possible from the public to relieve the victims of the war, both combatant and non-combatant. Afterwards, they extended their work by supporting the freedom fighters morally, and by providing them with what little material their hands could grab. Eventually, they became more involved in political life as they became more politically aware. They became active participants in the political process and some of their members joined the WSLF central committee, but still, their primary goal remained the supportive role, at which they excelled.

8.5 The Decline of the Somali State

After the war, the Somali government faced many challenges that were mainly the result of the war. Somalia's regional position was already weakened by the war because she did not only lose the war but also lost superpower patronage. Furthermore, the Ethiopian aggression against Somalia continued and Ethiopia's military became superior to that of the Somalis. On the domestic side, the public was extremely disappointed at the outcome of the war. The morale of the armed forces was devastated by the defeat and some military officers criticized the government's conduct of the war as well as its overall military policy and strategy. Furthermore, the economy was severely affected by the war and urgent measures were needed to save it from collapsing. In the following section, we summarise internal and external pressures that led to the decline of the state.

8.6 The Decline of the Somali State: The Ethiopian

Aggression

Because of her victory in the war, after the Soviet bloc countries intervened in her favour, Ethiopia became more aggressive. Since 1978, Ethiopian aircraft attacked many Somali towns, and bombed and strafed the population in these towns. The air raids frequently took place during the period 1978–84 and affected nearly the whole country, from Borama in the north to Elberde in the south, along the whole provisional border. The ensuing causalities were very high because of the Ethiopian use of napalm and fragmentation bombs and because of their indiscriminate nature.

The widespread and indiscriminate air raids did not spare anyone, but the victims of the Ethiopian bombing were mainly civilians everywhere. As an example, the Ethiopian aircraft attacked the central regions of Somalia in November 1980, and the bombings left a heavy loss of life and materials. In Dusamareb, the air raids killed 26 people and injured 22 more people. Over 200 houses were also destroyed or damaged. In Adado 33 people were killed, 39 were injured, and 374 houses were destroyed in the air raids. In January 1984, an aerial bombing of a school in Borama killed 37 schoolchildren and wounded hundreds more.

Ethiopia's aggression was not only confined to the air raids. Ethiopia invaded Somalia several times and captured some towns. The Ethiopian army crossed the border near Dolo on 19 October 1980, captured the town of Yed and hoisted the Ethiopian flag there. The Somali army later ejected them from that part of Somalia. The towns of Galdogob and Balanballe were captured and occupied in 1982 by Ethiopian forces and they remained under Ethiopian occupation for several years.

In an attempt to bring down the Somali government and destabilize Somalia, the Ethiopian government armed Somali dissidents. It gave them military training, arms, bases, and financial support. As we will see in the next section, Ethiopia succeeded in destabilizing Somalia and contributed to the collapse of the Somali state, by using Somali rebels.

8.7 The Decline of the Somali State: Internal Conflict

Only a few weeks after the withdrawal of the Somali Army from the Ogaden, the president's leadership was questioned. The first challenge of political authority came from the military establishment. On 9 April 1978, some Somali army officers unsuccessfully attempted to oust the government in a coup d'état. Most of the failed coup leaders were executed afterwards, but some managed to flee to Kenya, from where they then moved to Ethiopia and formed an armed resistance, namely the Somali Salvation Democratic Front (SSDF). The present interim president of Somalia, Abdullahi Yusuf became the first leader of the SSDF. The organization got substantial military and economic backing from the Eastern bloc countries and Libya, in addition to Ethiopian support. In collaboration with the Ethiopian army, the SSDF militants used to launch attacks on Somali villages in the central region and to broadcast hostile propaganda from a mobile radio station (Radio Kulmis). But because of its connection with Ethiopia and its narrow tribal base, the organization did not gain the sympathy of the Somali public, let alone its support.

Despite the apparent lack of support for the SSDF, the demand for a change of government gradually grew over time across the regions. Although the demand for change was widespread among the whole population, it was not channelled through national organizations, but through tribal and clan affiliations. Different clans began to form armed opposition organizations of their own. The Somali National Movement (SNM), which was formed in 1981, was – like the SSDF – a clan-based organization, and both of them sought the support of Ethiopia. The many other tribal opposition groups that were established afterwards such as the Somali Patriotic Movement (SPM), and the United Somali Congress (USC), were also all clan-based organizations and had ties with the Ethiopian regime.

The armed opposition contributed to the decline of the Somali state in two ways. First, they divided the population along clan lines, and thereby undermined the unity of the nation. They replaced the national aspiration with a tribal one and aroused hostile sentiments among the various clans. In other words, they exchanged the national identity for clan identity and gradually destroyed the identity of the Somali nation. The other way they contributed to the destruction was by their surrender to the Ethiopians. Through them, Ethiopia got access to valuable classified information about the Somali state, its make-up and its army, and because of their collaboration, Ethiopia was able to penetrate deep into the Somali state and manipulate Somali politics. The latter card, which the Somali armed groups provided to Ethiopia, became particularly useful leverage that Ethiopia still possesses and effectively uses.

The government's responses to the armed groups fighting for its overthrow also contributed immensely to the decline of the Somali state. The government not only refused to respond to the public's demand for change, but it used the same tactics as that of the opposition in dividing the society, by punishing the clans that supported certain opposition groups and rewarding those it felt to be loyal. As the public was divided along tribal lines by both the opposition and the government, the national spirit disappeared. It became evident that the two opposing forces were united in destroying the national consciousness, Somali solidarity and all other unifying factors of the nation.

8.8 The Decline of the Somali State: The Military

The Somali officials claimed that the US promised them it would provide Somalia's military needs should the Russian leave Somalia. That claim was, however, denied by the US government. Whether the US double-crossed Somalia, as some Somali officials claimed or not, it approached Somalia cautiously. Somalia hoped to sell the Russian bases in Somalia to the US at a high price, but these hopes were also dashed. Berbera was Somalia's most valued strategic post, because of its location and because of the advanced facilities that the Russians built there. President Siyad Barre offered Berbera to the US for a price of $2 billion but the US negotiator responded with an offer of $40 million, which Somalia in the end accepted.

Despite its strategic position and the West's desire to contain the communist expansion, Somalia did not get superpower patronage from the US in military terms for several reasons. The desire to contain the Soviet satellite in the Horn was real, but the US government gave priority to other regional considerations. The US opposed the Ogaden war and was not willing to give Somalia offensive capabilities. Furthermore, the OAU supported the Ethiopian position on the war and some African leaders, notably Nyerere of Tanzania, and other African diplomats undertook a campaign against Somalia. Thus, the US government was not prepared to confront the African leaders for the sake of the Somalis.

The military base at Berbera did not change the Somali-US relationship and the US remained a reluctant ally of Somalia. The Carter administration withheld even the defensive weapons the US government promised to Somalia, despite constant Ethiopian aggression against Somalia. It was only after the occupation of two Somali towns, namely Galdogob and Balanballe, in 1982 that the Reagan administration supplied Somalia with some desperately needed defensive weapons. Following the occupation of the Somali towns, American military aid was increased in 1983 and was budgeted for $40 million, but then it decreased to $36 million in 1986.

Compared with Ethiopia, Somalia became very weak militarily

because of the huge supply of military hardware to Ethiopia by the Soviet Union and its allies, both during and after the war, and the reluctance of the US to fill the military hole left by the Russians in Somalia. As Somalia's defence capabilities were reduced, the Ethiopian threat became real. The military vulnerability not only undermined the Greater Somalia dream but also jeopardised the sovereignty of the Somali state.

8.9 The Decline of the Somali State: The Political Economy

By the end of the 1970s, Somalia had experienced economic and political stagnation. The Ogaden war was the main factor that led to the stagnation, but other factors such as corruption and the 1974/75 drought also contributed to the poor performance of the economy. Following the war, both debt and foreign trade deficits had increased dramatically, the inflation rate also rose sharply and both the industrial and agricultural output declined. Besides that, not only was the socialist program in disarray but, when the Soviets left Somalia, the government began to dissipate enthusiasm for the very socialist ideals that never had popular support among most of the Somali people.

As a result of the political and economic difficulties that the country faced after the war, the government of Somalia turned to the West for help. The West offered economic assistance to Somalia through the Bretton Woods institutions (the International Monetary Fund (IMF) and the World Bank) on the condition that Somalia fulfils the standard IMF loan conditions. Because of its weak position, Somalia could not resist the offer. She adopted an IMF programme and took corrective measures to meet the Fund's conditions. The prime objective of the Fund programme was to provide a viable balance of payments position and a reduction in inflation, both of which were needed to ensure a more satisfactory and more sustainable rate of economic growth over the medium term. The policy instruments for achieving these goals were the exchange rate (devaluation) and domestic credit expansion (credit restriction). In other words, the money supply had to be tightened to reduce the rate of inflation and the Somali shilling had to be devalued to improve the balance of payments and reduce inflation.

In February 1980, a stand-by arrangement agreement was signed with the IMF, but not implemented until July 1981, although the government had carried out several corrective measures in 1980 to meet the IMF standards. The programme relied primarily on restrained fiscal and monetary policies, including interest rate increases. The stabilization policies pursued in 1980 were followed by a major adjustment effort, which the authorities launched in mid-1981. The effort was supported by two consecutive stand-by arrangements with the Fund (covering the period 15 July 1981 to 14 January 1984), aimed at stimulating domestic production, slowing the rate of inflation and reaching a sustainable external sector position over the medium term. To achieve these goals the government carried out corrective measures.

Devaluation was one of the two main policy instruments to improve the balance of payments and reduce the rate of inflation, and the Somali shilling was devalued several times during the 1980s. In mid-1981 the authorities devalued the Somali shilling by 50 per cent. The shilling was further devalued in mid-1982 by 17 per cent on the export side and 34 per cent on the import side in foreign currency terms. After a year, the dual exchange rate was unified, and the exchange rate made flexible.

Other corrective measures that the government took included the abolition of the imports system known as 'Franco Valuta', the liberalisation of private sector imports and the introduction of external accounts denominated in US dollars. To improve financial intermediation, encourage domestic saving, increase immigrants' remittances and discourage capital outflows, the government followed a flexible exchange rate policy and devised a bonus plan in which the government offered a 25 per cent premium in foreign currency terms above the official exchange rate for workers remittances and foreign capital sent into the country by Somali nationals.

Several price liberalization and marketing policies designed to encourage economic growth were also introduced. For example, producers' prices of major agricultural products increased by 17–50 per cent and producers' prices of bananas were raised 158 per cent; the monopoly enjoyed by the government agency dealing with cereal products was discontinued and producers were allowed to market their produce freely in the marketplace. Furthermore, the principle of economic pricing was adopted when, in 1983, the government decided that enterprises should sell at prices that reflected the costs as well as an adequate profit margin and abandoned the control of input and output prices for public goods.

In an attempt to reduce the budget deficit as required by the IMF, the government carried out a number of revenue-increasing as well as expenditure-reducing measures. The revenue-increasing measures included a 25 per cent tax on livestock exports, changes in custom valuation procedures, and the elimination of exemptions on import duties for some public and private enterprises and the conversion of major specific excises to an ad valorem basis. As a result of these measures, domestic revenue increased at an annual rate of about 42 per cent during 1981–83. By contrast, the annual growth rate of total expenditure was confined during 1981–83 to about 28 per cent and this decline in the level of expenditure was the result of austerity measures. As part of these measures, the government recruited fewer new employees, did not grant cost-of-living salary adjustment to civil servants, limited administrative and other expenditures, reduced capital outlays and, in 1983, decided to abandon the policy of guaranteed employment for high-school graduates.

The government prepared a medium-term recovery program, consisting of a public investment program for 1984–86, and phased a programme for policy reforms, but because of International Development Association (IDA) considered this programme too ambitious, the government scaled down its projects. In March 1984, the government signed a letter of intent accepting the terms of a new US$183 million IMF extended credit facility to run for another three years. But because of a proposed 60 per cent cut in the military budget, the agreement was cancelled at a Council of Ministers meeting in April by one vote.

Despite the breakup, Somalia had nowhere else to turn to, and it was not possible for her to take care of her economy alone. Because of this constraint and because of economic deterioration, the government went back to the IMF in 1985 and signed an agreement with the Fund in which the government agreed to take more unpopular measures, including further devaluation of the Somali shilling, further cuts in public spending and a reduction in civil servants. In both the 1985 and 1987 plans, the Somali government was instructed to permit further privatization particularly in the banking and industrial sectors. In the end, Somalia had carried out nearly all the policies required by the Fund and the World Bank to achieve the aims of the programme.

In June 1983, the government of Saudi Arabia decided to stop importing Somali livestock, the most important single export item of the Somali economy. Saudi officials claimed that rinderpest had been detected in Somali livestock, making them unsafe to eat. Despite this ban, the regional hostility and the drought that hit the country in 1983/84, the economy had improved during the period 1981–83, and the IMF claimed that this improvement was the result of the adjustment policies followed by the Somali authorities. The overall results of the programme, however, contradicted that claim, despite the encouraging signs in the first three years of the programme period. The estimated growth of GDP, which averaged 1 per cent a year during 1979/80, increased to 5 per cent in 1981 and reached 11 per cent in 1982. The rate of inflation fluctuated by falling in the first year and increasing in the second year. In the external sector, the current account deficit declined from 6 per cent of GDP in 1980 to 2 per cent in 1983 but the overall balance of payments deficit remained high although it had declined from $95 million in 1980 to US$93 million in 1983. The government also succeeded in reducing its overall budget deficit from 9 per cent of GDP in 1980 to 3 per cent in 1983. This somewhat successful story did not last long, and the overall result of the programme was devastating to the economy and to the stability of the Somali state.

The intermediate aims of the programme were to improve the balance of payments and reduce inflation in order to raise the real GDP, which was the ultimate goal of the programme. But none of these goals was achieved. Inflation reached nearly hyper-rate levels and the balance of payments deficit became larger, and the real GDP declined. Furthermore, unemployment increased sharply, public services deteriorated and all these and many other economic failures were blamed on the policies the Bretton Woods institutions instructed Somalia to carry out.

The expenditure reducing measures that Somalia carried out negatively affected the lives of the population, particularly the poorest. The hardest-hit services were health and education. Before the programme, the government provided free health and education services, and all high-school graduates were guaranteed either a position in higher education or employment. After the programme, the government was unable to provide these services as before and even forced to reduce the existing workforce. In 1985, 5 000 civil servants were dismissed as a result of IMF and World Bank pressures.

The devaluation of the Somali shilling neither reduced the rate of inflation nor improved the balance of payments as intended. Somalia was heavily dependent on imports for its food and other essential goods, and the effect of the devaluation was to increase the price of these imported goods, thus reducing the public's affordability of these goods. The price rise on imported goods led to overall price increases that severely reduced the purchasing power of the Somali shilling.

The economic deterioration and the consequent decline in public goods made the government even more receptive to the directives of the Bretton Woods institutions. In other words, Somalia not only became dependent on the IMF and the World Bank but also lost its authority over the management of the economy because all sectors of the economy were affected by the directives of the IMF and the World Bank. In addition to the decline in social services, the defence capability of the country was reduced because of the huge cuts in military expenditure. Because of their low wages and the high inflation rate, most of the soldiers could not live on their income alone and, as a result, many of them deserted the army to find better jobs. The required military hardware also became unaffordable because of the budget reduction. In short, Somalia's economy and sovereignty were undermined by the directives of the Bretton Woods' institutions.

9

New Liberation Movements and Different Challenges

New liberation movements (The birth of ONLF and Al-Itihad)

9.1 The Ogaden National Liberation Front

As we saw in chapter 8, the WSLF became to some extent a puppet organization controlled by the Somali government and the liberation forces became more detached from the leadership of the organization. On the one hand, the public's call for an independent organization to lead the struggle was not headed by the WSLF and Somalia. On the other hand, the grassroots were not prepared to compromise on the question of the independence of the leadership of the struggle. Thus, some sort of action from the opposition became inevitable, but the question was: What to do, given the circumstances?

On 15 August 1984 six members of the dissatisfied group within the WSLF movements met to discuss the stand-off between the grassroots and the WSLF leadership as well as the future of the struggle. At that meeting, the six men saw the need for an alternative representative organization and decided on the formation of a new organization, namely the Ogaden National Liberation Front (ONLF). Three of the men, Abdullahi Mohamed Sa'di, Sheikh Ibrahim Abdallah and Mohamed Ismail, were the WSLF representatives in Kuwait, the United Arab Emirates and Algeria, respectively. Of the other three, Abdirahman Sheikh Mahdi was the former chairman of the youth organization, Abdirahman Magan was a WSLF central committee member and Abdi Ibrahim Geele was from the WSLF trade union.

At the time of the formation of the ONLF, the struggle was suffering from a misconception about the Ogaden cause, which resulted from Ethiopia's portrayal of the conflict as a border dispute and the policy fusion of the WSLF and the government of Somalia. The successive governments in Addis Ababa worked hard to turn the colonial question into a border dispute between Ethiopia and Somalia and branded the latter as an aggressor. Because of the close relationship between Somalia and the WSLF, and the former's leadership of the struggle, the Somalis also contributed to the misrepresentation and helped Ethiopia's efforts to change the true image of the conflict. In both the regional and international forums Ethiopia successfully presented itself as a victim of Somali aggression, despite its illegal occupation of the Ogaden.

The ONLF's use of the name 'Ogaden' instead of Western Somali was partly necessitated by the need to eliminate that misconception. The name 'Western Somali' was confusing in that it was often understood as a region within proper Somalia and WSLF officials often had to explain the name in the international forums. The confusion about the name was exacerbated by the appearance on stage in the 1980s of several Somali movements opposed to the Somali government. The region is globally known as the Ogaden and the use of that name would in the ONLF's view not only remove the name confusion, but also the misconception about the cause. Following the footsteps of the Ogaden Liberation Front/Nasrullah, which was established in Hodayo in 1963, its founders decided to take all necessary measures to restore the proper image of the cause.

The public was frustrated with WSLF policies and was trying to find other ways of lifting up the struggle. For that reason, the people warmly welcomed the new organization. Despite the announcement of its formation and the warm welcome it received, the organization existed only on paper and the enthusiastic public were soon disappointed. Until 1992, when the ONLF held its first general conference and elected leadership, the organization did not have a formal organizational structure. Somalia banned the new organization immediately after the announcement of its formation. As mentioned above, the founders of the organization used to live in different parts of the world, but they were all either holding Somali passports or living in Somalia. Those who lived in Somalia could not reveal their identity to the public because of fear of persecution, and Somalia withdrew their passports from some of those living abroad. Furthermore, some of the founding members joined other organizations and temporarily disappeared from the struggle platform. This lack of leadership created a great deal of confusion among the activists, which in turn lead to a waste of resources.

Because of the lack of formal organization, during the 1984–1992 period, the liberation movements that supported the ideals of the ONLF acted on behalf of the organization, with each group or individual interpreting the programme of the new front in their own way. The existing support groups in Somalia such as the WSWLO and WSYLO changed their mantles and became ONLF grassroots and leaders.

Similarly, other support organizations such as the Ogaden Action Group in the UK, the Ogaden Welfare Association in Norway, the Ogaden Welfare Organization in Sweden and The Ogaden Relief association in Germany, were formed in the diaspora and became supporters and representatives of the invisible ONLF. The public waited eight years for the founders to organize a conference or bring an organization with a structure before the grassroots, whose agitation brought the birth of the ONLF took the initiative.

In late 1990 some support groups, mainly from Somalia and the Arab countries, began to move to the Ogaden and make operation bases there, aiming to establish a formal structure for the organization and lead the struggle from there. Thanks to their efforts and the self-mobilized grassroots, the ONLF got a foothold in nearly the whole region within a short period. The grassroots were ready and all that was missing was the leadership of the ghost organization. To fill that gap, the young intelligentsia who came from Somalia and abroad began to prepare a general conference inside the Ogaden.

In the general conference held at Garigo'an near Garbo on 17 January 1992, a central committee led by Sheikh Ibrahim Abdallah was elected. The former members of the WSYLO dominated the leadership. Over 98 per cent of the executive committee were from that youth organization, which remained the backbone of the liberation struggle since the 1980s. Among those honourable gentlemen from the WSYLO who laid down the foundation of the ONLF at Garigo'an, put its programme into practice and took leadership roles were 'Abdirizaq sheikh Mohamud, Abdirizaq Mohamed, Abdulqadir Sheikh Hasssan, Abdulqadir Hirmoge, Adbullahi Abdi Taflow, Abdullahi Qaji, Abdullahi Adan, Ahmed Mohamed, Ahmed Nur Mohamed Omar, Ahmed Mohamed Hussein, Hassan Aw'ise, Ilyas Sheikh Ali Siyad, Mohamed Sheikh Muhumed Irad, Ismail Sheikh Abdi, Kafi Yusuf Abdallah, Mohamed Abdi Yasin, Mohamed Sheikh Ibrahim and Siad Bedri'.[1]

9.2 The Ogaden Islamic Union (Al-Itihad)

The Ogaden Islamic Union, better known as Al-Itihad, was founded in 1983 in Somalia, but because of the hostile political climate in Somalia, it went underground. Unlike the ONLF, however, Al-Itihad did not originate from the grassroots of the WSLF. It began as a welfare Islamic

---

[1] Sheikh Ibrahim Abdallah, 2001, *Tuhfatul Awfiya, Limasirati Atahriri wata'ribi Fil Qarinil Ifriqi*, Horn of Africa Studies, page 429.

organization to alleviate the suffering of the Ogaden people in the refugee camps in Somalia and inside the Ogaden. But although the organization started its activities as a relief organization, its ultimate goal was to remove the cause of the suffering, namely colonization. The organization preferred a peaceful means to achieve its liberation goal, but it did not rule out the use of force should that be necessary.

The organization opened Islamic schools in the refugee camps in Somalia and began a secret mobilization campaign in which the youth were taught about the root causes of their plight and the need to liberate the land they came from. Military training was also part of the programme of the organization. In 1989 the organization sent a mission, headed by Sheikh Abdullahi Sheikh Ahmed Qasim, to the Ogaden region to assess the situation there. The mission visited all zones of the region and gathered extensive information material for the organization. Before the mission returned from the Ogaden, however, the Somali government collapsed and most of the refugees, including many of the Al-Itihad activists, went back home.

The refugees went back home empty-handed, and the country they returned to was hit by a severe drought. The same regime they fled from was still in power and the humanitarian situation there was very grave indeed. Like the other refugees, the members of Al-Itihad fled in different directions and became scattered over all parts of the world. The fall of the Mengistu regime, however, a few months later brought a breathing space for the people of the region. Soon after the fall of the Derg regime, led by Mengistu Haile Mariam, the Al-Itihad mission, which arrived in 1989, and those returned from Somalia met inside the Ogaden, and decided to revive the organization and bring together its dispersed members.

On 30 June 1991, the organization held its first general conference in Qabridahare. Nearly all the Al-Itihad activists who were inside the Ogaden at the time, as well as various other sections of the society, attended the conference. Sheikh Abdullahi Bade and Sheikh Abdullahi Sheikh Ahmed Qasim were elected chairman and vice-chairman, respectively. A consultative body and an executive committee were also elected. The conference approved the formation of military training centres and the establishment of Islamic schools in all parts of the region.

9.3 The Challenges

In addition to the difficulties that already existed, the struggle for the liberation of Ogaden faced new problems originating from the use of the

Ogaden cause as a bargaining chip by both the Somali government and Somali armed opposition groups, the collapse of the Somali state, the death of Somali nationalism and the dismantling of the Western Somali Liberation Front.

9.3.1 The Somali-Ethiopia Accord

The Ethiopian and Somali leaders, Mengistu Haile Mariam and Mohamed Siyad Barre met in Djibouti in January 1986 during the establishment of the regional organization the Intergovernmental Authority on Drought and Desertification (IGADD). In that meeting, the two governments agreed in principle to ease the tension between the two countries and not to support the groups opposed to their governments. This meant Somalia should refrain from supporting the WSLF and, in return, Ethiopia would withdraw its support from the SSDF and the SNM.

Two other meetings, in Addis Ababa and Mogadishu, to discuss the technicalities of the Djibouti Agreement followed the Djibouti meeting. A final agreement was reached between the two countries on 3 April 1988 in Mogadishu, in which the two countries agreed – among other things – to respect the sovereignty and the territorial integrity of the two countries and to reduce tension and hostility along the common border, by ceasing their support to each other's rebel groups. This agreement contrasted sharply with the previous policies of the Somali military regime, but this U-turn policy was not new to the country in a sense. All previous Somali governments used to cease their assistance to the liberation movements whenever they faced some difficulties. The liberation movements in the NFD and the Ogaden, as we saw in earlier chapters, were encouraged after independence, but when the going got tough, both the governments of Abdirizaq Haji Hussain and Mohamed Ibrahim Igal reversed their policies. Because of the correlation between the support for the struggle and the security of the Somali state/regime, and the prioritization of the latter, all Somali governments dismantled the liberation movements they helped to form. However, the Mogadishu Agreement was more dangerous than the previous ones because the previous governments were in a stronger position than Siyad's government in 1988.

The first to condemn the agreement was the WSLF, which most of the Western Somali people branded a puppet organization controlled by Siyad Barre. This time, however, the organization reacted forcefully and denounced the agreement, calling it a reversal of the Somali efforts to liberate the missing territories and unite the Somali nation. In response to the Mogadishu Agreement, the Western Somali Liberation Front issued a statement on 12 April 1988, in which it heavily criticised the Somali government and declared its defiance of the Agreement. The WSLF stressed further that it would continue the struggle until the Western Somali was liberated and that the agreement between the two countries did not concern the colonial question of the Western Somali and the struggle for its liberation.

The Ogaden National Liberation Front and all the other organizations of the liberation movements responded similarly. They showed their defiance of the Mogadishu accord and declared their determination to continue the struggle until liberation day. The agreement confirmed the ONLF and the grassroots' belief that the Somali government was not sincere in its support for the liberation struggle. Thus, the accord made it easier for them to mobilize the public for a free and independent liberation organization.

Despite the condemnation and the strong opposition to the plan by the Western Somali people, Somalia went ahead with the peace deal between the two countries, because of domestic and external pressures. The Somali government wanted to crush the rebels opposed to it by cutting off their main source of support. Furthermore, some western powers, particularly Italy, promised aid to both Ethiopia and Somalia if the two agreed on a peace deal, and Siyad Barre was determined to achieve both goals. Similarly, Ethiopia needed both the aid money and the defeat of the Western Somali liberation movements.

Diplomatic relations between the two countries were resumed, and to put the agreement into practice several confidence-building measures were taken from both sides. Among these measures were common border patrols, demilitarisation zones and exchange of visits by armed forces officials. Somalia fully implemented the agreement and eventually dismantled the Western Somali Liberation Front, but the Ethiopian government did not honour the peace deal. On the contrary, she blackmailed Somalia by arming and encouraging the SNM to attack the Somali government. Mengistu told the SNM, the main opposition group at the time, to either leave Ethiopia unarmed for other countries or return home with their weapons.

The money promised by Italy reached the two counties and each of them was given $250 million. But Somalia's other aim for the peace deal was not achieved. After having succeeded in dismantling the WSLF through the peace deal reached by the two countries, Ethiopia turned against Somalia to destroy it, and in so doing she armed the rebel groups to the teeth and asked them to leave Ethiopia. The SSDF's military wing dispersed, after its leader Abdullahi Yusuf was imprisoned by Ethiopia in the 1980s, but the SNM was strong at the time. The SNM chose to attack the north in May 1988 and the ensuing battles were fought inside the main northern cities.

The government reacted heavy-handedly to the rebel attacks and used all its might, including aerial bombing, to defeat the rebels. The fighting between the government forces and the SNM forces left heavy loss of lives and huge devastation. Thousands of civilians were among the casualties and some districts of the cities of Burao and Hargeisa were totally or partially destroyed. The government got the upper hand eventually, but the civil war continued, and other rebel groups were formed in other parts of the country. As a result of the peace deal in which Somalia tried to sell the just cause of the Ogaden for the termination of Ethiopia's assistance to the Somali rebels, and the brutal response to the SNM attack in the north, the government lost its credibility. Ethiopia continued its support for the SNM after the war in the north. The new organizations – the Somali Patriotic Movement (SPM) and the United Somali Congress (USC) also got Ethiopian support. More importantly, the peace accord brought nothing good to the Somali people. Tens of thousands of Somalis died in the fighting in the north, many more were made homeless and fled the country, whole districts were destroyed, the freedom fighters in the Ogaden lost their organization, the killing of Somalis by Somalis began and Ethiopia contemplated the systematic downing of the Somali state.

9.3.2 The Somali Armed Rebels

The activities of the Somali armed groups who opposed the rule of President Mohamed Siyad Barre and later fought among themselves after the fall of the Barre government, adversely affected the struggle for the liberation of the Ogaden directly through political and military cooperation with Ethiopia, and indirectly through the weakening and destruction of the Somali state as well as undermining the efforts for its revival. Like the government they opposed, the burying of the just Ogaden cause was the main thing that the Somali opposition groups offered Ethiopia to gain the latter's support. The opposition groups were given bases inside the occupied Ogaden and in collaboration with the Ethiopian forces, the Somali rebels conducted attacks against both the WSLF forces and civilians in the Ogaden. Hussein Muhumed Awnuh (Amusane), one of WSLF's best and most respected army commanders, and several of his aides were killed in an ambush carried out jointly by a Somali rebel group and Ethiopian forces. One of the main reasons why Siyad Barre sought the peace deal with Ethiopia was to contain the rebels, and because of them the Barre regime negotiated from a position of weakness and as a result was not able to resist Ethiopia's demand for the abandonment of the Ogaden cause.

The opposition not only weakened the Somali government and forced her to bend to the Derg regime, but they continued their anti-government activities until the Somali state collapsed. In opposition, they did not formulate an alternative form of government and when power fell into their hands, they did not take it over in an orderly manner but instead started fighting among themselves until the situation was out of control. They not only brought down the Somali government, but they destroyed the fabric of the Somali Nation. Because of their narrow clan affiliation, their collaboration with Somalia's chief enemy, the violent means they chose in reaching their goals and the inter-clan conflict they commenced, they dismantled the basis for nationhood. In short, they did not bring any public good with them and were united only in destroying the state and nationhood.

After the collapse of the Somali state, the armed militias engaged in internal wars among themselves and competed for the backing of Ethiopia in order to gain power. Ethiopia for its parts took maximum advantage of the situation, by fooling the selfish faction leaders and fuelling the war among the militias. The Ethiopian government armed the warring factions to fuel the war among them and at the same kept telling every one of the faction leaders that he was the only one who deserves the top post.

The fighting was not only between the Ethiopia sponsored groups and the minority opposed to its intervention, but also among the groups within the Ethiopian camp. Despite their common boss, Ethiopia backed militia leaders kept fighting each other because Ethiopia actively tried to create differences between the allied factions and to widen the gap between the opponents so that they remained weak, dependent and loyal. Because of their submission, in practice, Ethiopia controlled these faction leaders who became agents for Ethiopia in their respective regions. They not only relied on Ethiopia in winning the war against their faction opponents but also in suppressing the people in the areas under their rule.

On the political development, Ethiopia presented herself as a peacemaker, despite the contrary reality on the ground. Furthermore, she claimed that IGAD mandated her to preside over the Somali peace process. The Ethiopian aims in controlling the peace process were to prevent the revival of the Somali state, to get funds and assistance in the process, and to misrepresent the Somali crises in the international forums. The 1993 reconciliation conference, which Ethiopia hijacked and held in Addis Ababa, illustrates this point. The conference enabled Ethiopia not only to control the reconciliation efforts but also to widen the gap between the faction leaders and to penetrate deeper into Somali clan politics. Besides that, all the funds for the peace efforts from governments and non-governmental organizations were channelled through Ethiopia. The combination of the two roles (peace-making and conflict-fuelling), and the submission of most of the Somali faction leaders to Ethiopia, effectively brought most parts of Somalia under Ethiopian rule.

The Addis Ababa conference failed to produce results, despite the huge efforts by the UN and other international organizations, largely because of Ethiopia's intervention. After having got control of the reconciliation process, the Addis Ababa government took the initiative for future reconciliation efforts. Ethiopia launched another reconciliation conference of its own at the resort of Sodere, south of Addis Ababa, in 1996 to create a puppet government. Only the faction leaders backed by Ethiopia attended the conference. By the end of the conference, the faction leaders announced the establishment of a council with 41 members and a rotating chairman. The plan failed, and the council dispersed soon afterwards. The process or the outcome of the Somali peace conferences that took place after that meeting was, however, determined by Ethiopia.

The Addis Ababa government does not want the return of a proper government in Somalia. The present chaotic situation is the most preferable to her and a puppet government under her control is her second-best preference. Through the loyal faction leaders, Ethiopia still dictates the direction and future shape of Somalia. The Addis Ababa government used these warlords to fail the Cairo conference in 1997 and the Somali Transitional Government (TNG), which was formed in Arta, Djibouti and headed by Abdulqasim Salad Hassan. The TNG failed mainly because of external pressures, of which Ethiopia was the main facilitator. The present Interim Federal Government, which was established in Kenya, was largely an Ethiopian design. She heavily dictated the process, and the selection of the members of the parliament and the executive was not free from her intervention. Because of her involvement in the selection of the parliament and alleged bribes to some members of the assembly, her candidate for the presidency was elected. The prime minister and most of the ministers were hand-picked by Ethiopia. At the peace conference in Kenya, the main faction leaders also signed an additional protocol, worked out by Kenya and Ethiopia, in which they renounced any territorial claims to the neighbouring countries. This meant the abandonment of the Ogaden and NFD.

Ethiopia not only controlled the political process but has been militarily active on the ground since the latter half of the 1990s. In fact, without the blessing of the Ethiopian regime, it became difficult for the Somali warlords to hold power in their respective regions. Moreover, incursions into Somalia by Ethiopian forces became frequent after 1996, on the pretext of pursuing Somali terrorists or on rescuing a faction leader whose position is threatened by another. Ethiopia is now occupying the whole country on the pretext of protecting the interim government.

Ethiopia-backed faction leaders and their regional administrations also helped Ethiopia in the capture and killing of Somali dissidents from the Ogaden, who escaped into Somalia. The Ethiopia-backed regional administration in Hargeisa rounded up many civilians and handed them to the Addis Ababa regime for alleged membership of the Ogaden National Liberation Front. Others remained in Hargeisa jails on orders from Ethiopia. In collaboration with the faction leaders, the Ethiopian agents gunned down many people of Somali-Ogaden origin as well as from Somalia in Somali cities. The Addis Ababa regime's strategy has been to encircle the liberation movements fighting in the Ogaden and deny them their traditional escape land, and the faction leaders were given orders to wage war on the dissidents from the Ogaden and their hosts and inform them of any suspicious activities from these people.

Somalia, the main backer of the Ogaden struggle and the centre for the Greater Somalia dream became, in the 1990s, the centre for anti-Somalis because of the faction leaders. The control of Somalia by Ethiopia has been a very big blow psychologically to the Somalis already under Ethiopian occupation. The Ethiopians always try to downgrade the Somalis to a mere tribe and claim that the Somalis are not capable of ruling themselves. Thus, the failure of the Somali state and the submission of the Somali faction leaders to the Tigray government were interpreted by the Ethiopians as proof of their belief. This had a demoralizing effect on Somali nationalism and especially on liberation movements in the Ogaden. Indeed, the idea of bringing down Somalia under Ethiopian rule willingly instead of liberating the Ogaden, was a great gift to Ethiopia, an incomprehensible disaster to the Somalis in general, and a very humiliating act to the Western Somali people. In the words of the late Sultan Bihi Foley, a prominent freedom fighter who was part of the Somali delegation that went to London in 1955 for the independence negotiations of the former British Somaliland: "Seeking Ethiopia's support for the destruction of the Somali state is like requesting to be turned from human beings into monkeys, because by their submission to Ethiopia the Somali factions are trading freedom for enslavement."

9.3.3 The Death of Somali Nationalism

The main reason why the warlords behaved so badly was the death of the national spirit. Its absence was observable in all sections of society. Somali nationalism was one of the main ideological driving forces of both the domestic and foreign policies of the Somali state, but due to various adverse factors, it died out. Bad government, the failed search for the unity of the Somali nation, external intervention, irresponsible opposition and diminished moral responsibility were the main parameters that contributed to its death.

Despite the parliamentary system in the 1960s and the rapid progress in development in the first half of the 1970s, the system of government in the country was often distorted by corruption, tribalism, arbitrary judiciary and very oppressive policies in the last decade before the collapse of the government. Because of tribalism and corruption, citizens lost confidence in their system. The alienated public turned to their traditional clan ties to get their rights and they became more attached to their clan connection than to the system of government. As a result, the national consciousness was gradually replaced by clan spirit.

The search for the unity of the Somali people in the Horn backfired and brought them a lot of hardship. The lack of progress in the search for a united Somali nation and the heavy price the Somalis paid in that struggle negatively affected Somali nationalism. In particular, the economic deterioration and the political instability that followed the 1977/78 Ogaden war were significant factors that contributed to the weakening of the Somali state and, thereby, to the spirit of Somali nationalism. As the hardship became a reality, the people began to blame one another. The Somalis from the Ogaden were blamed for the difficulties that originated from the war. For their part, the Somalis in the Ogaden blamed the Somali government for the lack of progress in the struggle. Similarly, different clans accused each other of taking an undue proportion of the scarce resources. Blaming one another in times of difficulty is human nature, but submitting to the enemy who caused the hardship and abandoning the fundamental rights they were fighting for was neither in line with common sense nor imaginable, given Somali pride. The situation was further exacerbated by the exploitation of the clan system by both the opposition and the government.

As we saw earlier, the precarious situation was exploited by foreign forces that fuelled the internal conflict indirectly or directly to destroy the fabric of Somali society and statehood. In collaboration with local warring factions, Ethiopia worked hard to eliminate the Somali state. 'Both Ethiopia and the factions are responsible for the national disaster in Somalia. Ethiopia worked incessantly to eliminate Somalia from the face of the earth, and the faction leaders made its task of removing the Somali National flag from the world forums easier.'[2] Although it was not justifiable, Ethiopia's position was understandable, because in destroying Somalia she was pursuing her own national interest. In order to bury the Ogaden cause, the Addis Ababa government wanted to shift the battlefield from the Ogaden to Somalia. However, the Somali warlords, strangely, were not aiming at anything other than the demolition of their homeland. Had they had any sense of nationalism or patriotism, they would have neither acted that way nor sought the help of Ethiopia.

The Somalis are a nation united by religion, culture, common traditions and land. The civil war in Somalia shook all these pillars of the nation's identity. Respect for one another, a safe haven for children, women and the elderly in times of conflict, and all the other fundamentals of Somali culture and traditions were put aside during the civil war. Secularism, which flourished during the socialist period, bad systems of government and materialism reduced the practice of Islamic sharia, which the Somali culture is mainly based on. The good values which the Somali society inherited from the Islamic teaching such as peace, human dignity, honesty, generosity, etc., were profoundly affected negatively by these developments and resulted in moral decay.

9.3.4 The Elimination of the WSLF

The dismantling of the WSLF dealt a heavy blow to the Ogaden struggle. Despite the criticism of the leadership by the grassroots and the ONLF, the WSLF was the shadow government of the people in the Ogaden. It took many years to build the machinery of the Western Somali Liberation front and, in fact, it was a big organization by the time the Somali

---

[2] Mohamed Osman Omar, 2004, *Somalia, Between Devils and Deep Sea*, Somali Publications, page 19.

government began to dismantle it gradually. More importantly, it was the only organization that liberated parts of the country. With the help of Somalia, the WSLF succeeded in liberating over 90 per cent of the Ogaden in 1977–78 and that vivid memory still lives.

Despite the re-conquest of the liberated land by Ethiopia and its allies, the WSLF was a power to be reckoned with. At the beginning of the 1980s, the WSLF had an army of about 15 000, had representation in several countries, had a well-mobilized public under its control and was present in every district within the Ogaden region. By the time the Siyad Barre government signed the peace deal with Mengistu in 1986, the WSLF still had a strong army and was the only liberation organization that had a presence in the Ogaden. Thus, the loss of the Western Somali Liberation Front, which was once seen as the representative of the people, the liberator of the land, the protector of the population and the symbol of the struggle, was incredibly great to the Western Somali people.

The newly created liberation organizations, namely the ONLF and Al-Itihad, were unable to fill the vacuum left by the WSLF for some time. Before the 1990s these organizations did not even have a visible formal organization and they were not physically present in the region. It took years for these organizations to establish their organization in the Ogaden. The formidable WSLF army was not able to reorganize themselves and remain there as an entity because they were killed from the top, and the new liberation organizations did not have the capacity to take over the command of the forces before they disintegrated. The tragic loss of that strong force, which once liberated the land, was not easy to swallow. But realistically there was very little the confused grass roots could do to save it.

In addition to the tragic loss of WSLF machinery and the other challenges outlined above (the Somali civil war, the death of Somali nationalism, etc.), the liberation movements and the inhabitants of the region were negatively affected by the regime change in Ethiopia. The impacts of the latter are the topic of our next chapter.

10

The Ogaden After the Fall of the Derg

Regime change; deceptive self-rule; human rights; the economy; the environment; natural resources; hunger

10.1 Regime Change

The 1984 famine in Ethiopia unveiled the inhuman face of the Derg regime, which eventually paved the way for its downfall. The failure of the rains during July–September 1983 signalled a famine for 1984, but the warning was ignored then by the regime. The authorities were preparing for the revolution's tenth anniversary and the establishment of the Worker's Party of Ethiopia (WPE), and they were neither willing to release any information about the country other than a positive one, nor to divert attention and resources from the celebration to the alleviation of the suffering of the famine victims. The government did not want to reveal the disaster to the world, but concerned officials from the government's Relief and Rehabilitation Commission (RRC) leaked news of the famine to the international press, humanitarian organizations and diplomats. Commenting on this sad situation Harold G. Marcus, the historian, wrote:

> While one-sixth of Ethiopia's peoples were threatened with death and were fleeing their homes to seek food, the government prepared an expensive extravaganza to showcase the establishment of the new WPE. Before the event, the regime's media described only the prosperity and freedom that Mengistu and socialism had brought to Ethiopia. It lambasted the West for its imperialism, while praising its Eastern allies, especially the Soviet Union, for their help and support. The RRC's dilemma was thereby made worse, since the European Economic Community and the United States held the grain surpluses, whereas the Soviet Union was facing its own shortages and other Warsaw Pact nations had little extra to donate to the starving Ethiopians.[1]

Although the rains failed in June and July 1984, and by that time the people had died in the tens of thousands weekly, the government went

---

[1] Harold G. Marcus, 1994, *A History of Ethiopia*, University of California Press. page 206.

ahead with the celebration. Foreign dignitaries, mainly from the Soviet bloc, who attended the parade on 12 September, saw a city in celebration as the Derg kept the sad situation under the carpet. Only after the tragedy came into the open through the international press did the Derg regime accept the existence of the problem. The international community, particularly Western countries, responded quickly as news of the disaster reached them and they generously provided the desperately needed relief. Thanks to their efforts, the lives of millions of people were saved. Had the Ethiopian government not withheld the news of the disaster from the international community, many more could have been saved.

Before the famine scandal disappeared from press headlines, Mengistu began another sinister plan. Seizing on the famine disaster, the government in 1985 embarked on resettlement and villagisation programmes. It claimed that the purpose of the programmes was to deal with droughts in the long run and to provide social services. Sceptics, however, argued that the programmes were driven by military goals, and the aftermath observations confirmed this view. By removing people from the north to the south it wanted to achieve two things at the same time, namely, to drive out supporters from the movements in the north and to change the demography in the Ogaden and Oromia, to undermine the liberation efforts there. Over 800 000 were removed from their homes in the period 1985–86. The villagisation programme was another means of controlling the local population. It was more extensive than the resettlement programme in that it involved over ten million people across the country. Most of the villages created by the government did not get social, educational or health services, the provision of which the government claimed to have established. Furthermore, the government refused aid to the rebel-held areas in Tigray and Eritrea, confirming the critics' view that the government's response to the disaster was motivated by military considerations, rather than humanitarian concerns.

Meanwhile, the famine did not lead to a cessation of hostility between the government and the rebels in Eritrea and Tigray. The fighting continued and both the Eritrean People's Liberation Front (EPLF) and the Tigray People's Liberation Front (TPLF) made big headway in their struggle in the late 1980s, both militarily and politically. The two organizations forged an alliance in 1989 and their cooperation was a crucial factor in their success, both on the battle and diplomatic fronts. The EPLF defeated the Derg forces at Afabet in northern Eritrea in March 1988, and that victory was the turning point in the Eritrean struggle in that it boosted their confidence and paved the way for the liberation of entire provinces afterwards. Similarly, the TPLF with the support of the EPLF soundly defeated the Ethiopian forces near the town of Enda Selassie in February/March 1989. The government forces were not only defeated but they were also forced to withdraw from the whole of the Tigray region. The two movements cooperated again in the capture of the Port of Massawa in February 1990.

The defeat of the government forces had both external and internal implications. In reaction to the defeat, senior military officers mounted a coup in Addis Ababa on 16 May 1989 after Mengistu flew to East Germany. The coup failed, but it weakened the military government from within because of the arrest of 176 senior military officers including 24 generals, and the replacement of many other high commanding officers. On the diplomatic front, former US president Carter began to mediate between the EPLF and the government. The EPLF leader Isaias Afeworki visited Washington in May 1989. Afeworki 'was received by high-ranking officials at the State Department and by important congressional leaders, signalling the beginning of the end of the US policy supporting Ethiopia's territorial integrity in terms of Addis Ababa's definition of national unity'.[2] By the end of 1989, the Italian government invited the TPLF and the representatives from the government to Rome in a parallel effort to get the mediation under way. The mediation efforts were not successful because the liberation movements, which were advancing at high speed, did not wish to compromise, but the mediation efforts led to more involvement of the West and strengthened the ties between the Western governments and the guerrilla leaders. Afeworki also met US diplomats in Khartoum in 1990.

The democratic changes in the Soviet Union and Eastern European countries also adversely affected the Derg regime. During a visit to Moscow in July 1988, the Ethiopian leader was told that Soviet support for Ethiopia would not continue unless the Ethiopian government introduced substantial economic and political liberalization. Furthermore, Gorbachev refused Ethiopia's request for additional military assistance and told Mengistu to find a negotiated settlement to the Eritrean problem. Mengistu went to China afterwards to seek military assistance from Peking, but the Chinese support was not forthcoming either, because they had their own economic revolution and the socialist ideals on which the Derg sought the Chinese help had already been abandoned there.

To get a replacement for the military assistance, which the Russians

---

[2] Harold G. Marcus, 1994, *A History of Ethiopia*, page 215.

threatened to terminate, Mengistu secretly established relations with Israel. The Derg regime was also hoping the Jewish lobby in the US would persuade the US government to cease its hostility towards the Addis Ababa government, and instead support it. Israel, for her part, wanted Ethiopia's cooperation in her struggle against the Arab countries and to facilitate the emigration from Ethiopia of the Ethiopian Jews (the Flasha). The secret deal came into the open when, in 1989, the liberation movements in Tigray and Eritrea detected Israeli advisers in the Ethiopian army field units and the Israeli mission in Addis Ababa became visible to the public. The arrangement enabled Israel to get the Ethiopian Jews into Israel, but attempts by the Ethiopian and Israeli officials to change Washington's position on the Derg regime through the Jewish lobby in the US congress failed. The US government had already made up its mind and established contacts with some rebel movements, and was not willing to save the Mengistu regime.

The cooperation between the two main guerrilla organizations, the EPLF and the TPLF, increased as they scored more victories against the government forces, and both began to position themselves for the takeover of power. The EPLF was a secessionist movement, whose main aim was to turn Eritrea into an independent state. Unlike the EPLF, the TPLF wanted to take the reins of power in Ethiopia and preserve Ethiopian unity. The TPLF preferred Eritrea to remain part of Ethiopia, but the Eritreans were not willing to compromise on the independence issue. After pressure from the US and TPLF, however, they accepted that the independence referendum is delayed for two years to give the new government time to consolidate power and deal with the anti-secessionist forces.

As part of its preparation for the takeover of power, the TPLF formed an umbrella organization, namely the Ethiopian People's Revolutionary Democratic Front (EPRDF). The main components of the EPRDF were the Tigray People's Liberation Front (TPLF), the Ethiopian People's Democratic Movement (EPDM) and the Oromo People's Democratic Organization (OPDO). The two latter opposition groups were from the Amhara and Oromo ethnic groups respectively and were both formed by the former group. The TPLF could not persuade the Oromo Liberation Front (OLF), the main Oromo Liberation organization, to join the EPRDF, although it made a loose alliance with the OLF.

Both the EPRDF and the EPLF made big advances as their military successes continued unabated during the period 1990–1991. Because of the rebel advances, US mediation efforts were brought into the open. Assistant Secretary Herman Cohen, who led the mediation efforts, invited representatives from the EPLF and the Derg regime to Washington in late February 1991. The talks in Washington did not make progress, but the two sides agreed to meet again after each one had presented its position. Mengistu, however, fled the country before the date of the next meeting. On 21 May Mengistu flew to Zimbabwe via Kenya, where he was given asylum. Before he left the country, Mengistu designated his vice-president, Tesfaye Gebre Kidan, as acting president. By that time, the Derg defence lines were falling apart everywhere and the EPRDF forces were in control of Tigray, Wollo, Gonder and parts of Shoa. The guerrilla forces bypassed Addis Ababa because the US government advised them not to enter it at that stage.

By the end of 1990, Somalia descended into chaos after the government was overthrown by rebel groups. The US was determined to avoid a similar situation taking place in Ethiopia. To avert the collapse of the Ethiopian state the US administration began talks with the government and the opposition to help them set up a government to replace the Derg. On 27 May 1991, Assistant Secretary Cohen invited the government, the EPLF, the EPRDF and the OLF for talks in London. The EPLF accepted the postponement of the referendum on independence for two years and the OLF agreed to cooperate with the EPRDF but did not join the organization. The Ogaden National Liberation Front requested to take part in the talks but was rejected by the US on the grounds that it was not controlling any territory. By the time the conference convened, the EPRDF's forces surrounded the capital but were advised by the US not to enter it. However, while the talks were going on, Acting President Tesfaye Gebre Kidan informed the American Embassy in Addis Ababa that his government was going to surrender to the EPRDF. With American consent, the EPRDF forces entered Addis Ababa on 28 May 1991 under the order of its leader, Meles Zenawi, who emerged from the London talks as the new leader of Ethiopia. A few days later, the southern regions including the Ogaden came under EPRDF forces. In Eritrea, the EPLF liberated the whole territory by the last week of May, and it designated itself as the provisional government of Eritrea on 23 May 1991.

The EPRDF leader, Meles Zenawi, arrived in Addis Ababa on 1st June from London and on arrival in the capital, he assumed the position of Acting Head of State. He immediately held press conferences and briefed the diplomatic corps on plans for the future of the country. He also addressed the nation over radio and TV. Zenawi promised, among other things, immediate restoration of law and order throughout the country and the introduction of democracy and a free-market economy. On 6 June Zenawi announced the formation of a provisional government headed by Tamrat Layne, the Leader of the EPDM. On 26 June Zenawi announced that a national conference to form a Transitional Government would convene on 1 July.

As scheduled, the national conference was held in July, but although some other organizations attended the conference, such as the Oromo Liberation Front and the Afar Liberation Front, it was dominated by the victorious EPRDF. The conference elected an 87-member council of representatives, which in turn established a transitional government and confirmed Meles Zenawi as the transitional president and Tamrat Layne as the transitional prime minister. The conference also introduced a Transitional Charter, which was approved on 22 July 1991, and which recognized all basic principles of human rights, including the right of self-determination for all nations in the empire state of Ethiopia.

10.2 Deceptive Self-Rule in the Ogaden

The Ogaden was one of nine states declared autonomous by the transitional authorities and the present constitution, with wide-ranging powers including the power to administer, legislate, levy taxes and duties, establish state police and even lead the state to secession if it fulfils the condition for secession as set up in the constitution. The nine autonomous states are Somali, Tigray, Afar, Amhara, Oromia, Benshangul/Gumuz, Southern Nations, Gambela and Harari. According to the transitional charter and the constitution, which was approved and replaced it in 1994, the state governments are sovereigns in their respective territories, and except in defence and foreign policies, the state governments are responsible for the running of their state affairs in coordination with the central government. Another important element of nationality empowerment was the use of the regional languages as official languages in addition to Amharic, which is the national language. The exercise of these sovereign powers would start from the day the states elected their representatives to the state council.

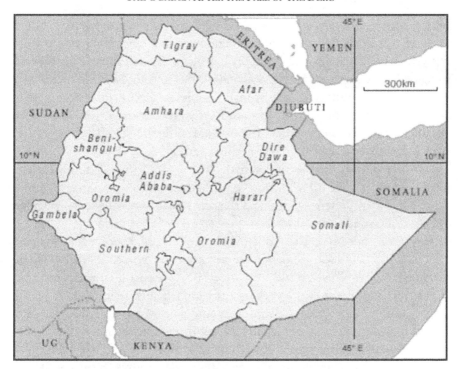

Map 10-1: The current administrative regions of Ethiopia

The new democratic approach from Addis Ababa changed the mood of the population by changing their long-held pessimism about the political development in Ethiopia into one of optimism because none of the above-mentioned democratic commitments was imaginable under the previous regimes. In particular, the self- determination promise made the Western Somali people extremely excited and forward-looking. With unprecedented enthusiasm, they welcomed the new government and cooperated with it fully in maintaining peace and order. The transitional authority formed in 1991 promised to hold elections within a year and end the transitional period within two years after the elections. According to the transitional arrangement, the constituencies were to hold elections for both the federal parliament and the state parliament at the same time. To realize the human rights and political freedoms promised by the new regime, all political parties in the Ogaden began to register as required by the new government and prepare themselves for the elections and exercise of power.

The optimism, however, did not last long; the new regime came up with some of the usual Ethiopian repression policies before they had finished lecturing about the new democracy. In a short time, the gap

167

between what the new regime proclaimed and its actions on the ground became too great to be reconciled. The new democratic system, which the government claimed to have brought, was accompanied – and even preceded – by suppression of political parties and indiscriminate killing. To their disappointment, the Somali people in the Ogaden region saw signs of the unpromising reality and what to expect from the Addis Ababa regime. However, they had no alternative but to see through the whole deception saga unfolding before them.

To take part in the election scheduled for 1992, the existing political parties such as the ONLF and Al-Itihad organized themselves into different constituencies within the region. These constituencies, and the public at large, also contributed to peace and order to make the elections as smooth as possible. The Addis Ababa government, however, was not serious about democracy and it seemed that the lip service it paid was intended to get Western aid and the time to consolidate power. The Western governments were very receptive to the new regime's successful propaganda of introducing democracy and rule of law to Ethiopia. The Western governments' economic and political support to the Tigray-led regime enabled Zenawi to consolidate power in the Ogaden and elsewhere, using very inhuman measures. The regime knew about the self-determination aspiration of the Somali people in the Ogaden, which was not acceptable to the new regime despite the clause in the Charter which permitted secession.

To suppress the people's aspiration, Zenawi began to manipulate the politics of the Somali state, by encouraging the formation of tribal-based parties in order to divide the inhabitants of the region along clan lines. Over a dozen such parties were formed with the help of the EPRDF. Having created some clan-based parties, the majority of which existed only on paper, the regime turned against Al-Itihad, the strongest liberation organization in the region at the time. Despite legal recognition of the organization as a political party by the transitional authority, the existence of Al-Itihad was not acceptable to the regime and it decided to eliminate it before the elections.

In a surprise military operation, similar to the one the government had taken against the Oromo Liberation front in 1992, Tigray forces attacked the Al-Itihad headquarters in Halooye in order to destroy the organization from the top. On 11 August 1992, they conducted a well-planned attack on the organization's headquarters without provocation, killing 26 people including its chairman, Sheikh Abdullahi Bade and vice-chairman Sheikh Abdullahi Ahmed Qasim. Despite the killing of the top leaders of the organization, Al-Itihad was too strong to be crushed by the

EPRDF. They quickly regrouped, elected new leadership and waged a jihad against the occupation.

From the day they declared the war on Al-Itihad and its sympathisers, the familiar status quo, which the Ogaden region has known since its occupation, fully returned. On the pretext of fighting the Al-Itihad, which they branded a terror organization, they stepped up the usual Ethiopian oppressive and destructive policies – collective punishment, extra-judicial killing, detention, the looting of livestock and the rape of women, etc.

There was a heated debate within the ONLF on whether to continue the cooperation with the new regime, following the attack on Al-Itihad and the ensuing war between Al-Itihad and the government. The hard-liners argued that enough evidence, which showed the deception of the Tigray-led government over democracy and self-rule, was seen and urged armed struggle to be resumed. Despite the state-of-war situation, the ONLF eventually decided to take its struggle through the ballot boxes, as long as the regime permitted that for the reasons below.

Although it was clear to many that the Ethiopian regime was not sincere about its democratic and self-rule policies, the public at large was confused about these issues. The regime did not cease talking about them, the claim was written, and preparations for elections got underway. Thus, the moderates argued that opting for an armed struggle before the democratic channels were tested would not be a sellable product to the public. Equally, to go to war while the regime was promising the peaceful attainment of what they were fighting for would not have been a sensible thing to do, as it would have given the government both internal and external support and undermined the credibility of the ONLF. Furthermore, the region was experiencing hunger and food shortages following drought and the return of huge numbers of refugees after the fall of the Somali state in 1990. Considering all these issues, the ONLF had no choice but to lead the struggle through the ballot box.

The first general election to be held in the Ogaden took place in December 1992. Over a dozen parties, most of them clan-based, contested the election. With mediation from local elders and politicians, a ceasefire was reached between the government and the Al-Itihad by the end of 1992, but the organization did not take part in the election. The ONLF won a landslide victory, by winning over 80 per cent of the seats in the state assembly. Although it won a clear majority, it chose not to govern alone and wanted to share the state government seats with other parties to make it a broader government.

The state parliament met for the first time in Dire Dawa on 21 January 1993 and the first thing on their agenda was to approve the new coalition government, led by the ONLF. Abdullahi Mohamed Sa'di and Siyad Badri, both from the ONLF, became the president and vice president respectively, while Mahdi Ahmed Warsame from the IGLF (Issa and Gurgura Liberation Front), became the secretary. After the state parliament approved the government, it turned to the next item on its agenda: choosing a capital for the state. The state parliament chose Dire Dawa, but within minutes of the decision, the central government in Addis Ababa sent a fax annulling the decision on the grounds that Dire Dawa was a disputed city.

The Sa'di's government lasted only about seven months due to internal conflicts within the ruling ONLF and central government intervention. For different reasons, the central government and the ONLF leadership together sacked that first government. The ONLF branded its own government weak and a puppet, whereas the central government accused it of incompetence and the misappropriation of public funds. A government supported by the ONLF, under the leadership of Hassan Jire Qalinle, took over the power in the region. Qalinle was from the Western Somali Liberation Front (WSLF), which later changed its name to the Western Somali Democratic Party (WSDP). The ONLF and the WSLF/WSDP agreed on 21 July 1991 to work together and to strive for self-determination for Somalis in the Ogaden.

Seizing on the new human rights and democratic commitments proclaimed by the

Addis government, the ONLF and the WSLF/WSDP wanted to pursue their self-determination goal through democratic means. As far as human rights were concerned, both the National Transitional Charter and the new constitution, which replaced it afterwards, clearly endorsed all basic human rights and obliged Ethiopia to ratify all human rights treaties. In addition, Article 39 of the Constitution provides the nationalities in the Ethiopian empire the right to secede from Ethiopia if the majority of the inhabitants in a particular state decide to do so. Article 39 is about "The Rights of Nations, Nationalities, and Peoples", and is formulated as follows:

1. Every Nation, Nationality and People in Ethiopia has an unconditional right to self-determination, including the right to secession.
2. Every Nation, Nationality and People in Ethiopia has the right to speak, to write and to develop its own language; to express, to develop and to promote its culture; and to preserve its history.
3. Every Nation, Nationality and People in Ethiopia has the right to a

full measure of self-government, which includes the right to establish institutions of government in the territory that it inhabits, and to equitable representation in State and Federal governments.

4. The right to self-determination, including secession, of every Nation, Nationality and People shall come into effect:

(a) When a demand for secession has been approved by a two-thirds majority of the members of the Legislative Council of the Nation, Nationality or People concerned;

(b) When the Federal Government has organized a referendum which must take place within three years from the time it received the concerned council's decision for secession;

(c) When the demand for secession is supported by majority vote in the referendum;

(d) When the Federal Government has transferred its powers to the council of the Nation, Nationality or People who have voted to secede; and

(e) When the division of assets is effected in a manner prescribed by law.

5. A "Nation, Nationality or People" for the purpose of this Constitution, is a group of people who have or share large measure of a common culture or similar customs, mutual intelligibility of language, belief in a common or related identities, a common psychological make-up, and who inhabit an identifiable, predominantly contiguous territory.[3]

The article explicitly endorses unlimited self-determination, but was the government genuine about this commitment? To find out, in January 1993 the author of this book interviewed the Ethiopian Foreign Minister, Seyoum Mesfin, in Stockholm, Sweden. The interview concentrated on the issue of self-determination for the Somali region and the applicability of the clauses in the Transitional Charter permitting secession to that region. The interview revealed the truth about the government's hidden agenda concerning the much-talked-about article, which deals with the right of self-determination up to secession for Ethiopian nationalities and was conducted as follows.

Author: Is it true that there is an article in the Transitional Charter, which permits secession to nationalities in Ethiopia?

Mesfin: Yes, there is an article in the Charter, which gives the nationalities the right to secede, and in the constitution soon to be drafted a similar article will be included.

Author: If the recently elected state parliament in the Somali state declares self- determination for the Somalis in that region, will your government respect that decision?

---

[3] The Ethiopian Constitution 1994, Ethiopar. Net.

Mesfin: No, we will not respect that, because that is not what they were elected for, and we know that the people in the region do not want to secede.

Author: The members of the state assembly are the representatives of the people, but if you do not accept their decision, on the grounds that the inhabitants do not wish to secede, would you allow a referendum to be held to see what the people want?

Mesfin: No, we will not allow a referendum to be held, because we know the feeling of the people in the region. For the first time in their history, they consider themselves to be Ethiopians.

Author: You said that there is an article in the charter which allows self-determination, and we know that an Ethiopian region, namely Eritrea will soon become an independent state. While you are at the same time denying the right of self-determination to the Somali region through democratic means, how do you reconcile these conflicting positions? Does the article apply only to particular nationalities?

Mesfin: The two issues are quite different; the Eritreans have been fighting for their cause over thirty years and the Eritrean issue has been resolved through military means.

Author: The Somalis have been fighting for the same thing much for longer than the period the Eritreans were fighting, but unlike the Eritreans they are not in control of their region militarily. Does this mean that the article will be applicable to the Somalis only after further bloodshed from both sides and after the Somalis liberate their land?

In apparent anger, the Minister twisted his face, and walked away right after the last question, saying, "This is not the right place for a discussion on issues like this. See you in places like Jigjiga."

The Somali people in the Ogaden had no representation in the commission that was appointed in 1993 for the drafting of the constitution, but the constitution the commission came up with was well received by the inhabitants of the Ogaden, mainly because the constitution recognised basic human rights, including the right to decide the region's destiny. The constitution made Ethiopia a federal republic, composed of nine autonomous states, based on national and ethnic backgrounds. On 8 December 1994, the federal parliament ratified the new constitution, which replaced the National Transitional Charter and became the basis for the parliamentary elections held since 1995. However, by the time this constitution was officially approved, the Somali people in the Ogaden had it tested.

At a press conference in Addis Ababa on 28 January 1994, the ONLF called for a referendum on independence for the region. On 25 March 1994, the state assembly almost unanimously approved a motion sponsored by the ONLF, calling for a referendum to be held on self-determination in the Somali region. However, instead of respecting the democratic rights exercised by the Somali state council and honouring its commitments, the EPRDF-led government began to dismantle the democratic process, starting with the removal of the elected state government and the changing of the state capital (Godey).

Following the council's decision to hold a referendum, the central government dismissed Hassan Jire Qalinle and his deputy Ahmed Ali Dahir on 30 April 1994, without consulting the regional council, and since that time Zenawi has handpicked the members of both the council and the administration of the region. The regime in Addis Ababa also changed the state capital from Godey to Jigjiga in the same year. The reason given for the removal of the state government was the same as that given at the time of the overthrow of the Sa'di's administration; that is, incompetence and misappropriation of funds from the regional budget. The same charges were also labelled against all the successive handpicked regional administrations that followed suit. No reason was given for the change of the capital, but since Jigjiga is closer to Addis Ababa and Godey is within the stronghold area of the liberation movements, security considerations were the most probable reasons behind the move.

After having sacked the first elected regional government, Zenawi began to create the first of several puppet organizations, through which he ruled the region after the overthrow of the Qalinle administration. The central government brought together some small parties in the region, most of which were clan-based, and united them under one umbrella organization, namely the Ethiopian Somali Democratic League (ESDL) on 12 February 1994. The government planned to rule the state through the ESDL and eliminate the liberation-minded parties such as the ONLF and Al-Itihad from the political scene.

On 27 May 1995, the government formed a new organization, calling itself the new ONLF. The motive was to undermine the ONLF and the struggle and to strengthen the Ethiopian government's manipulation of the Somali region's politics. The so-called new ONLF and the ESDL were declared the winners of the 1995 elections boycotted by the ONLF, Al-Itihad and the public at large. The two-puppet organization started merger talks in January 1997 and the process ended in July 1998 with the integration of the ESDL and the Tigray-formed ONLF, establishing the Somali People's Democratic Party (SPDP), which replaced them. The SPDP remains the only party represented by the Somalis at both the regional and federal level and its leaders are handpicked by the central government.

The dissolution of the democratic representation did not lead, however, to political stability or peace as the government proclaimed it was promoting. The Addis Ababa government frequently changed the regional authorities, to the extent that the seat of the regional president is nicknamed the 'unsittable' chair. All the Zenawi-nominated leaders before the present one were dismissed, accused of public fund irregularities and incompetence, and ended up in jail. Because of their predictable common fate, one such leader is reported to have told his successor to improve the prison service for his own sake, before he joins his predecessors in the prison cells. As predicted by Ahmed Makahil Hussein, Id Dahir was, in fact, imprisoned and joined his predecessors, although he ignored Hussein's advice to improve the condition of the prison and cooperated fully with the central government.

The government often accused the Somali regional authorities of corruption and there is some truth in that. The state authorities are both corrupt and incompetent in many ways and no one in the region is denying that, but the inhabitants do not pay attention to the central government's allegations because they know the government is not sincere. They lost trust in the whole system of government and are not expecting any good from the central government for several reasons.

It is common knowledge that the central government has been withholding the region's share of the national budget on the grounds that the regional authorities do not utilize it on time. The budgets allocated for the Somali region are alleged to have been transferred to Tigray. The corrupt authorities in the Somali region get only a small fraction of the state's budget, most of which they misappropriate, and the rest is embezzled by the central authorities. The corrupt leaders in the region are not elected by the people but nominated by the central government. The Addis Ababa government dismantled the democratic institutions and replaced the elected people with nominated ones of her choice. Thus, the accusation that the administration is not able to submit the budget on time is not acceptable, since the central government is working all the time against the formation of representative and credible authorities and is deliberately undermining efforts to rebuild the state institutions.

Besides that, the administration of the state authorities is confined to Jigjiga, as the government is not in full control of most of the Ogaden region, and the regional authorities are detached from the population. The fraction of the budget received by the state authorities does not reach beyond Jigjiga, because of the authorities' limited power and corruption as well as the Addis Ababa government's attitude towards the region. As a result, vital social services such as health and education are not available in most of the region, let alone economic development. Despite the promise of the introduction of democracy, self-rule and economic development by the Zenawi regime, the Ogaden remains the most deprived region in Ethiopia, and there is no sign of improvement soon, given the harsh economic and political climate in the region. As Dr Abdi Aden Mohamed – the former Deputy Health Minister – explains, the political atmosphere in the region makes it impossible for a responsible leader to operate or make any impact. His testimony also reveals the fact that the Ethiopian government deliberately attempted to exterminate the inhabitants, by hiding massive epidemics of cholera that hit the region during 1993/94:

> I became Deputy Minister of Health for Ethiopia, representing the Somali region, in 1991. I remained in that post until the end of 1994, hoping that somehow change would come and I could contribute my part to represent my people's interests in the government. My endeavours to bring changes resulted not only in active resistance, but also put me on a blacklist as a sympathizer of the ONLF. Besides my security, staying in that post will only have given the false impression that our region remained represented in the central government. Worst of all, the Ethiopian premier ordered me to hide from the United Nations (UN) agencies, embassies and the rest of the world, the outbreak of the massive epidemic of cholera that killed thousands in the Somali region during 1993/94. Among the reasons for which he gave me that order were: "Let those who are opposing us disappear in the dark of the night", "This will compromise our export commodities", and so on. When the UN agencies and embassies got the information, the regime condemned me for the humanitarian appeal to the UN agencies and others for help, and starting from that moment, I remained considered as the enemy of the regime.[4]

10.3 The Human Rights Situation: The General Picture

The Ethiopian parliament ratified all the important human rights documents including the International Bill of Human Rights, which consists of the Universal Declaration of Human Rights, the International Covenant on Economic, Social and Cultural Rights and the International Covenant on Civil and Political Rights. Other major international human rights treaties ratified by Ethiopia include the International Convention on the Elimination of All Forms of Racial Discrimination, the

---

[4] Dr. Abdi Adan Mohamed, 2001, *The Forgotten and Neglected Somali Region in Ethiopia*, Ogaden Online, pages 4–5.

International Convention on the Suppression and Punishment of the Crime of Apartheid, the Convention on the Prevention and the Punishment of the Crime of Genocide, the Convention on the Right of the Child, the Convention on the Elimination of All Forms of Discrimination against Women, the Convention against Torture and other Cruel, Inhuman or Degrading Treatment or Punishment, and various slavery conventions.

In addition to these treaties, the constitution of today's Federal Democratic Republic of Ethiopia offers detailed basic human rights guarantees and provides for the incorporation into domestic laws of all human rights treaties to which Ethiopia is a party. But this pledge of implementing the human rights standards by the Ethiopian government contradicts its practice. Both local and international human rights observers have documented gross infringements of rights in Ethiopia, but for the sake of convenience, we take only a few examples from their findings. We begin with the comments of the Ogaden Human Rights Committee (OHRC):

> Despite the Ethiopian government's ratification of all these important international human rights treaties, the OHRC, which monitors the human rights situation in the Ogaden, confirms the deterioration of the human rights situation in the region, and believes that the Ethiopian government's accession to the treaties was merely intended to mislead the international community, in order to avoid international public censure over its human rights record, and to get more aid from donor countries, which demand the improvement of human rights situation in the Third World Countries which receive their aid.[5]

Observations of other human rights organizations, both local and international, which monitor the human rights situation in Ethiopia, are similar to that of the OHRC. The Human Rights Watch Africa commented in its December 1997 report about the human rights situation in Ethiopia as follows:

> Despite frequent statements about its commitment to the enforcement of human rights standards in the country, the Ethiopian government's actual practices, detailed in *Ethiopia: the Curtailment of Rights* released by Human Rights Watch today, significantly deviate from these principles. The government daily violates the civil and political rights of Ethiopian citizens by denying them the basic freedoms of speech, assembly and association. The practices of arbitrary arrest, ill-treatment and torture in detention continue under the Ethiopian People's Revolutionary Democratic Front

---

[5] Ogaden Human Rights Committee, 1997, *No Rights, No Democracy*, OHRC, page7.

(EPRDF), which took power in May 1991 after defeating the Derg military dictatorship.[6]

Violations of human rights are today widely observed in all parts of Ethiopia, but as the OHRC documents, the human rights abuses inflicted upon the Somalis in the Ogaden date back to the Ethiopian occupation of the first part of the Ogaden over a century ago. All the successive Ethiopian regimes from Menelik to the present one enforced oppressive and inhuman policies and infringed all rights in the Ogaden. Although Ethiopia does not reject in principle the universality of the human rights standards and has ratified all the major international human rights treaties, it deliberately violates all kinds of human rights in the Ogaden. The inhabitants of the region are not only treated as second-class citizens in their own country but all their fundamental human rights are denied.

The Ogaden case presents one of the most consistent cases of human rights violations in the world. Not only the rights that are essential for the maintenance of human dignity such as cultural, economic, social and political rights are denied, but also the basic rights of life and liberty, which most people take for granted, are infringed. The Somalis in the Ogaden are constantly terrorised, massacred, abducted, detained, imprisoned, tortured, displaced; their properties are confiscated or destroyed and their land is mined by the forces of the Ethiopian government. During previous regimes, the military garrisons were the only visible signs of Ethiopian presence, and it is no exaggeration to say that the present regime turned these military garrisons into concentration camps. Since 1994 the current regime has embarked on a terror campaign, which effectively eliminated all rights.

Having removed the elected authority, the Tigray government imposed a curfew throughout the region, limiting the movement of the people. The aim was to isolate the region, before the start of the terror campaign. By mid-1994 the campaign was effective, as the news of the casualties from each district showed. The terror campaign involved, among other things, extra-judicial killings, abduction, torture, detention without trial, rape, looting of livestock and poisoning of watering wells. These punitive measures were taken against the individuals singularly and collectively against the whole society. The tragedy is thoroughly investigated and documented by the Ogaden Human Rights Committee, and the author strongly recommends the reader to see the reports of the OHRC and other international human rights organizations' reports on

---

[6] Human Rights Watch, 1997, Press Release, Human Rights Watch Africa, page 2.

the subject. Here we merely outline some of the above-mentioned common crimes that take place on a daily basis.

10.4 The Human Rights Situation: Extrajudicial Killings

Innocent people are killed daily in the Ogaden, for allegedly supporting a particular banned organization such as the ONLF, or merely opposing some of the government's policies. The victims are not only murdered in the detention camps and other secret locations but are also publicly executed in broad daylight on the streets and in the markets of the towns. The Ethiopian armed and security forces brutally kill their victims. They kill fathers before their families, and whenever defeated by the liberation forces somewhere in the Ogaden bushes, they kill the inhabitants of the nearest town indiscriminately as an act of retaliation. Furthermore, Ethiopian soldiers often exhibit the bodies of the people they kill on the streets and anyone who attempts to bury these murdered people meets the same fate. Commenting on the killing that goes on in the region, Dr. Abdi Aden Mohamed (former Deputy Health Minister) stated:

> The Tigray Peoples' Liberation Front (TPLF) soldiers in the region are themselves the courts, judges, prosecutors, executioners, the police and you name it...!!!, that is to say, all the powers in the region are in their hands. They kill people indiscriminately at their own will, without the rule of law, since they have the green light to do, so unchecked by those in Addis Ababa.... These evil Ethiopian soldiers executed members of my family in the town of Degahbour in early 1994, by their usual method of collective punishment and killing measures. The remaining relatives were denied access to bury them, and their corpses were left in the open to decay, while wild animals like hyenas, foxes, wild dogs and vultures were allowed to eat the corpses. Traditionally, the Ethiopian soldiers butcher our people in those ill-fated manners and leave the corpses in the open, watching to see if there are sympathizers and anyone who does so gets the same ordeal. When I complained to the premier, he told me: "Wait! We are teaching those who oppose us an unforgettable lesson." These are some of the most common and wild inhuman tactics that they use to terrorize and intimidate the people of this region.[7]

10.5 The Human Rights Situation: Detention and Torture

Detention practice is so widespread in the region that it became part of

---

[7] Dr. Abdi Adan Mohamed, 2001, *The forgotten and neglected Somali Region in Ethiopia*, page 5.

the inhabitants' daily routine, and it is unusual to find someone in the Ogaden towns who has not experienced this kind of treatment. Thus, the people of the region do not ask themselves whether they go to the detention centres, but only how long they will stay there, what type of torture they will face and whether they will come back alive from detention. Many of them perish in detention centres, because of the harsh torture. Torture is extensively used in the Ogaden by the Ethiopian government, despite its signing of the human rights treaties forbidding it. The Ogaden Human Rights Committee investigated the method of torture used by the Ethiopian government in the Ogaden and summarised it as follows.

> Torture methods employed against detainees by the Ethiopian armed and security forces in the Ogaden are numerous. Among them are:
> indiscriminate beatings with gun butts and barrels, heavy sticks or iron bars
> gang-raping of women, and child molestation
> beatings on the soles of the feet and testicles
> burning of victims with cigarettes
> deprivation of sleep and food
> death threats, with loaded guns pointed at the head
> suffocation of detainees by burying them alive, which causes death in many cases
> forcing detainees to drink urine or salty water
> suspending from the roof upside down
> denial of sanity
> leaving victims in a prostrate position under the burning sun for long periods, with their hands and legs tied together behind the back.[8]

10.6 The Human Rights Situation: Disappearances

The disappearance of people is also very common. People are often abducted secretly from their homes and military detention camps and are taken to unknown places. Thousands of people have been reported missing since the Tigray-led government come to power in 1991. Suspicion of liberation activities involvement is the main reason for the abduction of these people, and given the brutality of the Tigray-led government, the chance of finding them alive is very minimal. Some of the people are reported to have been transferred to detention centres in other parts of Ethiopia but presumably, most of them are dead, although

---

[8] Ogaden Human Rights Committee, 1997, *No Rights, No Democracy*, OHRC, page 2.

their families are still waiting in hope that the unexpected reunion may take place one day.

So far, Ethiopia managed to keep the international community in the dark about its grave human rights violations in the Ogaden by misleading it, and it intends to do so in the future. Ironically, 'the Ethiopian government, which violates the very basic human rights of all citizens in the empire-state of Ethiopia, including the Ogadenis, poses itself as a champion of Democracy and Human Rights in Africa'.[9]

10.7 The Economy

The two main livelihoods in the Ogaden, namely pastoralism and farming dominate the subsistence economy. There is no industrial sector, and the service sector is very small. As there is no proper government in the region, the public sector is very trivial. Livestock and agriculture are the only significant sectors that matter and the utilizable wealth in the region is in private hands in the form of mainly livestock or agricultural products. Infrastructure is absent as there are no modern telecommunication networks, such as telephone and postal services. There are no roads, modern facilities are unknown in the region and there are not many skilled workers in the region.

Although not yet utilized, the region is rich in natural resources and its economic development potentiality from a resource point of view is not as bleak as it seems. Given its abundant resources and the small size of its population, the Ogaden is, in fact, potentially a rich country. It has natural resources, which include gas, oil and minerals. It has a large fertile land and it is one of the world's leading livestock regions. Despite this potential wealth, the Ogaden is one of the poorest regions in Ethiopia, because of the oppression and the war waged against its inhabitants by the Ethiopian regimes.

Since Ethiopia occupied the Ogaden, violence has persisted there, and the successive Ethiopian regimes have pursued similar oppressive policies. Thus peace, stability, security and justice are unknown phenomena in the region. The warfare situation and repression led to, among other things, displacement of people and misallocation of resources, which in turn affected the economy and the human environment negatively in several ways. These adverse effects include disruption of production, capital outflow, brain drain, dependency, deforestation and health problems. These effects are related and impact

---

[9] Ogaden Human Rights Committee, 1999, *The Graveyard of Rights*, OHRC, page 15.

one another.

Since the warfare situation is a permanent phenomenon, so its displacement continues a process that does not end. Large numbers of people are always on the move after being forced to leave their homes. Some of these displaced people travel to other countries and continents and others move from one place to another within the region. Displacement occurs very often in the region and most of the inhabitants have experienced it; in fact, large parts of the population never settle because of the warfare situation. Displacement creates unfavourable economic conditions, and it hinders development by removing people from their utilizable resources and making them dependent on aid. Instead of producing the food they need, they have to depend on handouts they receive at refugee camps.

Misallocation of resources took the form of diverting factors of production, labour and capital from economic to war activities. At present, Ethiopia is not only waging wars in the Ogaden and Somalia, but other wars are also going on in other parts of Ethiopia, and the country has a hostile relationship with Eritrea since the beginning of the war between the two countries in 1998. Able men are removed from their farms and pastures in order to fight on behalf of the government in the Ogaden or elsewhere, waging a war instead of producing food. Others join the liberation movements to escape conscription or to fight for what they believe is their right. Most of the little capital in the region goes to the war in one way or another. The government collects taxes regularly from the farmers and the pastoralists to finance its wars and the freedom fighters are fed by the inhabitants. According to the OHRC, the government sometimes even prevents farmers from cultivating their land on the pretext of tax. For example, in 1996 the government imposed a new tax of 500 birrs on each farm, and those who could not pay the tax were evicted from their farms. The government also confiscates their livestock for alleged collaboration with liberation movements.

Livestock and farming dominate the Ogaden economy. Both of these resources depend on rainfall and there are no reservoirs or water-keeping damps in the region. Thus, because of the frequent droughts and the lack of precautionary measures, these important sectors of the economy are very volatile. Very often, livestock dies from lack of water or pastures, and farmers leave their fields uncultivated for lack of water.

Efforts to develop an alternative urban economy failed because of the violence and the inhuman practices of the government. For fear of looting and other violence-related losses, many business people are forced to flee from the region with whatever they had to more peaceful places in the world. In addition, the violence and the suppression disrupt supply lines and restrict the movement of both goods and people. It is not only money that leaves the country but also human resources, especially the few educated people. Those who could contribute most to the development, namely the professionals and the intellectuals, are among the most hunted groups.

In short, the poor economy is in awfully bad shape, and the prospect of improving it in the near future is very bleak, given the present harsh conditions, the lack of concerted effort by regional or international actors to change the situation, and Ethiopia's determination to further destroy what is left of it.

10.8 Environmental Degradation

There are many existing conventions and declarations on the environment to which Ethiopia is a signatory, but the 1972 Stockholm Declaration is perhaps the most important one of these treaties because Principal 1 of this declaration proclaims the solemn responsibilities of governments to protect and improve the environment for both present and future generations.

As the principle made clear, the states have the responsibility to ensure an adequate environment for the present as well as future generations. However, the options available to states regarding compliance with these conventions vary with the causes of environmental stress, the nature of the economy, climate, and the capital and technology available to them.

Ethiopia is one of the least developed nations in the world, with a very fast-growing population. The environmental problems in the Ogaden and Ethiopia include resource depletion, soil erosion, urban air pollution, deforestation and the disappearance of species. Poverty and government policies are the main causes of environmental stress in Ethiopia. Poverty pollutes the environment in several ways. Those who are poor and hungry will often destroy their immediate environment to survive: they will cut down forests; their livestock will overgraze grasslands; they will overuse marginal land, and in growing numbers, they will crowd into congested cities. Like the other sub-Saharan African countries, Ethiopia suffers the vicious cycle of poverty leading to environmental degradation, which leads in turn to even greater poverty.

The Ethiopian government has not developed significant policies aimed at the protection of the environment and its short-sighted policies have been the chief cause of environmental degradation in the country.

These policies have affected the environment negatively in two ways, directly and indirectly through poverty. Government policy, which is one of the main causes of environmental problems in Ethiopia, is also a cause of poverty. The chronic underdevelopment of the Ethiopian economy is the result of, among other things, political instability, constant wars, economic mismanagement, violation of property rights and diversion of resources from development efforts to war efforts.

The origins of the Ethiopian state explain its violent nature. The Ethiopian empire was formed through the barrel of the gun and without the will of the various nationalities which it consists of. It is the product of conquests and occupations, and its artificial existence is maintained by force. It owes its existence to military violence, occupation and oppression, and it is always at war with its own people.

Poverty, injustice, environmental degradation and conflict interact in complex and potent ways. The main instruments of the military violence policy pursued by the Ethiopian regimes for the maintenance of the artificial empire are massacre and suppression. The results of such policies are unending wars, mass movement of refugees, disruption of economic production and social organization, all of which in turn lead to environmental stress.

The Ogaden region suffers from other environmental damages in addition to the environmental problems it shares with the rest of Ethiopia. In the Somali region, the environment provides the livestock, which is the backbone of the economy, with grassland, water, etc. It also provides the people with, among other things, the air they breathe, agricultural land, water, fuelwood, and shelter. In the future, when the country develops its industry, it will supply the economy with raw materials, which will be formed into consumer goods by the production process, and energy, which fuels this transformation.

Despite the importance of the environment to the economy and the life of the population, environmental consciousness has not yet emerged in the Ogaden region. The main reasons for the lack of environmental concerns in the region are the warfare situation created by the Ethiopian state, and ignorance, which is also mainly the result of the inhuman policies of the Ethiopian regimes.

The armed conflict and the oppressive policies created major obstacles to sustainable development. They made large claims on scarce material resources. They pre-empted the human resources and wealth that would be used to combat the collapse of environmental support systems, underdevelopment, and poverty. In addition, wild animals and forests disappeared as a direct result of the war. The animals were either hunted by the hungry Ethiopians or caught in the crossfire. Many of the animals that survived fled to the relatively peaceful neighbouring countries such as Kenya. Deforestation is also largely the result of deliberate military actions. For fuel use and for fear of attacks by the liberation movements, who may hide out in forests near the towns, the Ethiopian forces systematically cut and destroyed forests and shrubs.

10.9 Illegal Exploitation of Natural Resources

Since 1945, when Haile Selassie offered the then US president Franklin D. Roosevelt an exploitation concession to the American Sinclair Company in exchange for US support for the Ethiopian takeover of the Ogaden from Britain, successive Ethiopian regimes have been trying to exploit the Ogaden's natural resources such as fossil fuels and minerals for their own economic and political ends, and have been carrying out gas and oil explorations over the years. The international oil companies Agip, Shell, Mobil, Gewerkschaft Elwerath, Hunt oil company, Sinclair and Tenneco are some of the companies that undertook different geological surveys in the Ogaden in the 1950s, 1960s and early 1970s and one of these oil companies, namely Tenneco was the first to discover the Calub and Hilala Gas Fields in 1972. After the overthrow of Haile Selassie in 1974, the Russian oil company, Soviet Petroleum Exploration Expedition (SPEE), replaced these companies and conducted explorations in the Ogaden basin in the 1980s. The Soviet company made further discoveries of gas and other related liquids in the early 1980s and surveyed the Calub and Hilala fields. Although the estimation figures of the quantity of gas in the Calub and Hilala gas fields vary, all companies that surveyed the fields agree that they are among the largest in the world. According to a Canadian Oil Company, Alconsult International Ltd, the Ogaden basin contains 4 trillion cubic feet of gas and 13.6 billion barrels of associated liquids.

The present regime has intensified the efforts and is planning to extract natural gas from the explored fields. Since the present regime came to power in 1991, over a dozen oil companies from all parts of the world made exploration and survey agreements with the Ethiopian government. These companies include Hunt Oil of America, SI–Tech International Ltd (SIL) of Jordan, ZPEB of China, Petronas and PEXCO of Malaysia, Gail India Ltd and Gujarat State Petroleum Corporation Ltd of India, and Lundin Petroleum of Sweden. International financial institutions and some Western governments are also drawn into the deceptive project. The International Development Association (IDA), the African Development Bank and the government of the Netherlands have contributed financially to the project.

The exploitation of energy resources is a delicate business because it involves both risks and gains over time. Costs-benefit analyses are therefore necessary before exploring to ensure optimal use of the natural resources. The optimal result can be achieved only when the estimates of the social benefits exceed the social costs. However, social cost-benefit analyses of this type are extremely limited because of, among other things, the uncertainties related to their estimations, the stock size of the natural resource under consideration, the long-term rate of return, and environmental consequences. Further, the violence, instability, and suppression that prevail in the region increase the risks, which in turn add to the uncertainties and the costs.

The main social costs of fossil fuel exploitation projects are exploration, extraction and environmental. All these costs are not easy to estimate because they fluctuate wildly and are affected by variables that are not all quantifiable. Estimates of the total natural gas-in-place of ultimately recoverable reserves are also not easy to determine. This uncertainty and risk have the effect of increasing both the extraction and the environmental costs. The revenues of the energy resources depend on volatile world prices, floating interest rates and extraction and environmental costs as well as risk costs, and all these factors are in turn affected by uncertainties.

Given these difficulties, a decision on energy resources exploitation requires extensive research, preparation and public debate. In addition, Ethiopia does not have the technological, financial, infrastructural and administrative capacity to extract fossil fuels, and the international financial institutions and oil companies have been discouraged by the constant armed conflict there. Despite these constraints, Ethiopia is determined to exploit the Ogaden resources today. Economic problems and her new geopolitical designs, following the collapse of the Somali government and the secession of Eritrea, are the driving forces of the new determination.

The aim of the Ethiopian government is not to maximize social welfare or to alleviate some of the region's social and economic problems, but merely to get finance for the war it wages in the Ogaden and elsewhere in the Horn and to overcome some of its economic problems such as the foreign exchange shortages and the ever-widening deficit. The government, therefore, did not need to conduct a feasibility study or assess the economic viability of the project.

Ethiopia, which is one of the poorest countries in the world, spends millions of dollars annually on its internal and external conflicts. The country was stricken by a severe drought, which affected over eight million people in 2000–2002, and is prone to drought and famine. Furthermore, Ethiopia owes a large interest-bearing debt to the international financial institutions despite the debt relief announced in 2005 by some of those institutions, and she imports large quantities of armaments and other goods and services. In addition, her export earnings, mainly from crops, have been decreasing over the years because of war, drought and unfavourable terms of trade. As a result, the country is in a foreign exchange shortage crisis, and both the deficits of the balance of payments and the budget are growing at high rates. The way out of these crises, according to the Addis Ababa government, is the exploitation of the Ogaden's natural resources.

Because of the totalitarian nature of the state, a public debate and a consultation with the true owners of the resources, namely the Somali inhabitants, are not expected. In line with its occupation and the oppressive policies, it minimized as much as possible the flow of information to the public about the exploitation project, by denying the Somali inhabitants access to the exploration sites and by restricting the movement of people in the area designated for the exploration. The Calub Company, which runs the project, does not employ the Somali people, the government does not allow them to be in or around the drilling and extraction areas, and there are no other possible sources of information available to the inhabitants of the Somali region.

Ethiopia became a landlocked country after the secession of Eritrea, and this development coincided with the collapse of the Somali government. This led to the revival of her old imperialist policies. Now she wants to incorporate Somalia into the empire, by either establishing a puppet government there or by imposing direct rule from Addis Ababa through some Somali warlords. According to her calculation, by pretending to be a peacemaker and by fuelling the clan war, she will be able to conquer Somalia and at the same time get credit from the international community for putting an end to the anarchy there.

The present regime in Addis Ababa expects that the control of Somalia and the financial and military aid it receives from the West through its claim of combating Muslim extremists in the region will give it unconditional access to the sea and will enable it to defeat the freedom fighters in the Ogaden, both militarily and politically. Whether it can realise these dreams depends on the reaction of the Somalis in both the

Ogaden and Somalia.

But as far as the exploitation of the Ogaden's resources is concerned, Ethiopia is not waiting for the success or the failure of her new geopolitical designs. She has already begun a share-selling game with some foreign investors and oil companies. She has also set aside a large portion of her income for oil and gas exploitation and she has requested financial assistance from international financial institutions. According to reliable sources, a Russian company drilled natural gas fields in Calub and Hilala, during the reign of the Derg. The gas is ready for use and finding ways of transporting it is part of the short-term exploitation plan of the present regime.

Natural gas is not something that can be easily transported, and the Ogaden infrastructure is almost non-existent. Additionally, there is an armed conflict in the region and therefore a responsible government would not dream of transporting such gas at this stage. But as its record shows, a barrel of gas is more important to the Ethiopian regime than the possible damage to the health of the people, the resources and the environment.

On 24 April 2007, a commando unit of the Ogaden National Liberation Front stormed an oil exploration site in Obale, a village near Dagahbour. In a press release on 25 April, the ONLF claimed to have killed nearly 200 Ethiopian soldiers in that operation and to have removed seven Chinese workers from the place to ensure their safe return. The seven Chinese were handed over to the International Committee of the Red Cross (ICRC) afterwards. For its part, the Ethiopian government admitted the operation but reported the killing of 74 workers, including nine Chinese workers. Whatever the claim and counterclaim, the incident highlighted the extent of the indigenous inhabitants' opposition to the illegal exploitation of their natural resources. According to the ONLF, the foreign companies have been warned and the Obale operation could have been avoided had they listened to the repeated warnings of the ONLF.

10.10 Hunger in the Ogaden

The Ogaden has been hit by droughts several times since 1991. There were droughts in 1993/94, 1996 and 2000–2002 but the severest was the one that hit the region in 2000, after three years of rainfall failure. The bulk of the livestock, upon which the pastoralists depend almost entirely, perished in 2000. All the animals, including the drought-resistant ones such as camels, have died on a massive scale, although the mortality rates among them varied. Cattle mortality was higher than that of other animals and was estimated at 90% of the total. The mortality figures for camels varied from 5–10 per cent and for sheep between 10 and 20 per cent. Grain production also ceased in the last three years because of little or no rainfall.

Having lost their main sources of livelihood (livestock and grain production), the people could not survive. They too began to die, and shocking scenes of starving people captured TV screens all over the world. The starving people were not only the weak groups such as the children and the elderly but people of all ages were affected by the famine. The TV pictures from the town of Denan of helpless parents watching their children dying as they held them, or of parents and children dying of hunger and malnutrition together, shocked the world. But the tragedy was not confined to Denan. Millions of people in the whole region were affected by the drought and the ensuing famine and whole communities were lost as a result.

Thanks to the TV cameras that brought the famine to the attention of the world, the response was quick and positive. But the relief aid came too late for many, because of political and technical obstacles. Despite her appeal for help, the Ethiopian government did not intend the relief donated by the international community to reach its destination. As usual, she wanted to use the bulk of the aid for other purposes—mainly military—and for that reason, she tried to hinder it from reaching the starving population. Lack of or poor infrastructure, which is mainly blamed for the Ethiopian state, and the government's determination to maximizing aid on the Ogaden famine crisis, were the main obstacles that slowed the speed of the relief aid from reaching the needy in time. On the pretext that roads and transportation infrastructure were lacking, the government delayed the relief shipment and, as a result, many more lives were lost.

Following the 1984 famine, Ethiopia developed an early famine warning system administrated by its Disaster Prevention and Preparedness Commission (DPPC), which effectively works in other parts of Ethiopia, but is absent in the Ogaden. For example, the DPPC released its food stocks in Tigray during the early stages of the drought and thus the organization was able to avoid food shortages in that region during the 2000–2002 famine.

Although the drought was the main contributor, it was not the only cause of the famine. Other long-term factors have contributed to the famine. The other main causes, which are all man-made, are state-sponsored violence, oppression, poverty and environmental stress. In the above sections, we saw how warfare, injustice, poverty and environmental degradation interacted. The combined results of these factors are widespread poverty and environmental stress, which in turn led to further deterioration of the economy. The population is increasing, but the economy is declining, and this means fewer utilizable resources and more mouths to feed. Thus, there is an increase in the demand for the use of the utilizable resources of livestock and agricultural land. Overgrazing of rangeland and the overuse of agricultural land lead to environmental stress and the land becomes less productive. As there are no possibilities of production diversification and intensification, this will lead to further increase in livestock and expansion of the cultivated land and further environmental degradation. The famine is the product of this cycle of violence and oppression leading to economic decline, which in turn causes environmental degradation and further economic deterioration.

Farming in the region is not only affected by the general factors outlined above but as the incidence in Godey, in which farmers were refused to cultivate their land indicated, their activities are very limited. It seems that the consensus among the successive Ethiopian regimes is that the Ogaden region should remain part of Ethiopia at all costs and the policy instrument of achieving that aim is to starve, terrorise and repress the people of the region. These policy instruments have already ensured, among other things, chronic underdevelopment, starvation and environmental and health damages.

To summarize: all basic human rights are violated in the region; in fact, the inhabitants are terrorised and there is no way the scared society could develop its subsistence economy amid warfare and repression. In addition, overexploitation of natural resources resulted in productivity decline and exerted more pressure on the environment. Thus, the famine was inevitable, and the region will remain prone to famine as long as the terror and the systemic destruction of the infrastructure (if any) and the environment continue unabated.

11

Widening the Scope of the Struggle

Al-Itihad; the Ogaden Human Rights Committee; the Ogaden National Liberation Front

In reaction to the terror, suppression and war waged by the Zenawi regime against the Somali people in the Ogaden, the freedom fighters stepped up their struggle and resumed the armed resistance in 1994. The resistance against oppression took both organized and unorganised forms, as in the past; however, the organized resistance took pluralistic shape after the fall of the Derg. Many resistance movements were set up both at home and abroad, during the late 1980s and1990s, with the aim of ending the occupation in one way or another, but most of these organizations were formed to support the main political organizations. Of the many organizations that were established, three emerged as prominent regarding the resistance struggle, and suffice it to examine these three main organizations here. The three are the Ogaden Islamic Union, which later changed its name to Western Somali Liberation Union (better known as Al-Itihad), the Ogaden Human Rights Committee (OHRC) and the Ogaden National Liberation Front (ONLF).

Al-Itihad is an Islamic resistance organization that aims to liberate the region from the Ethiopian occupation. As its name suggests, the organization is guided by the Islamic teachings both in its organizational structure and the method of its struggle. Decolonisation is also the goal of the Ogaden Human Rights Committee, but it wants to achieve that goal through peaceful means, by uncovering the repression, humiliation and terror that prevails in the region and presenting it to the international community, so that outside pressure and international intervention might force the Addis Ababa government to change its occupation policies. The ONLF is a nationalist organization that aims to liberate the Somalis in the Ogaden from the colonial yoke, by both political and military means. Unlike the other two, the ONLF claims to have succeeded the previous liberation movements and is also claiming sole political representation of the Ogaden in the international forums. In the following sections, we will go through the performance of these three organizations and their contributions to the resistance struggle.

11.1 Al-Itihad

As we saw in chapter 9, Al-Itihad was formed in 1983 as an underground organization in the refugee camps inside Somalia, but its first general conference that formally established the organization and its leadership took place inside the Ogaden in June 1991. Although the organization never ruled out the use of force if necessary and already undertook armed resistance, initially it attempted to achieve its goals through peaceful means. Complying with the central government's decree that demanded the registration of all political parties in Ethiopia, Al-Itihad registered itself as a political party in October 1991, delivered its political programme and even revealed its military wing. Trying to realize the democracy and respect of human rights promises made by the Tigray-led regime in Addis Ababa, the organization first attempted to carry out its mission through peaceful means. However, it soon came under fire from the Ethiopian armed forces.

Ethiopian government forces ambushed the resistance movement's headquarters on 11 August 1992, killing its top leaders and two dozen other members of the movement. Encouraged by operations that she had conducted against other organizations (The Oromo Liberation Front and Issa and Gurgura Liberation Front), which effectively destroyed or weakened these organizations, the government decided to eradicate Al-Itihad before it became a strong organization. The organization's members quickly regrouped and elected Sheikh Abdulsalam Osman Abdulsalam as the new leader to replace Sheikh Abdullahi Bade, who was killed in the Ethiopian raid together with his deputy Sheikh Abdullahi Sheikh Ahmed Qasim. The government forces continued their offensive. However, after nine big battles with the Al-Itihad resistance movement in which, according to Al-Itihad, the rebels emerged victorious, the government agreed to a ceasefire by the end of 1992.

The ceasefire was broken by the Ethiopian government in 1994 when it launched a political and military campaign against Al-Itihad. After it branded the organization an Al-Qaeda-type terrorist organization, the Ethiopian government sought the help of Western governments in dealing with what it called the threat posed by Al-Itihad to the stability of Ethiopia and the Horn of Africa. Using all its military power including aerial bombing, the government also conducted a military campaign in parallel to the political one. The Ethiopian political front was successful in that it secured military and financial assistance from the West, particularly from the US government and the Ethiopian government admitted the help given to it by the US in fighting the Al-Itihad. Despite the huge Ethiopian force and military and financial assistance from the West, the military offences failed to achieve their goals. Using the well-known guerrilla tactics of hit–and-run, the Al-Itihad forces defeated the Ethiopian government forces and the campaign ended in failure.

By October 1995, Al-Itihad was so powerful that its forces were active in all parts of the region, particularly in the west and north. The organization paralysed the transport links between Addis Ababa and the Somali region after it almost got control of rail and road transport links between Dire Dawa, Harar and Addis Ababa. Everywhere in the region, Al-Itihad forces were on the offensive, putting the government under great pressure.

In response to the growing power and activities of Al-Itihad inside the Ogaden, the Addis Ababa government invaded Somalia in 1996, claiming that Al-Itihad is supported by Somalia, a country without an effective central government since January 1991. The motive was to divert attention from its internal problems and turn the Ogaden issue into one of international terrorism. The Ethiopian government succeeded in this deception, at least in the short run, and eventually, Al-Itihad was added to the US list of terrorist organizations after September 11, 2001, although by that time Al-Itihad was no longer in existence as an organization.

Because of internal conflicts that involved both power struggles and disagreements over the political direction of the organization, Al-Itihad descended into chaos, which eventually resulted in its disintegration. By the end of the 1990s the organization disappeared from the Ogaden region, having dismantled itself.

Despite its disappearance, the organization left its mark on the social, armed resistance and political fronts of the region and these marks are unlikely to vanish soon. The organization undertook many social activities, conducted a guerrilla war, which resulted in heavy losses on both sides, and the conflict got the attention of the international media. The achievements and failures of the organization are mirrored in those fronts.

The organization started its activities as a welfare organization in the late 1980s. Its social programme included establishing Islamic schools, relief work such as feeding the poor, taking care of the orphanage and the weakest members of society. Given its limited resources, the organization did a commendable job on socially related issues. Many people got the chance to attend school through this organization and that was probably its biggest achievement on the social front.

According to Al-Itihad leaders, the organization was victorious in its military campaigns as is evidenced by the heavy losses inflicted on the Ethiopian side. The organization claimed that between 1992 and 1998 it killed 13,500 government soldiers, compared to the 750 Al-Itihad fighters killed by the Ethiopians. The organization also claimed to have captured or destroyed 124 vehicles and to have emerged victorious from most of the 394 armed engagements with the Ethiopian forces during that period.

On the political front, Al-Itihad also claimed it was furthering the cause of the Somali people in the Ogaden, by contributing to the publicization of the conflict and by cooperating with its counterparts in Oromo, Afar and other parts of Ethiopia. It also boasted of its relations with Islamic movements worldwide and of taking the cause to new territories and countries throughout the world.

There is no doubt that Al-Itihad is missed in the region as far as its social welfare network and resistance are concerned. However, the military and political victory declarations are disputed. Although it is true that the organization dealt a heavy blow to the Ethiopian forces militarily and the conflict became more publicized, the disintegration of the organization and Ethiopia's political, financial and military gains suggest the contrary.

Al-Itihad did not only cease to exist as a fighting force, but it disappeared as an organization, after nearly a decade in armed resistance. The Ethiopian government claimed to have destroyed it, a claim that could hardly be refuted, given its absence from the region. Unsubstantiated reports of revitalised Al-Itihad returning to the region have been circulating recently, but it is too early to confirm these reports. Whatever the claim or counterclaim, the absence of Al-Itihad from the region contradicts its victory claims.

The political gains of the Ethiopian government from its conflict with the Al-Itihad no doubt greatly outweigh those of the Somalis in the Ogaden region. It is not disputed that the conflict was publicized and quoted in the international press; however, unfortunately, the publicity that the conflict got during the military confrontation between the Ethiopian government and Al-Itihad was negative for the Ogaden cause and positive for the Ethiopian government's goals. Al-Itihad and other liberation movements began their struggle to liberate the inhabitants of the Ogaden region from the colonial yoke, but Ethiopia always misrepresented the conflict to mislead the international community, using whatever argument it thought fitted the situation of the day. During the time of the OLF/Nasrullah in the 1960s and the WSLF struggle in the 1970s, it presented the conflict as a border dispute between Somalia and Ethiopia, accusing the former of being an aggressor. It, too, turned the Al-Itihad resistance struggle into a terror war, in which it presented itself as a victim of international terrorism and branded Al-Itihad a regional terrorist organization backed by major international terrorist organizations. On that claim, it sought the help of the world community in dealing with it. Because of the international situation regarding terrorism, the ears of Western governments were very receptive to Ethiopian propaganda. The West, particularly the US government, responded quickly to the Ethiopian request and gave it political backing as well as military and financial assistance, before listening to the other side of the conflict.

Because of the above-mentioned marks the organization left in the region and the ongoing international war on terrorism that made the organization a target, the inhabitants of the region are divided over the usefulness of Al-Itihad to their cause, both in the past and the future, should the organization revive itself. Considering Ethiopia's use of the terrorism issue as a diplomatic card and the US government's position on the organization, the critics argue that the organization's damaging image to the cause outweighs its contributions. Al- Itihad's supporters for their part stress the organization's contribution to both the struggle for freedom and to the social network, adding that the present diplomatic obstacles created by the Ethiopian regime and exacerbated by the unfavourable international climate, can be overcome, and should not be allowed to deter the determination of the people to end the occupation, which is the chief cause of their misery.

Both sides have valid points, but historical records worldwide show that the definition of terrorism is not only a disputed one, but it also changes over time. There are many examples of liberation organizations that were branded terrorists by the Western powers, but afterwards accepted as partners. These include the PLO and the ANC, and the reverse is true for the Mujahidin in Afghanistan. The rejection of the elected government of Hamas in Palestine also shows the illogicality of the definition of terrorism. Thus, the idea of relinquishing resistance whenever the occupier with the help of some other powers labelled that movement a terrorist is itself self-imposed oppression. The Ogaden conflict is about colonialism and the war is between the resistance movements, whatever form they take, and the colonizer and any attempt to change the true picture of the issue should be rejected by the whole society.

11.2 The Ogaden Human Rights Committee (OHRC)

The Ogaden Human Rights Committee was founded inside the Ogaden on 13 June 1995. By that time, the terror campaign that began in 1991 and intensified in 1994 was at a very high peak. Under the shadow of terror, repression and all kinds of human rights violations, which made the region nearly inhospitable, the OHRC emerged to defend the human rights of the victims of injustice and abuse.

The immediate goals of the OHRC, as the organization stated, are: 'to monitor and promote the observance of internationally accepted human rights standards in the Ogaden. It investigates all allegations of human rights abuses, and when it is satisfied that the claim is authentic, documents it.'[1] The organization's work is not only confined to recording individual cases, but as its appeals and recommendations often show, it also highlights the big picture; that is, the general absence of human rights in the region and its chief cause, namely the occupation.

The programme of the organization consists of human rights awareness and observance promotion measures. In the former, the organization informs the people of their rights and in the latter, it records abuses and takes possible appropriate steps in putting violations to an end. However, the organization does not have leverage over Ethiopia and can influence the situation only through international interested bodies. The organization is even banned, and it does not have open communications channels with the Ethiopian government to inform the regime of its responsibilities regarding the human rights issue. Furthermore, the organization is not only outlawed but its members are hunted by the Ethiopian security forces worldwide. In 1997 an Ethiopian agent attempted to kill the OHRC's coordinator, Abdulkadir Sulub, and his family when he tried to burn the coordinator's home in Switzerland.

Despite the ban and the prosecution, the organization has underground activists all over the region, and the victims of human rights abuses get the support of the organization through its local representatives. The OHRC helps individual victims of human rights abuses in two ways. It records proven abuses inflicted upon the individuals and at the same time informs them of their rights. Due to the over century-long repression, terror, lack of basic education, isolation,

---

[1] Ogaden Homan Rights Committee, 1999, *Graveyard of Rights*, OHRC, page 3.

and the international community's neglect of its duty in the Somali region, most of the inhabitants are unaware of their rights or have lost hope of justice. Furthermore, victims of human rights abuses and their relatives are threatened with further punishment if they speak of their experiences to anyone especially to humanitarian organizations, and that real threat makes it even more difficult to spot the signs of abuse. Despite the difficulties, many victims and their families come forward and give testimonies although some of them do not reveal their identity for fear of reprisal.

Awareness promotion of human rights is essential for both the revelation of abuses and observance of human rights, and this can be done most effectively through education. Education, both as a right and as a means of raising human rights consciousness, is especially important to all societies. This important right is one of the many fundamental rights denied in the Ogaden and the fight for its restoration is being given priority by the organization.

The reports compiled by the OHRC are distributed worldwide and are available to anyone interested. The OHRC confronts the Ethiopian government directly about its inhuman practices through diplomatic missions and indirectly via international bodies such as the human rights organizations that also use OHRC reports when conducting their own investigations. In the many reports that the organization issued since its establishment, thousands of individual cases of different types of human rights violations are recorded. The OHRC summarized its latest Report on 20 February 2006. An abstract from that summary is as follows:

> The report documents human rights violations in the Ogaden, including illegal imprisonment without charge or trial, enforced disappearances, torture, extrajudicial executions, abduction, forced labour, hostage-taking, abusive dismissals, ethnic discrimination and religious persecution carried out by the Ethiopian government. The OHRC has documented so far: 2036 extrajudicial killings; 2940 disappearances cases; 1870 rape and child molestation cases; 15332 cases of unlawful private property confiscation; and demolition of 9484 houses owned by innocent civilians. The violations took place between the years 1992 and 2005, in rural areas as well as urban areas. To the best of the Ogaden Human Rights Committee's knowledge, no one has been charged for this horrendous crime.[2]

The Ethiopian government has not yet paid due attention to the reports of the OHRC and other international human rights organizations

---

[2] Ogaden Human Rights Committee, 2006, *Mass Killings in the Ogaden*, OHRC, page1.

such as Amnesty and Human Rights Watch, and the international community has not yet intervened on behalf of the victims, despite the endless appeals to do so by the OHRC. Nevertheless, it is not only the documentary part of the work of the OHRC that is very important. Its peaceful approach to the liberation struggle contributes immensely to the restoration of the true image of the Ogaden cause and the struggle for the liberation of the occupied Somali region by presenting the realities on the ground. In collaboration with the Ogaden Natural Resources and Environmental Organization, the Ogaden Human Rights Committee also contributed to the environmental protection efforts and through these two fronts is expecting to reach its ultimate goal.

Since colonization is the chief cause of the human rights problems in the Ogaden, decolonisation is the key solution to these problems. Decolonisation is not, however, a precondition for action towards the improvement of human rights problems. On the contrary, action aimed at the improvement of these problems will lead to the achievement of the intermediate goal of independence and the ultimate goal of the well-being of the Somali people in the Ogaden. The OHRC aims to realize all these goals and it intends to achieve them through peaceful means. Given the violent nature of the Ethiopian state, a peaceful resolution does not look probable at least in the short run, but in the long run, Ethiopia cannot afford to ignore the will of the international community for several reasons, should the latter choose to intervene for the sake of human rights.

The human and environmental problems that the OHRC is involved in are local, national, regional, and international, and improvements to these problems require efforts at all these levels. Peace and security of the nations, respect for human rights, protection of the environment and sustainable development are closely linked to each other, and the world community recognizes this linkage. Because of this recognition, economic interdependency among the nations and the international nature of human rights and environmental issues, international cooperation in tackling these problems is increasing.

Since the end of the cold war, the world has changed from an ideological and geo-political framework to a geo-economic one in which the trading blocs and trans-national institutions, particularly the economic and financial ones, are playing a leading role. Different regions of the world have established trading blocs that have developed common human rights policies. Both regional and international institutions are also established to deal with these issues.

The New World Order is a capitalist order. As a result of the demise of the Eastern bloc, and its foreign aid and military protection, other economic models have virtually ceased to exist. The big economic powers such as the US, Japan and Germany dominate the capitalist world system and will continue to have the biggest input in international economic policy. The Bretton Woods institutions also became more powerful; indeed, the power of the International Monetary Fund to impose a singular economic model throughout the world will be unrivalled, and without the approval of the World Bank, a Third World country will not have a chance of receiving any loans from the capitalist world. This concentration of power in the first world will in turn lead to an increased dependency on the Third World. In reality, the least-developed countries, of which Ethiopia is one, have no say at all on international economic policy.

Development assistance is also becoming more conditional, as a result of the New World Order and also because of, among other things, the new international approaches towards human and environmental problems. Donor governments nowadays demand that development assistance recipients respect human rights and protect the environment, and in many cases, an improvement on these problems is conditional on development aid. The World Bank and the IMF have also shown signs of redirecting their programmes towards higher sensitivity to environmental concerns, and are expected to incorporate some human and environmental rights safeguards into their lending conditions.

Seizing on the increased dependency of the Third World on Western aid donor countries and the new global approach to human rights and environmental problems, the OHRC and its sister organizations are determined to contribute to the efforts. The OHRC believes that the revelation of the inhuman practices of the Ethiopian regime will eventually enable it to persuade the donor countries to make sure that Ethiopia either reverses its inhuman and environmentally devastating policies and safeguards human and environmental rights or cut the development assistance they give to her. Recently, there have been some encouraging signs in that direction. Several countries have expressed their concerns about the deterioration of human rights and some, like Britain, went as far as cutting direct economic assistance to the Ethiopian regime. The OHRC welcomed the British move and appealed to other donor countries to follow suit. Although it is not enough, the British move raised the hope that the international community will take its responsibility and in defence of humanity step up the pressure on the Ethiopian regime.

11.3 The Ogaden National Liberation Front (ONLF)

Although established in 1984, the ONLF lacked formal organizational structure until January 1992, when it held its first General Conference in Garigo'an near Garbo, Ogaden and elected a central committee headed by Sheikh Ibrahim Abdallah. After the collapse of the Mengistu regime, the ONLF activists returned to the Ogaden to secure a foothold in the region. At the time, the Ogaden region was experiencing food shortages that resulted from a drought, refugee returnees from Somalia following the Somali civil war, and the lack of a caring government in Ethiopia.

Although the political programme adopted by the ONLF conference concentrated on the liberation efforts of the Ogaden region, the above-mentioned difficulties constrained the political manoeuvrability of the organization and its options were in reality very limited, despite the rhetoric. Their opponent, the EPRDF government, was not in full control of the region and was trying to consolidate its authority. From these weak positions, the two organizations tried to reach out to each other and eventually made an agreement to cooperate in 1992. The two agreed to cooperate on the security and the local administration ahead of the election scheduled for 1992, and each organization in its own way strengthened its position in the region. The cooperation declaration with EPRDF enabled the ONLF to extend its power base through the enlargement of its grassroots and was successful in winning the hearts and minds of the majority of inhabitants in the region, whereas the EPRDF government used the peace declaration to consolidate its power in the region by increasing its military and security apparatus.

Throughout the peace declaration period, there was mutual suspicion between the Ethiopian government and the ONLF, and that mistrust came to the surface when the Ethiopian government forces attacked the Al-Itihad bases in 1992 and began the abduction, imprisonment and killing of Somali political leaders, including ONLF central committee members. Despite these signals from the regime, which indicated to the contrary, the Tigray-led regime in Addis Ababa continued the preach of its promise to introduce democracy, respect for human rights and the rule of law to Ethiopia, and for several reasons the ONLF wanted to see the theatre game through before an eventual break-up.

Given the difficult economic and humanitarian situation in the country, as well as its small military capabilities, the ONLF was not ready to terminate its relations with the EPRDF. Furthermore, the population was bombarded with propaganda from the Ethiopian government claiming not only a better life within the empire but even a peaceful break-up with Ethiopia. The ONLF itself was divided, with hard-liners dismissing the EPRDF promises as mere propaganda intended to confuse the people and distract attention from the real issue while consolidating power, whereas the moderates preferred to continue the cooperation with EPRDF, and described the idea of dismissing the government's promises in advance as political suicide. Mindful of the life situation of its people, eager to take advantage of political change in Ethiopia, aware of the diversity of opinion within the ONLF on how to approach the new regime and conscious of the need for peace and stability, the ONLF, in the end, chose to carry out the liberation struggle through the ballot box. The organization, however, never ruled out armed resistance, but it wanted to use that option as the last resort.

Having decided to pursue its political programme; that is, the realization of the Western Somali people's rights and national aspiration through peaceful and democratic means, the ONLF prepared itself for the upcoming election. The delayed election was held in December 1992 and the ONLF won a landslide victory. It won over 80 per cent of the seats in the regional assembly. Despite its big majority in that assembly the ONLF chose to form a coalition government, in which it occupied the presidency and vice-presidency, and the IGLF took the secretary post. Other, smaller, parties were also given a share in the heads of departments. The ONLF-led administration, under the leadership of Abdullahi Mohamed Sa'di, did not last long, however. It soon came under fire from both the central government, on charges of corruption and from the ONLF leadership itself, on charges of incompetence and distraction from the liberation path. For their part, the regional authorities accused the central government of undermining regional autonomy by its flagrant interference in regional affairs and claimed their refusal to bend to the central government as being the root cause of the stand-off. After only about seven months in office, the Sa'di administration was replaced by another ONLF-dominated administration but headed by a small party. Hassan Jire Qalinle, who became the new president, was from the Western Somali Democratic Party (former WSLF) but his deputy, Ahmed Ali Dahir, and most of the heads of departments belonged to the ONLF.

The former president (Abdullahi Mohamed Sa'di), the vice-president (Siad Badri) and the secretary (Mahdi Ahmed Warsame) were arrested by the central government and imprisoned in Addis Ababa. The men were held there for about ten months without having been charged or tried.

In the meantime, the ONLF continued to pursue its liberation efforts peacefully within both the regional and federal levels in collaboration with other parties in the regional assembly. Using the new democratic channels, it attempted to realize the fundamental human rights, including the right of self-determination, advocated by the Transitional Charter. To that end, it mobilized regional assembly members before introducing a bill demanding a referendum on secession. At a press conference held by the ONLF in Addis Ababa on 28 January 1994, the organization called for a referendum on self-determination for the Ogaden region. The referendum issue was discussed in the regional parliament's session in Jigjiga on 25 March 1994 and the regional assembly almost unanimously passed a resolution demanding a referendum on independence to be held.

Alarmed by the demand for a referendum on independence and the resoluteness of the Somali people in the Ogaden region, the central government reacted in a very hasty and harsh manner. It violently put down pro-secession rallies, carried out widespread arrests, starting with top leaders, and began to dismantle the democratic institutions. The referendum demand uncovered the true face of the central government regarding human rights and national aspirations and shortened the lifespan of its deceptive propaganda in that regard. The central government realized its underestimation of the Somalis in the Ogaden and as a result began to reverse the political process in the region, by taking direct control of all aspects of political life and giving the military a green light to kill, in order to quell the national aspiration.

To kill the national aspirations, the central government introduced measures aimed at changing the political landscape and began a military campaign intended to terrorise the population and uproot the liberation fronts. As a first step, it dismissed the regional authorities and imprisoned the president, vice-president and many other politicians. Like their predecessors, the two top leaders were held in prison without charge for many months. The president died a few months after his release and his ordeal in the underground prison in Addis Ababa is believed to have been the chief cause of his death. Having replaced the elected authorities with puppet ones of his own creation, Zenawi changed the capital of the region from Godey to Jigjiga, to bring the regional authorities closer to Addis Ababa, both geographically and politically. In the long run, the central government decided to change the political landscape by creating an EPRDF-type organization directed by the EPRDF but carried out by people with a Somali background. The government's aim with the creation of the puppet umbrella organization was to replace it with the ONLF, the chief political organization of the region.

The organization the government created to replace the ONLF for the leadership of the region was the Ethiopian Somali Democratic League (ESDL). The central government undertook several steps to achieve its goal of uprooting the ONLF and replacing it with the ESDL. First, it declared war on the ONLF; second, it abolished many of the ONLF's stronghold constituencies; and third, it attempted to divide the movement by creating a false ONLF of its own.

Not only was the ONLF dislodged from the political leadership of the region, but the Ethiopian government declared war on the organization. On 22 February 1994, the ONLF leader, Sheikh Ibrahim Abdallah, was attacked by the Ethiopian government forces while addressing a crowd in Warder. Eighty-one civilians who came to listen to the speech of their leader were killed, but the leader escaped unharmed, thanks to the many civilians who staged themselves as human shields to defend him. On 17 April 1994, the EPRDF government launched a large-scale military offensive against the ONLF positions and detained many suspected supporters of the ONLF. After the Warder incident and the ensuing all-out war against the ONLF, the organization had no choice but to resume the armed struggle. The ONLF quickly regrouped and dug down in self-defence all over the region, despite its small force at the time. Though all odds were stacked against the ONLF, the movement put up stiff resistance and the Ethiopian government again learned that it underestimated the strength of the ONLF.

In parallel with the military campaign, the EPRDF government continued its political offensive. It did not content itself with the creation of the ESDL but formed another organization that it called the new ONLF on 27 May 1995, and claimed it to have replaced the old one, which it claimed to have destroyed. The so-called new ONLF organization declared that it would cooperate with the central government and participate in the upcoming election, which the true ONLF and its supporters boycotted. To deny the ONLF any influence in the political process, many of its stronghold constituencies were abolished. Although the 1995 regional elections did not take place in most of the constituencies because of insecurity resulting from the war between the liberation movements (the ONLF and Al-Itihad) and the Ethiopian government, The ESDL was declared winner of the June 1995 elections and the so-called new ONLF was declared the second-largest party in the regional assembly.

Because of the attack on the ONLF, the dismantling of the democratic institutions and the terror that followed, the Somali people in the region rallied behind the liberation movements. The ONLF was a movement consisting of various groups with different views on wide-ranging issues; however, its military confrontation with the Ethiopian government was a unifying factor and the movement became more united as a result of the armed resistance.

Although the bulk of its members both in and out of the region were united in their confrontation with the EPRDF government, the organization remained remarkably diverse in many ways for several reasons. Ordinary as well as central committee members were dispersed all over the world and the successive leaders of the organization and many of the executive committee remained outside the region for most of the time. This geographical barrier not only reduced the effectiveness of the leadership, but it also led to subcultures and different attitudes towards liberation work.

Despite these internal difficulties and the external challenges examined in chapter 9 the ONLF, under both Sheikh Ibrahim Abdallah and Admiral Mohamed Omar Osman, made great headway in the liberation efforts. In the former period, the organization not only survived the intensive military campaign aimed at its elimination during 1994–1996, but it emerged victorious against all odds. Under Sheikh Ibrahim, the ONLF has shown that it can resist without outside help. Somalia, the traditional support base of the Ogaden liberation movements, was no longer in existence as a functioning state. The Ethiopian government was in many ways even in control of Somalia through its satellite warlords, and Ethiopia not only emerged as a regional superpower but was fully backed by the US, the only remaining superpower on earth. Given the political, diplomatic and economic support of the West to Ethiopia, the well-equipped huge Ethiopian forces, the near-starvation situation in the Ogaden and the small force of the resistant movements, Ethiopia not only expected that it would eradicate the ONLF, but it also contemplated an early surrender. Afterwards, the Ethiopian government realized that it had once again grossly underestimated the resolve of the ONLF and Somali people in the Ogaden.

On the battlefield, too, the Ethiopian government learned the limits of its overwhelming military power after the ONLF taught the Ethiopian forces unforgettable lessons. During the first two years of the conflict, the Tigray forces were on the offensive, thinking that they could eliminate the organization. In fact, they even prematurely announced in 1994 that they had destroyed the organization. But after many battles, in the majority of which the Ethiopian forces were badly defeated, the

Ethiopian forces changed their tactics from offensive to defensive. The battles were too many to count in that period, but the ONLF emerged victorious. The holding of the second ONLF general conference inside the Ogaden was an indication of the military success of the ONLF forces over its enemy forces.

In the second conference which took place in September 1998 inside the Ogaden, the organization changed its leadership. Admiral Mohamed Omar Osman replaced Sheikh Ibrahim Abdallah as chairman. Mohamed Omar Osman selected an executive committee of 11 from the 51 central committee members the conference elected. Changes were made to the make-up of the executive committee, because of death or other reasons. The central committee members during the admiral's period include Abdullahi Mukhtar Hussein, Abdirrahman Sheikh Mahdi, Abdirizaq Sheikh Mohamud, Abdulqadir Hirmooge, Ahmed Mohamed Jabhad, Deeq Abdi Rasin Mohamed Sirad Dolal, Mohamed Ismail Omar, Mohamed Abdi Yasiin, Salahu-Diin Ma'aw and Sulub Abdi Ahmed.

Although the organization proved its resistance capabilities, it was diplomatically isolated until the late 1990s, its armed forces were effectively militant but very small, had few weapons, limited access to potential supply lines, and did not have the backing of any country. Besides that, the organization suffered from an exclusion image within the Somali context, which arose from name similarity between the largest clan in the region (Ogaadeen) and the regional name (Ogaden) as well as the widespread clan fighting in Somalia, which also affected the Somali clans inside the Ogaden.

Under the leadership of the admiral, the ONLF lifted itself out of diplomatic isolation and greatly increased its military capabilities. The admiral's personal contribution as a heavyweight politician as well as a known figure throughout the Horn of Africa was instrumental in reaching out first and foremost to neighbouring countries. The organization made tacit deals with various regional administrations in Somalia and through these deals, the organization got access to the outside world as well as to transit bases in the Horn neighbours.

On 21 May 2006, the ONLF entered into an alliance with five Ethiopian opposition groups, namely the Ethiopian Peoples Patriotic Front (EPPF), the Oromo Liberation Front (OLF), the United Ethiopian Democratic Forces (UEDF), the Sidama Liberation Front (SLF) and the South Ethiopian Peoples, Justice & Equality Front (SEPJE), forming an umbrella opposition organization called the Alliance for Freedom and Democracy (AFD). The move was intended to widen and strengthen the front against the regime in Addis Ababa.

The ONLF's much-publicized relationship with Eritrea is no doubt one of the most important relationships the organization has with the outside world. Because of the similar colonial history of the Ogaden and Eritrea and the current hostility between Ethiopia and Eritrea, the two found common ground. The relationship between the ONLF and the Eritrean government is based on mutual interests and their cooperation covers a wide range of issues. The defeat of the regime in Addis Ababa is in the mutual interest of the Somali people in the Ogaden and the Eritrean people, and the realization of this common interest was the main factor that motivated the cooperation of the two. To defeat the common enemy, Eritrea opened its door to the ONLF, supporting it with both technical training and some of the much-needed military hardware. The Eritrean assistance was important in upgrading the military capabilities of the ONLF as well as in increasing its diplomatic and political manoeuvrability.

The increased military capabilities are felt inside the Ogaden, as evidenced by the defeat of the Ethiopian forces throughout the region and the abandonment of their positions in rural areas. Not only did the ONLF militants contain the enemy forces inside the main urban centres, but their fighting morale deteriorated to the point that they avoided going to places when they suspected an ONLF forces presence, and they began to defect to the ONLF in large numbers. The huge defeat of the Ethiopian forces by the ONLF's operation, codenamed Manded, in April 2005, which the international press reported, and the failure of its much-publicised operation in 2006 which involved several divisions of its best army, revealed the ONLF's new military power.

According to Radio Horiyo, the Mandad operation aimed at weakening enemy forces in the Qorahay and Dolo districts, and the fighting took place between the ONLF units and the Ethiopian forces on 15 April 2005 at Alen and Garas Qalo. The ONLF claimed to have killed 60 Ethiopian soldiers and captured 2 Ural trucks. In retaliation, the Ethiopian forces conducted massacres in Shilabo, Farmadaw and Qabridahre on 29 June, 26 October and 15 November 2005, respectively. In Shilabo six civilians were killed and many wounded, in Farmadaw seven were killed and 15 wounded and in Qabridahare over 30 people died and 45 were wounded. The village of Fooljeex was also burned by the Ethiopian forces on 21 November 2005.

In May 2006, the Ethiopian government sent tens of thousands of its troops to the region, in what she called a sweeping operation. The military offensive was partly prompted by the need to convince foreign oil companies that she was trying to make deals over the exploitation of the natural Ogaden resources, that she is in control of the region and that it is safe to conduct exploration there, and more importantly to weaken the ONLF. To the disappointment of the Ethiopian government, the ONLF forces got the upper hand and government forces were defeated everywhere in the region. According to Radio Horiyo, the ONLF forces clashed with the occupation forces in nearly all districts of the region, with the heaviest battles taking place in Godey, Nogob, Qorahay, Jarer and Danood and the ONLF forces emerged victorious. Again, in revenge the Ethiopian government turned against the civilian population, killing them indiscriminately and burning the villages near the battlefields. Sasabane in the Dagahbour district was the latest to be burned after two Ural trucks with 120 soldiers on board were burned by the ONLF near that village.

The ONLF nowadays conducts raids into the main towns and in the main military headquarters, including military airfields. The downing of aeroplanes and the recent operations inside Qabridahare and Dagahbour are evidence of the increasing strength of the organization. The organization downed a military attack helicopter in Gebo- Gebo, Qorahay district, on 18 July 2006 and a similar helicopter was destroyed in a military operation conducted by specially trained ONLF fighters, inside the town of Qabridahare on 12 November 2006. On the same day, a similar commando operation was conducted by specially trained units of the organization in Dagahbour. Radio Horiyo reported high tolls of Ethiopian soldiers in both operations.

The new military power of the ONLF is also reflected on the political and diplomatic fronts. The ONLF is today a major actor in the Horn of Africa, and that position is recognised even by the Ethiopian regime. The Ethiopian leader rarely holds a major speech or press conference nowadays without mentioning the ONLF, sometimes stating that his government is ready to enter negotiation with ONLF, as he did on 17 July 2005, and sometimes threatening to eradicate the organization. (He vowed in his press conference on 4 August 2006 to wipe out the organization.) In his last address before the parliament in October 2006, he listed the ONLF among what he called the destabilizing forces in Ethiopia and at the same time declared his willingness to engage in peace negotiations with the resistance movement. The new recognition in the Horn of the ONLF as a major player changed the image of the organization in many ways. Both the Ethiopian opposition and the regime in Addis Ababa – for the first time in the history of the region –

recognize the ONLF as a contender and possible future partner.

In the international arena, the ONLF has made contacts with several Western governments, including the US and some European countries. The recent Ethiopian organizations' alliances agreement, which included the ONLF, is the result of Western governments' attempts to find an alternative administration to the EPRDF government. Although this could have an image and political problem for the ONLF, because of the ambiguity of the agreement regarding the liberation issue, it showed the importance of the ONLF within the Ethiopian context. The organization is raising itself on the national, regional and international stages, but still, it has a long way to go and needs much more effort to reach the desired position.

The ONLF has become a locomotive for the pan-Somalism against Ethiopian occupation and interference and greatly improved its image by altering much of the exclusive perceptions some sections of the Somali people held about the organization. The Somali people are grateful to the ONLF for the anti-colonial leadership it has shown and recognize the importance of the organization in that regard. Sections of the Somali society within the Ogaden region that had suspected the organization of clan affiliation gradually began to accept the ONLF as a national liberation organization, because of the organization's universal defence of the Somalis and their territories.

Despite the improvements, many people, including its supporters, still see the ONLF as a club for a particular group or section of the Somali people in the Ogaden. Thus, the organization needs a lot of persuasion and more goodwill in order to eliminate that exclusion image. The organization has been led for the most part by leaders in exile, and that contributed immensely to the group phenomenon and incoherence that characterized the ONLF, both of which in turn adversely affected the efficiency of the work of the organization, and the ONLF leadership needs some drastic measures to reduce the size of its exile leadership to improve its efficiency.

During the transitional period, the ONLF was very ambiguous both in dealing with the EPRDF government and on its stance regarding the secession issue. The main factors which led to the lack of clarity in its position were misinformation, from the central government, the hard economic and social conditions in the Ogaden and – above all – the lack of visible strategy from the organization on how to deal with the Tigray-led government. To many intellectuals within the ONLF, the deceptive game was clear from the outset, but the organization was not able to articulate its position until the regional ONLF-led administration was overthrown, and the central government declared war on the organization.

After the armed conflict started, the ONLF developed a clear strategy on how to carry the liberation programme forward and it made its standpoint regarding any peace deal with Ethiopia very clear. The ONLF declared its readiness to enter peace negotiations with Ethiopia, on the condition that the talks take place in a neutral country and in the presence of a neutral arbiter from the international community. The ONLF stuck to this straightforward position it had adopted, and that standpoint boosted its image as a transparent and serious actor. Given the unreliability shown by the Addis Ababa regime as well as the need to draw the attention of the international community to the conflict, the ONLF standpoint is in the right position.

The recent ONLF agreement with the Ethiopian opposition, however, overshadows the liberation goals of the ONLF and its position for peace talks in several ways. Some of the organizations within the alliance oppose the secession of any region within Ethiopia. Second, the formation of the alliance was originally initiated by some Western governments who see the need to get credible opposition capable of forming an alternative administration. Secession is not on the agenda of these governments. The ONLF opponents, including the Addis regime, interpreted its membership of the alliance as an abandonment of the organization's secession goal. Meles Zenawi failed in his latest attempt to divide the ONLF and its supporters in the diaspora through the Ogaden elders, but tirelessly he is still trying to divide the organization. Claiming that he could offer more to the Somalis in the Ogaden than the alliance, he launched a new deceptive peace mission, involving the elders and members of his regime. Because of the history of the present regime in Addis Ababa, the divide-and-rule tactics of the Zenawi regime are doomed to failure. However, the ONLF should look ahead beyond the present regime and take precautionary measures now to avoid the repetition of the situation in the early 1990s.

Although there is always a need for improvement, the ONLF has come a long way. Given the many internal and external challenges and the huge Ethiopian power it faces, the organization has done well against all odds and the prospect of achieving its aims are very good. As the political representative and defender of the Somalis in the Ogaden region, the organization has made milestone steps in its liberation efforts. Due to the centrality of the Ogaden issue to the Horn conflicts and the recent ONLF political, military and diplomatic successes, the organization has also become a major actor to be reckoned with in the Horn of Africa.

12

Epilogue

The effects of the Ethiopian occupation of Somalia on the struggle; the struggle in retrospect; the prospect for conflict resolution

In this chapter, we will take a look at the struggle for freedom both backwards and forwards, summarising its past failures and successes and the reasons behind them, and assessing the future rate of its success. We begin the chapter with a brief examination of the effects of the recent Ethiopian occupation of Somalia on the struggle, review the positive and negative results of the history of the struggle and end it with predictions about its future.

12.1 The Effects of the Ethiopian Occupation of Somalia on the Resistance

In December 2006, Ethiopia fully invaded Somalia and on 28 December the capital city of Somalia, Mogadishu, came under Ethiopian occupation. The occupation of Mogadishu by the Ethiopian forces is not only a big obstacle to the revival of the Somali state and the liberation of the Ogaden, but it is also the mother of all humiliations, the symbol of the end of statehood in Somalia, the death of Somali pride and a complete victory for Ethiopia. The occupation of Mogadishu, the capital city of Somalia, the centre of the Greater Somalia dream and the former base of the liberation movements, was psychologically a big blow to Somali pride.

Ethiopia was in control of many parts of Somalia through the Ethiopian-sponsored Somali warlords, and its troops were stationed in other parts of the country such as Baydhabo and Galkayo before the latest invasion, but in December 2006 it decided to take over the whole country when it got the green light and assistance from the US government, and after it captured the central and southern regions of Somalia. With the capture of Dusemereb, Baledweyn, Jawhar, Mogadishu, Merka, Bu'alle and Kismayo, Ethiopia completed its control of Somalia from Borama to Raskamboni. Ethiopia is now in full control of Somalia and has the blessing of the US to do whatever she wants in

Somalia.

The latest Ethiopian invasion of Somalia was prompted by the rise to power of the Union of Islamic Courts, an organization aimed at restoring statehood in Somalia. The organization took over the power in Mogadishu in June 2006, after it defeated the US- and Ethiopian-supported warlords. The organization was able to restore law and order in the capital and many of the regions that came under its control within a short period. Because of its Islamic outlook and national agenda Ethiopia felt unease about the organization from the outset. It did not hide its feeling and decided to kill the new Somali spirit before it took over the whole country.

The situation was exacerbated by the US and Kenyan governments' active involvement in the invasion. The US government not only blessed the Ethiopian invasion, but it took part in the operation financially and militarily. On the pretext of tracing Al-Qaeda suspects, its navy has been blockading the Somali coast since the start of the invasion, its air force bombed Somali towns and some units of its combat troops landed on Somali soil. The government of Kenya, too, supported the Ethiopian aggression. Kenya not only closed its border with Somalia to prevent refugees from entering Kenya, but its troops entered Somalia to assist the invading forces. Furthermore, the Kenyan government rounded up Somali people in Nairobi and other Kenyan towns and handed them over to the Ethiopian occupation army in Mogadishu. Some ONLF officials who were on a private visit to Kenya were among those handed over to Ethiopia.

Leaving emotions aside, the Ethiopian invasion of Somalia will have adverse effects on the stability, freedom and human rights and the economy of the whole of the Horn of Africa region. What Ethiopia did in Somalia is the reverse of what she was required to do. Instead of occupying her neighbour on the pretext of supporting Somalia's government, Ethiopia was supposed to put an end to her occupation in the Ogaden, introduce a rule of law in Ethiopia and stop fuelling the civil war in Somalia. As a result of the invasion, Ethiopia's economy will be affected negatively by the occupation, despite American financial support to Ethiopia, and her invading army will probably be defeated. Of course, the brunt of the occupation will be borne by the Somalis.

The Somalis in the Ogaden and Somalia are interdependent economically and, because of its land-locked geographical location, the Ogaden is dependent on Somalia's coast. In other words, Somalia provides supply lines to the Somalis in the Ogaden region. It used to be the safe haven for Somali Ogaden dissidents when Somalia had a functioning government, and recently it was the escape route through which they passed when fleeing the Ethiopian forces. Among Ethiopia's aims in occupying Somalia were to encircle the freedom fighters in the Ogaden and cut their supply lines, but as history shows, it can neither sustain the occupation in Somalia nor can it crush the resistance in the Ogaden. Thus, the occupation might delay justice in the Ogaden and prolong the suffering of the people in the Horn of Africa region, but it is unlikely to benefit Ethiopia in the long run.

12.2 The Resistance in Retrospect

In this section we will review the main achievements and setbacks of the struggle and in doing so we need to answer two questions, namely, why has the struggle not yet achieved its aims and how were the resistance movements able to sustain the centuries-long struggle? The answers to these two questions will cover the ups and downs of the struggle. However, as we have examined most of these achievements and setbacks in earlier chapters of the book, we will not go through them in detail; instead, we present them in summary form.

12.3 The Resistance in Retrospect: Setbacks

Because of the long period of the struggle, different setbacks affected the struggle over the decades and centuries. However, there were some common problems that all different resistance generations faced, and which hampered the progress of the struggle for freedom. The main blocking bricks of the struggle for self-determination have been the interference of external powers in favour of the occupation, neglect of the rights and the plight of the Somali people in the Ogaden by the international community, misconception about the struggle and shortage of resources.

The struggle started as a reaction to the expansion and threats of the Christian kingdom of Abyssinia, and the occupation of the Ogaden by that kingdom was made possible by the support of the main European powers. These foreign powers not only helped Abyssinia conquer the Ogaden, but their support was also crucial in maintaining the occupation. As we saw in chapter one, the Portuguese supported the Abyssinians with both weapons and fighting force in their attempt to conquer Adal. Likewise, France, Russia, Italy and Britain all helped Menelik to conquer the Ogaden in the late nineteenth century. The next reoccupation of the Ogaden region by Ethiopia, which took place after the Second World

War, would not have been possible without the backing of these powers, particularly Britain, Russia, France, Italy and the USA. In 1946, the British foreign secretary advocated in the British parliament unification of the Somali lands, first under British rule and then under a future Somali state, but he abandoned the proposal before presenting it to the UN when he recognised opposition to his proposal from the big European powers, particularly Russia. Britain was in control of the Ogaden at the time and had she been sincere enough, she could have kept the territory under her control until independence, but she was not wholehearted about the proposal. The transfer of the NFD to Kenya in 1963, and the British support for the OAU policy of accepting the colonial boundaries, confirmed British hypocrisy about the self-determination issue of the Somalis. The British handover of the Ogaden region to Ethiopia without consulting the inhabitants, and the backing of that British move by the other members of the four-power commission (France, Russia and the USA), highlighted the conspiracy and the cruelty of these powers against the Somali people. Ethiopia's claim on the Ogaden was based solely on its earlier occupation in the late nineteenth century and in that occupation, too, the same powers helped Menelik.

Although Ethiopia has changed alliance several times, both the superpowers and other big European powers all supported Ethiopia's efforts to colonize the Ogaden. The US replaced the European powers in backing Ethiopia's colonial policies in the Ogaden in the 1950s and 1960s, and the first half of the 1970s. Russia, whose support for Ethiopia predates the scramble for Africa and who always cared about Abyssinia because of the common Orthodox faith, was the chief superpower patron of Ethiopia in the period 1976–1990. With the help of Somalia, the WSLF succeeded in liberating over 90 per cent of the Ogaden in the 1977/78 Ogaden war, but a Russian-led evil alliance brought back the occupation. On the pretext of combating international terrorism, the Ethiopian government got the backing of the US in combating Al-Itihad, a resistance movement that fought against the occupation in the Ogaden during the 1990s. From the sixteenth century up to now, Ethiopia has enjoyed the backing of the contemporary superpowers in its pursuit to conquer, colonize, repress and subjugate the Somali people, and that support has been the biggest bottleneck of the struggle.

The world community failed to carry out its duty toward the Somali people in the Ogaden region, in legal, political and human rights terms. The UN neither opposed the occupation of the Ogaden in the first place nor did it criticise the inhuman policies of the occupiers. Since the UN was controlled by the same world powers that helped Ethiopia conquer the Ogaden, Somali attempts to liberate their land and free their people were never backed by the United Nations. Over a million people fled the Ogaden region during the 1970s; however, Somali attempts to bring the root cause of the plight of the Somali people in the Ogaden, namely the occupation to the Security Council did not materialize. In the words of Louis FitzGibbon: 'The United Nations has evaded its duty.'[1]

It was not only the UN that failed the Somali people in the Ogaden, but other world bodies and regional bodies such as the international human rights organizations, the OAU, the Arab League and the Organization of Islamic Conference all let down the inhabitants of the region, either by supporting Ethiopia's occupation or becoming indifferent to the suffering of the people.

Despite the unspeakable level of human rights violations in the Somali region of the Ogaden, and the huge number of refugees and displaced people that resulted from the repression of the Ethiopian forces, the human rights organizations did not react to that tragedy in a proportional or acceptable manner. They neither campaigned for the freedom of the inhabitants of this occupied territory as they did in other parts of the World, (East Timor, Darfur, etc.) nor did they report enough about the gross violation of human rights that took place on daily basis. Even within the Ethiopian context, their reports of human rights violations are short compared to what they reported elsewhere in Ethiopia.

The OAU was expected to be at the forefront of the fight against the occupation because of the continent's experience with colonization but, unfortunately, the organization sided with the colonialist state of Ethiopia in the case of the Ogaden. Ethiopia was instrumental in creating the continental organization and because of her role in that regard, her high standing within the continent due to the survival of Ethiopia from the scramble for Africa, the preservation of her independence and her determination to keep the territories she occupied, she was able to manipulate the charter of the organization to her own advantage at the formation stage of the organization by adding an article requiring the acceptance of the colonial boundaries as future boundaries.

Ethiopia successfully sought the support of Christian world powers, on the grounds that she was a Christian kingdom surrounded by Muslims and pagans and got their backing. This help enabled her to both occupy and maintain the occupation in the Ogaden. The Somali people shared their faith with the member countries of the Arab League, and the

---

[1] Louis FitzGibbon, 1985, *The Evaded Duty*, Rex Collins Ltd, page 17.

Organization for Islamic Conference, but although the Somalis were not as smart as the Abyssinians diplomat-wise, these Islamic countries did not support the Ogaden cause and some of them even sided with Ethiopia.

Misconception about the Ogaden cause has been a major obstacle to the struggle in getting recognition from the governments of the world and their citizens. The misconception surrounding the Ogaden cause is mainly due to deliberate misrepresentation by Ethiopia aimed at misinforming and confusing world public opinion to win the diplomatic war. Lack of general knowledge about the history and the situation of the region, and Ethiopia's poor image, also contributed to confusion about the conflict.

As we explained in earlier chapters in this book, Ethiopia portrayed the Ogaden problem as a border dispute between Ethiopia and Somalia, accusing the latter of being both expansionist and aggressor. Partly because of ignorance about the Ogaden history but mostly because of Ethiopia's successful diplomacy, which proved superior to that of the Somalis, the Ogaden conflict did not reach the citizens of the world in its true nature. Ethiopia persuaded most of the OAU member countries to be on her side of the conflict after it portrayed itself as a victim of Somali aggression and persuaded the African leaders to add to the charter of the organization an article that recognizes the legitimacy of the colonial borders. The fact that Ethiopia is one of the poorest and most backward black African countries also made it easier to mislead and seek the sympathy of the world, despite its colonial practices. When people hear of colonization, the first thing that comes into their minds is the classical colonization involving extra-regional powers. Ethiopia is not only a black African country, but it is also a failed state that cannot even feed itself. Thus, it is hard for an outsider who does not know the facts about the Ogaden to imagine such a country colonizing other black African nations. Because of this image problem, world public views have not been malleable and extra efforts are required by the occupied Somali people in the Ogaden to persuade the world's public that Ethiopia is, in fact, one of the worst colonizers.

The Ogaden region is poorer than Ethiopia in terms of both human and material resources, a disadvantage that has partly hindered the struggle to achieve its goal so far. Ethiopia has a population of over 70 million compared to the small population of the Ogaden, which is estimated (genuine censuses were never taken) at about 4–5 million. Besides that, the Ogaden population lags behind that of Ethiopia in terms of educational, economic, social and political development.

Because of these imbalances, Ethiopia was able to isolate the region from the rest of the world, and the inhabitants were unable to lift the isolation imposed on them through political or conventional warfare by the regime in Ethiopia, except during the brief period of the 1977/1978 Ogaden war in which over 90 per cent of the region was freed.

The geographical location of the region, and its terrain, have also been unfavourable factors to the armed resistance. The Ogaden is a land-locked country that does not have access to the outside world, because of its geographical location and – more importantly – because of the political isolation imposed on it by successive Ethiopian regimes. Furthermore, the open terrain of the Ogaden region is not suitable for successful guerrilla operations. There are not many large forests in the region and, unlike most of the other parts of Ethiopia, there are few mountainous areas, and thus there are not many proper hiding places from airplane bombers and heavy artillery.

12.4 The Resistance in Retrospect: The Achievements

Despite the above-listed and many other trials, the struggle not only survived but has been making gradual progress over the decades, and in recent years it has made big advances. The struggle has had many ups and downs during its many-centuries-long history. Although some resistance movements that carried out the struggle disintegrated and disappeared, new ones replaced them and the struggle always continued in one way or another; that is, resistance organizations died and changed over time, but the struggle continued. The continuation of the resistance despite the setbacks is the core achievement of the struggle since all the positive results of the struggle interact with that variable. Thus, examining the parameters that lead to the continuity of the struggle is the same as looking into its gains over the decades, and therefore we need only to review the factors that contributed to the continuity of the struggle. The main factors that contributed to the renewability of the struggle and thereby to its achievements are the society's dream to live in freedom and dignity, persistent repression, self-reliance and ideological flexibility. These factors also interacted with one another and, in turn, positively influenced the liberation struggle.

Society's dream to retain its freedom and live with dignity has been one of the main root causes for the start as well as the continuity of the struggle for freedom. Because of their firm belief in preserving their inalienable fundamental human rights, the Somali people in the region could not accept subjugation and the infringements of their rights and, as a result, they began to mobilize themselves to defend those rights as they came under attack. Thus, the vision for the struggle for self-determination originated from the dream to live in freedom. The vision itself has been guided by, among other, things nationalism, religion and above all the need to safeguard human rights, all of which fuelled the struggle machine by providing rationale and spirit for the liberation efforts. Although the struggle for liberty made both retreats and advances, these pillars of the vision ensured its continuation.

Since the occupation of the region by Ethiopia, the Somali people in the Ogaden have been living under constant terror, repression and all kinds of human rights abuses. The inhuman policies of the successive Ethiopian regimes led to the alienation of the inhabitants and forced them to take armies in self-defence. The resistance started as a reaction to the occupation and the consequent repression and is fuelled by the unending atrocities committed by the Ethiopian regimes daily. In fact, it was said the occupation policies of the successive Ethiopian regimes were so harsh that a decent person could not stay in the region without becoming part of the resistance. The resistance became part of the daily routine of the inhabitants; however, the degree of participation remains a function of the level of atrocities. In other words, the harder the Ethiopian government hits the population, the higher the determination to resist and the stronger the involvement of the resistance.

Self-reliance is another characteristic that the Western Somali People's struggle gained, especially in the last two decades. Although they seek the support of the international community in ending the occupation, they know from experience that the thing at stake is their freedom and nobody else's. They know too that it is no use to make their liberation efforts dependent on the support of the international community. Reminding themselves of the Somali proverb *Xabaal ninkeed baa looga tegey*, which literally means 'the dead body is left in his graveyard', they continued the resistance, despite the lack of credible backing. Thus, though any help is welcome, it is not taken into consideration by the Somali people when planning the liberation strategy in the Ogaden. The Western Somali people used to depend on Somalia for support during the 1960s and 1970s, but that is no longer the case; in fact, the struggle is doing better now than it did during the period when it enjoyed Somalia's support.

The flexibility of the resistance movements also contributed to the continuation of the struggle in that the movements were able to renew themselves to face the new challenges of the time. When strategies and tactics did not work, the leadership of the struggle often jettisoned them and adopted new ones. They even went as far as changing the liberation organization in 1984, when some members of the WSLF abandoned their organization and formed the ONLF.

The recent intensification of the activities of liberation movements and the extension of the scope of struggle has made it almost impossible for the struggle to disappear easily before reaching its goals. The traditional liberation movements that led the struggle all made progress in their efforts to liberate their land and free their people, though the rate of their success varied. The ONLF, which assumed the leadership role of the political and militarily aspects of the liberation struggle after having succeeded the WSLF, has been making great headway recently in that regard, as detailed in chapter 11. The organization is operating in many parts of the world that were not reachable to its predecessors and it achieved a lot internally through its self-reliant attitude and bottom-up mobilization.

In addition to these improvements at the leadership level, the struggle was growing horizontally in that more organizations joined the struggle and brought with them new ideas, methods and tactics, and opened new fronts. The struggle nowadays is represented in most of the capitals in which Ethiopia has diplomatic stations, as well as in many others in which Ethiopia is not represented. Conducting the struggle in a pluralistic manner, the various organizations are all challenging the Ethiopian authorities everywhere in the world Ethiopia might seek political, economic or military assistance and are all striving for the same goals. These freedom fighters are there as human rights activists, revealing the inhuman practices of the Ethiopian regime in the Ogaden region to the world, as environmental pressure groups warning of the ecological dangers of Ethiopia's illegal exploitation of the Ogaden natural resources, as resistance movements representatives persuading the world to support their just cause and as refugees, reminding the international community of the plight of the Ogaden people and demanding the examination of the root cause of their plight, namely the occupation.

Because of the above-mentioned and many other strengths that the struggle possesses, it is no exaggeration to say that it has reached a point of no return. So, the question is: what is the likelihood of the success of the struggle, given its present situation? The answer to this question is the topic of our discussion in the next section.

12.5 Prospect for Conflict Resolution

Given the strong determination of the Somali people in the Ogaden that does not accept anything less than full freedom and, at the same time, Ethiopia's obsession with the occupation of the Ogaden, a resolution to the conflict in the near future does not seem probable. However, the realization of the freedom dreams of the Western Somali people through peaceful or military means seems unavoidable in the long run. Due to the nature of the Ethiopian state, the illegality of the Ethiopian occupation of the Ogaden and the resolve of the Somali inhabitants a resolution to the conflict in one way or another is expected in the long term.

12.6 Prospect for Conflict Resolution: The Nature of the Ethiopian State

The Ethiopian empire is a collection of different nationalities, most of whom have nothing in common except humanity and the colour of their skin, brought together by force. Not only was the empire formed through the barrel of the gun, but its control is also maintained by force. So the question is given: the fact that Ethiopia is a failed state could it afford to maintain the empire by force? The answer to that question is negative. Ethiopia could neither maintain the different nationalities under its rule by subjugation nor could it suppress the aspiration of the people for a long time to come. From political, economic and military perspectives it is unlikely to keep control of the different nationalities that were forcefully lumped together.

Although the successive Ethiopian regimes did their utmost to maintain control of the Ogaden and other territories under Ethiopian occupation by suppressing national aspirations, resistance to the occupation never died. On the contrary, the people's resistances were on the increase, and it seems that the suppression policies produced the opposite effects from a political point of view. In many ways, the Ethiopian empire resembles the former Soviet Union. The formation of both empires was not voluntary; both contained different people with no common cultural, religious, linguistic or common heritage. Furthermore, the successive Ethiopian governments have been very similar to that of the old Soviet Union in terms of totalitarianism, repression and lack of freedom. Because of these similarities of the two empires, the fate of the Ethiopian empire is expected to end up in the same manner as that of the Soviet Union.

After many decades or centuries of control, the Soviet Union gave up its occupation policies, after it realized that it could not maintain control of the occupied territories anymore, and accordingly allowed them to decide their future destiny. If the superpower Soviet Union could not preserve its union and Russia could not hold the Ukraine after 300 years of control, it is very hard to imagine Ethiopia preventing its empire from collapse or keeping control of the Ogaden in the long run. The experiences of the Soviet Union and Yugoslavia showed that it is possible to maintain control of nations physically for a period of time, but that one could never kill the spirit and the will of nations, no matter how long the suppression is maintained.

Economically Ethiopia is not capable of sustaining the level of military force needed to continue to control or defend the territories under fire. A country with a per capita income of $120 per year would not be able to finance the high cost of the ongoing wars that cost millions annually. Ethiopia is one of the poorest nations on Earth, and according to the United Nations Human Development Reports, Ethiopia is ranked 170 out of 174 countries in the human development index (1975–2006). The economy is also deteriorating because of, among other things, the warfare situation and recurrent droughts and, as a result, its ability to finance the internal wars will diminish further.

Militarily, too, Ethiopia could not continue fighting forever. The Ethiopian soldiers gradually understand the senselessness of the war against the very people they were supposed to defend, are experiencing the harsh reality of life in the military service, which bound to deteriorate further because of the likely reduction in military spending, and are becoming more aware of their lack of basic rights. In short, they are becoming weary of the war, and the recent large defection of the Ethiopian soldiers to OLF, ONLF and neighbouring states is evidence of the evaporation of their faith in the system and of winning the war. Civil servants and politicians have also been defecting to the West in large numbers.

12.7 Prospect for Conflict Resolution: The Illegality of the Occupation

The Ethiopian occupation of the Ogaden was unlawful and that illegality remains the core argument against the occupation. In proving the illegality of the Ethiopian occupation of the Ogaden, however, we need to review the situation of the territory before the occupation, as well as the application of legal practices regarding decolonisation to the Ogaden situation. Prior to the scramble for Africa, the status of territories within the continent varied. Some were subject to state sovereignty, some were open areas not yet acquired by any state (*terra nullius*), and others were in between; that is, neither state territories nor open territories for acquisition.

Before the Ethiopian occupation, the Ogaden was neither under the rule of any power nor was it 'available for acquisition as being a *terra nullius*, i.e. open territory to be freely taken over by anyone.'[2] Although the Somalis did not have a state of their own in the modern sense, they were a nation ruled by small, decentralised kingdoms and tribal leaders, and were in control of their land and people. The Sultanates of Ajuran, Obbia, Majerten and Adal are examples of the emirates that directly or indirectly ruled various territories within the Somali nation. The emirate of Harar which succeeded Adal, and which Menelik destroyed in 1887 with help of the main European powers that came for the scramble of the continent, ruled parts of the Somali lands, including the Ogaden region. The sultanate of Ajuran ruled parts of the Ogaden and southern Somali territories.

The European colonizers who ruled some of the Somali territories (Britain, Italy and France), made treaties with the Somali tribes before and after the occupation, and that is further evidence that the Somalis were in firm control of their lands and were not freely obtainable. However, unlike the Europeans, Ethiopia did not make treaties with the inhabitants of the Ogaden and that difference in approach reflects Ethiopia's many centuries of expansionist policies and the fall of Adal. For centuries Ethiopia wanted to expand its boundaries eastward and southward, but because of the Adal-led resistance, that dream did not materialise until Ethiopia finally destroyed that kingdom with the help of Europeans. After eliminating Adal, she did not need to seek permission to invade the Ogaden, and because of the modern weapons she obtained from Europeans, she became more emboldened and aggressive.

The history of the conflict between Adal and Abyssinia is recorded by local, regional and international historians. Not only is the conflict recorded, but also the geographical boundaries of Abyssinia before its expansion in the late nineteenth and twentieth centuries are documented by explorers such as Sir Richard Burton, colonial authorities, both Europeans and Ethiopians, and contemporary geographers. The maps and documents produced by these witnesses all showed the southern boundary of Ethiopia as the river of Awash. (See map number 3.)

In his book *First Footsteps in East Africa*, published in 1856, Burton

---

[2] Louis FitzGibbon, 1985, *The Evaded Duty*, pages 21–22.

describes his observation of the region. He travelled from Aden to Harar via northern Somali lands and visited among other places Zeila and Berbera in 1854-55. 'In that book Burton gives an account of his journey from Aden to Harar in 1854–55, and he makes no mention of any Ethiopian presence in northern Somalia, nor does he note any links between the Somali tribes and the Ethiopians, neither is any reference to Ethiopians either as minority residents nor even as traders. Had they been present one may be sure that Burton would have noted.'[3]

Menelik's circular letter of 10 April 1891, which he sent to the heads of state of Britain, France, Germany, Italy and Russia, during the scramble in the Horn, was another indication of the beginning of his conquest of the Ogaden. 'The circular was a future expansion programme, indicating the beginning of the process of conquering the Ogaden and other territories. Furthermore, Italy informed Menelik of the partition plan and advised the emperor to set out his territorial claims, and the Italian government suggested that the list should include the Somali and Danakil lands. Accordingly, Menelik demanded his share of the partitioned Somali lands and the other European powers encouraged his expansionist plan.'[4]

During the scramble in the Horn, the three European colonizers of the Somali lands (Italy, France and Britain), signed various treaties with Ethiopia. Although the treaties endorsed Menelik's expansionist policies by agreeing with him boundaries on the basis of his extended new frontiers, the treaties showed that the Ogaden was not part of Ethiopia before the partition of the Somali lands. The four colonizers (Ethiopia, Italy, Britain and France) that occupied the Somali lands made border agreements among themselves after the partition. In 1894 Italy signed a boundary agreement with Britain on behalf of Ethiopia, because at the time (1889–1896) Italy was considering Ethiopia itself as an Italian protectorate and for that reason, Italy in particular supported Ethiopia's expansionist policies. Britain by then recognized the Italian version of the Wichale Treaty, on which the Italian claim was based. After the Adowa defeat in 1896, Italy recognized Ethiopia's sovereignty and all the European colonizers of the Somali lands made boundary agreements with Ethiopia in 1897, after it occupied nearly the whole of the Ogaden region.

The names of places and people in the Ogaden region also provide

---

[3] Louis FitzGibbon, 1985, *The Evaded Duty*, page 26.
[4] Louis FitzGibbon, 1982, *The Betrayal of the Somalis*, Rex Collins Ltd, page 27.

other evidence of Ethiopia's lack of connection to the region. The places all bear Somali names and the Ogaden region itself is named after a Somali clan.

Even Haile Selassie of Ethiopia confirms in his autobiography of 1976 (Oxford University Press edition) the fact that Ogaden was not part of the Abyssinian Empire before the partition. The emperor's father, Makonnen, became the ruler of Harar after Ethiopia occupied it in 1887. While describing his father's operations in the Harar region in the Ogaden, Haile Selassie stated:

> When my father conducted military expeditions in the Harar region, he did so leaving behind in Shoa my mother…When the war was over and the country began to be pacified, he let her come to Harar. He then secured the Ogaden, region, which had not yet been incorporated within Harar province.[5]

The European colonizers signed treaties with the various Somali tribes. Some of the clans in the Ogaden were among those who signed protectorate treaties with Britain (see Appendix 3). The treaties between the Europeans and the Somalis indicate that the Somalis were in control of their land before the partition and that the Europeans came before the Ethiopians. The European powers returned the Somali territories to their rightful owners except for the NFD, which Kenya occupied after the British left there, and Ethiopia should follow suit and pull out from the Ogaden. Ethiopia is not different from the overseas colonizers that ended their occupation of the Somali lands. Like these European powers, Ethiopia is obliged under the UN charter to end the occupation and transfer all powers to the people of the region. Being an African state does not exempt her from international law on decolonisation.

All the above-mentioned evidence shows that Ethiopia first occupied the Ogaden during the scramble in the Horn and that it has no connection with the region other than the occupation. Besides that, the lack of statehood in the Somali lands before the partition does not give Ethiopia possession rights in the Ogaden, as the ruling of the International Court in similar cases showed.

In October 1975, the International Court was called upon to examine whether in the period beginning 1884 Western Sahara was a territory belonging to no one (*terra nullius*). According to the advisory opinion of the court, the Western Sahara territory could not be regarded as terra

---

[5] Edward Ullendorff, 1976, *The Autobiography of Haile Selassie 1, My Life and Ethiopia's Progress (1892–1937)*, Oxford University Press, page 14.

nullius, because it has been inhabited by tribes or peoples having a social or political organization. Because of the similarities between the Western Sahara region and the Somali lands prior to the occupation, the ruling of the court could be applied to the Ogaden as well.

12.8 Prospect for Conflict Resolution: The Principle of Self-Determination

In this section we will examine the principle of self-determination from international and regional legal viewpoints as well as from Ethiopia's constitutional rights, taking examples of precedence in both the international and Ethiopian contexts.

The principle of self-determination has been recognised as a legal concept in dealing with the issue of independence of nations and all peoples and is affirmed by a series of UN resolutions. The right to self-determination of the people, which is the fundamental principle of international law, has been incorporated in two UN covenants. The principle is enshrined in Article 1 of the United Nations Charter, in Article 1 of the International Covenant on Economic, Social and Cultural Rights and Article 1 of the International Covenant on Civil and Political Rights, as well as other international and human rights instruments. The International Covenant on Civil and Political Rights provides for the right of peoples to self-determination besides the right of ethnic, religious or linguistic minorities to enjoy their own culture, to profess and practise their own religion or to use their own language. The principle is stated in the covenants as follows:

> All peoples have the right to self-determination; by virtue of the right they freely determine their political status and freely pursue their economic, social and cultural development.[6]

The UN General Assembly passed several resolutions affirming the concept of the right to self-determination and providing interpretation on its practical application. Resolution 1514 (XV) of 14 December 1960 was among the resolutions formulated by the General Assembly concerning the decolonisation of territories. The Declaration on Granting of Independence to Colonial Countries and Peoples that the resolution contained made it particularly significant. The declaration was based on Article1 (2), Article 55 and 73–74 of the Charter (see Appendix 5). The articles affirm the principle of self-determination and provide

---

[6] UN Charter, UN website (www.un.org).

practical guidelines in the implementation of the principle. The declaration requires that governments take steps to implement that principle as outlined in the charter. Administrative governments of non-self-governing territories are not only obliged to uphold the principle of self-determination of nations and all peoples who have not yet attained independence but are also required to assist them in attaining the goal of independence. The necessary steps required by administrative governments in assisting territories to attain their freedom are listed in Articles 73 (a)–(b) of the UN charter and are stated as follows:

Article 73
Members of the United Nations which have or assume responsibilities for the administration of territories whose peoples have not yet attained a full measure of self-government recognize the principle that the interests of the inhabitants of these territories are paramount, and accept as a sacred trust the obligation to promote to the utmost, within the system of international peace and security established by the present Charter, the well-being of the inhabitants of these territories, and, to this end:

a. to ensure, with due respect for the culture of the peoples concerned, their political, economic, social, and educational advancement, their just treatment, and their protection against abuses;

b. to develop self-government, to take due account of the political aspirations of the peoples, and to assist them in the progressive development of their free political institutions, according to the particular circumstances of each territory and its peoples and their varying stages of advancement;[7]

The principle of self-determination is not confined to 'classical colonialism' involving overseas possessions, but also to all non-self-governing territories as emphasised by the UN charter and resolutions of the General Assembly. Stressing that it applies to 'all peoples and territories that have not yet attained independence' Resolution 1514 in particular clarified that point. However, unlike the case with 'classical colonialism', the practical applicability of the principle was not clear-cut in the first place concerning the definition of non-self-governing territories, and for that reason, the General Assembly gave further criteria for the applicability of the principle in the latter situation. Whether the principle is applicable to a certain non-self-governing territory depends on whether it qualifies as 'a unit of self-determination'. According to Resolution 1541(XV), the principle applies to any 'territory which is geographically separate and is distinct ethnically or culturally from the

---

[7] UN Charter, UN website (www.un.org).

country administrating it'.[8]

The Ogaden satisfies the legal criteria of a unit of self-determination because the Somali people in that region are completely different from the Ethiopians in terms of culture, ethnicity, religion and geographical location. Because of these distinct characteristics, the illegal occupation and the indescribable inhuman policies that resulted from the occupation, the Somali people in the Ogaden no doubt qualify to be accorded the right to self-determination from an international legal point of view.

According to both the OAU Charter and the Constitutive Act that abrogated and replaced it after the establishment of the AU, the organization is required to defend the sovereignty, territorial integrity and independence of OAU/AU members. Respect for borders existing on the achievement of independence and non-interference by any member state in the internal affairs of another are also among the principles of the organization enshrined in both the documents. However, in the new document (the Constitutive Act) a new principle, which allows collective interference in the internal affairs of a member state, is added. The principle gives the Union 'the right to intervene in a Member State pursuant to a decision of the Assembly in respect of grave circumstances, namely: war crimes, genocide and crimes against humanity'.[9]

The rules safeguarding the colonial boundaries, territorial integrity, and forbidding interference in internal affairs, that are contained in both the above-mentioned documents as well as the Cairo Resolution of 21 July 1964, are not relevant to the Ogaden conflict, despite their use of Ethiopia in its quarrel with Somalia in the Horn conflict. First of all, the principles concern sovereign member states only, and as Ogaden is neither an independent state nor a member of the organization, the rules do not apply to it. Furthermore, the Ogaden is still under occupation and therefore it does not have borders left by its colonizer. The colonial powers have not agreed on boundaries even among themselves after the partition of the Somali Nation. Ethiopia and Italy failed to agree on the boundaries and, as a result, the Somali-Ethiopian border has not been recognised as an international border by colonial powers and it remains provisional as far as the Somalis are concerned.

The OAU/AU principles of non-interference in internal affairs and territorial integrity collide with the principle of self-determination and the

---

[8] Louis FitzGibbon, 1985, *The Evaded Duty*, page 48.
[9] AU Constitutive Act, AU website (www.africa-union.org).

bill of rights. The people's rights to self-determination and the preservation of human rights are more important than the preservation of the territorial integrity of a state. Thus, from an international legal point of view, these OAU/AU principles about decolonisation are meaningless. These principles of the African organization even contradict the stated objective of the OAU/AU. According to Article II of the Charter, the organization aims, among other things, 'to eradicate all forms of colonialism from Africa, and to promote international cooperation, having due regard to the charter of the United Nations and the Universal declaration of human rights'.[10]

According to article 103 of the UN Charter, the UN principle and rules override other international agreements and laws if they come into conflict. The Article is formulated as follows:

> In the event of a conflict between the obligations of the Members of the United Nations under the present Charter and their obligations under any other international agreement, their obligations under the present Charter shall prevail.[11]

The new principle in the Constitutive Act, however, is relevant to the Ethiopian situation. The Ethiopian failed state is at war with its subjects and all kinds of human rights violations are practised by the Ethiopian authorities in the Ogaden and elsewhere in the empire. Although it stops short of what is needed in terms of decolonisation, the principle is in the right direction, because for the first time the organization indicates the possibility of failed member-states and the need to correct them.

The Ethiopian state itself, at least on paper, recognized the need to review its make-up by the introduction of Article 39, the establishment of nationality-based regional administration (including the Somali region) and the granting of independence to Eritrea. A lengthy discussion is given in chapter 10 about Article 39 and its applicability; thus, it is sufficient to mention here only its importance in legal and symbolic terms. On paper, the constitution allows different nationalities to administer themselves and even to secede if the majority of the inhabitants wish independence from Ethiopia, and that recognition is important because it not only explicitly recognizes the self-determination rights of the different nationalities in the empire but also implicitly affirms the inevitability of the dismemberment of the empire sometime in the future.

---

[10] OAU Charter, AU website (www.africa-union.org).
[11] UN Charter, UN website (www.un.org).

Eritrean independence is a particularly important precedent in the question of self-determination in the Ogaden. The histories of the two nations are very similar in many ways. Both were under Italian occupation in the 1930s, followed by British occupation during the Second World War, and ended up with Ethiopian occupation during the 1950s and 1960s. Both nations fought long wars against Ethiopia to restore their independence, but Eritrea gained its independence in 1993, whereas the Ogaden is still under occupation. From a legal point of view, in both international and national contexts, Eritrea is the most relevant precedent for the question of the independence of the Somali people in the Ogaden.

12.9 Prospect for Conflict Resolution: The Determination of the People

Inspired by the freedom dream, emboldened by the justness of the cause they are fighting for, convinced of the attainability of their freedom and self-determination goals, angered by the unspeakable injustice inflicted upon them by the occupiers, encouraged by the dynamics of their resistance and conscious of the sacrifices needed to liberate the country, the Somali people in the Ogaden are more than ever determined to carry out their struggle for self-determination. With ever-increasing optimism about the outcome of their efforts, they are marching forward to free themselves from the colonial yoke.

Given their determination, the just cause they are fighting for and the weakness of the Ethiopian empire, the liberation of the Somali region of the Ogaden seems inevitable. But whether the Ethiopian regime realizes the unavoidability of the termination of the occupation of the Ogaden and acts accordingly to prevent more loss of lives is uncertain. Certainly, from the perspective of the Ogaden Somalis, the resolution to the conflict is in the hands of the Ethiopian government and the Ethiopian regime in their view should come to its senses, give up its colonial dreams and end the occupation in the Ogaden peacefully to avert more bloodshed and to prepare a better life for future generations, both in the Ogaden and Ethiopia.

Appendix 1

Corespondence between Menelik and the British consul at Aden after Menelik's occupation of Harar

On 20 January 1887 Menelik sent the following letter to the British Consul at Aden:

From – MENELEK, King of Shoa and of all the Galla, good and bad,
To – The English Consul at Aden
How are you?

By the Grace of God, I am well. Amir Abdillahi would suffer no Christian in his country.

He was another 'Gragne', but by the help of God I fought him, destroyed him, and he escaped alone on horseback.

I hoisted my flag in his capital and my troops & co., occupied his city. Gragne died:

Abdillahi was in our days his successor.

This is not a Muslim country as every one knows.

The British Consul at Aden replied to Menelik's letter on February 10 1887 as follows:

From – Major F. M. HUNTER, Political Agent and Consul for the Somali Coast,
To King MENELEK, Negus of Shoa, Efat and the Gallas, & c.

After compliments – We have received Your Majesty's friendly letter informing us that you captured and occupied Harrar and hoisted your flag there.

There can be no need to recall the terms of the treaty concluded with Her Majesty the Queen in 1841 by your Majesty's predecessor King Sahela Selassie, Negus of Shoa, Efat and Galla.

Your Majesty may rest assured of the continued friendship of the British Government, and we hope that under Your Majesty's protection may revive and the trade route be safe.

On all the Somali Coast from Ghubbet Kharab, and especially at Zeila, Bulhar and Berbera, where our troops are now stationed, we shall always be glad to further Your Majesty's interests.

Appendix 2

Extracts from British government officials and other independent reports on the Abyssinian atrocities in the Ogaden

Report No 1

The Deputy Assistant Political Agent in Bulhar, David Morrison, reported to the Assistant Resident at Berbera, on February 1 1891 that he received the following information from a kaffila that returned from the Ogaden:

About twenty-five days ago the Abyssinians came to the Ogadeyn country. The force was 7000 (?) strong. Their intention was to proceed to Merka and take possession of it. Merka, I am informed is inhabited by the Jaberta people (Rer Gibelad and Gibelmadow), whose Governor is named Suliman, a nephew of the late Sayyid Barghash, of Zanzibar. The country is rich and well cultivated.

While on their way along the River Soolool and at Harah Abdullah, they found the Ogaden Malangoor, whom they looted of 600 sheep and goats and 10 bullocks, all of which they killed and ate. They also looted one camel belonging to Ali Yusuf Rer Hosh Yunis and killed one Malingoor and wounded another.

After this, they proceeded on their march and met the Ogaden Rer Amadin-al-Galadooray. There they attacked an Ayal Yunus Kafila, killing Hassan Mahomed Rer Mah Gedid (brother of Jama Mahomed, Havildar of Police), Adan Abdi Miad Gedid and one Ogaden Rer Ali Esak, looting the entire kafila. They also attacked the Rer Amadin and looted two kraals containing camels (male and female), cows, bullocks, sheep and goats, and killed twenty men. After this they proceeded to Hamar and Merka. The Abyssinians said it was their intention to go to Merka and there make a settlement.

The Ayal Yunus wish to know if any compensation will be given for the loss sustained in life and property.

Harah Abdullah is thirteen days from Bulhar and four from Harar in southerly direction. Galadooray is only three days from the Webi. Morrison wanted to know the reaction of the British Government to the Abyssinian invasion.

Major C.W.H. Sealy, Acting Political Agent and Consul, Somali Coast replied:

With reference to the report No. 39 dated February 1. 1891, from Morrison in regard to the action of the Abyssinians, the Ayal Yunus should be informed that it is not a matter in which we can interfere.

Report No 2

In this report the British Acting Political Agent and Consul, Somali Coast, Captain H.M. Abud, reported the cruel killing in the Ogaden. The report was sent to the Political Resident at Aden and was stated as follows:

In continuation of my letter n. 841, dated the 29th August 1894, reporting that Ras Makunan, Governor of Harrar, had informed me of his intention to dispatch an expedition to the Ogaden to punish the tribes for certain misdeeds, I have now the honour to report that it would seem that the expressed intention has been fulfilled as constant representations are being made to the Assistant Resident at Berbera of the cruelty and oppression that is being exercised by the Abyssinians on the Ogaden. As an instance of the cruelty exercised it has been sworn to by a man at Berbera that the Abyssinians had skinned his brother. That this is true can hardly be doubted, as the man was actually seen by Major Mainwaring, South Wales Borderers, and Mr. Christie who have lately returned from shooting in the Ogaden. These gentlemen, moreover, state that they actually say [saw] a boy whose private parts had been cut off by the Abyssinians.

I would suggest that, now that this part of Somali land has been placed in the sphere of Italian influence, the attention of the Italian Government might be drawn to the utter ruin and the revolting cruelty that is going on in the Ogaden at the hand of the Abyssinians.

Report No 3

On December 3, 1894 the British Political Resident at Aden, Brigadier-General John Jopp, sent the following report to the Government of Bombay, Political Department:

This Residency is now powerless to check those atrocities in the Ogaden.

Before the protocol of May 1894 was published, although Abyssinian raids were more or less constant, such revolting cruelty, though habitually practised in Abyssinia proper, was almost unknown in this part. British influence extended so far inland and the knowledge that our officers on the coast would take measures acted as deterrent.

Now all is changed. The Abyssinian Government know the range of our authority is now limited, and the Governor of Harrar who on two or three occasions being addressed in friendly manner by the Political Agent and Consul, Somali Coast, bringing to his notice the extortion committed by his people, has invariably replied that "the country belongs to King Menelek," and more or less resents our interference.

The Ogaden, by the new Protocol, is now in Italian sphere of influence, but there is not an Italian official within the hundreds of miles, not even I believe in Harrar, who could intervene to induce the Abyssinian authorities to keep proper check over their soldiers who traverse the country.

I attach notes of an interview that Captain Abud, Assistant Resident, had with Mr. Felter, a merchant residing in Harrar, and who lately arrived in Aden, on the subject of Affairs in Abyssinia for what it is worth.

He is actually an agent employed by the Italian Government and is paid as such, and has the title of Resident though this is not publicly avowed.

As touching the action of the Abyssinians in Ogaden, he stated that the expedition returned on the 14th November, and that his wife saw slaves tied to the horses' tails. It is well known that the prisoners of war (natives) in Abyssinia are sold although Abyssinia had signed the Brussels's Act.

On referring to the late case of skinning a man alive he said that the Abyssinians did worse than that, and that every week Queen Taiton had two or three virgins killed and their entrails examined for omens.

Report No 4

Lieutenant-Colonel C.W.H. Sealy, political Agent and Consul, Somali Coast, said in a Memorandum (No.438, dated Aden, February 14 1895), quoting Mr. Gillett who returned to Aden from the Ogaden:

He informed me that the Abyssinians were still carrying out their apparent object of subjugating the country on, and south of, the Webbe Shebeyli. The procedure appears to be this: first, a somewhat small force goes and collects tributes from the villages; if unsuccessful, they are backed up by a second and larger force behind them, and behind all is Menelek's own force.

As far as I could learn from native sources at Berbera, while recently on the coast, it is not now the Ogaden who are suffering from the Abyssinians, but Galla tribes further south and south-east and south-west of the Webbe Shebeyli. For, whereas Mr. Gillett said quite recently the

Abyssinians continued their atrocities (such as cutting off women's breasts and pilling up the heads of victims in pyramids &c.) the Ogadens who came into Berebera with caravans reported that those atrocities had ceased, as the Ogaden were paying up the tribute demanded by the Abyssinians. The inference is that the victims referred to by Mr. Gillett are Gallas, not Ogaden.

Report No 5

Dr. Donaldson Smith, an American, who visited a village called Sesabene near Dagahbour in 1894, reported the Abyssinian atrocities there as follows:

You may imagine my chagrin when I heard, a few days afterwards, that they have just been raided by the Abyssinians under Makonnen. Their animals have all been driven off, the boys and girls taken as slaves, and the elder people killed or mutilated.

We earnestly wish they (the Abyssinians) as savages bearing arms against other poor defenceless Africans, should have such a drubbing that they could not forget it and try to extend their sway further. Let these good people who take an interest in uncivilised nations cast a thought on the black neighbours of the Abyssinians who are in the worst plight.

Report No. 6

As Sir Alfred Pease who visited the Somali lands in 1897 put it, the British Government neither protected the Somalis nor allowed them to acquire weapons to defend themselves:

We (British) have prevented them (Somalis) from acquiring arms and ammunition and having deprived them of all means of self-defence…have left them at the mercy of raiding Abyssinians who have no other employment than that of making raids on Gallas and Somalis.

Appendix 3

Supplementary treaties between Britain and Somali clans

Britain signed various supplementary treaties in 1886 with several Somali clans. The terms of these treaties were the same and were stated as follows:

Article I

The British Government, in compliance with the wish of the undersigned Elders [Clan inserted here] hereby undertake to extend to them and to the territories under their authority and jurisdiction the gracious favour and protection of Her Majesty the Queen Empress.

Article II

The said Elders of [clan inserted here] agree and promise to refrain from entering into any correspondence, agreement or treaty with any foreign nation, or power, except with the knowledge and sanction of Her Majesty's Government.

Article III

This treaty shall come into operation upon the first day of February One Thousand EIGHT Hundred and Eighty-Six.

> (Signed) F. M. Hunter Major
> Political Agent, Somali Coast
> [The Name of Elders here]

As Louis FitzGibbon reported in his book *The Betrayal of the Somalis*, Britain signed treaties not only with clans that inhabit both sides of the border, but it also signed a similar agreement in 1896 with some of the clans in the interior of the Ogaden and Jubaland. The text of that treaty is as follows:

I, Ahmed Murgan, Chief of the Ogaden Somalis, do hereby place myself, my people, and country, with its dependence, under the protection of Her Britannic Majesty the Queen, and do hereby declare and I will not, nor shall my successors or any of my people, cede or alienate any portion of my territories or dependencies, or make any treaties with any foreign state or person, without the previous knowledge and sanction of Her Majesty's Government.

Commercial arrangements between me and the non-natives shall be subject to the approval of Her Majesty's Representative, who shall regulate all disputes, and by whose advice I will be guided in all my relations with-non natives.

[Signature in Arabic]
Witness
[Signature in Arabic]

Appendix 4

British and Italian frontier treaties and agreements with Ethiopia in 1897 and 1908

I. Treaty between Great Britain and Ethiopia
   Signed by the Emperor Menelek II, and by Her
   Majesty's Envoy, at Addis Ababa, May 14, 1897
   Ratified by the Queen, July 28, 1897
   Her Majesty Victoria, by the grace of God, Queen of Great Britain and Ireland,
   Empress of India, and His Majesty Menelek II, by the grace of God, King of Kings of Ethiopia, being desirous of strengthening and rendering more effective and profitable the ancient friendship which has existed between their respective kingdoms.
   Her Majesty Queen Victoria having appointed as her Special Envoy and Representative to His Majesty the Emperor Menelek II, James Rennell Rodd,
   Esq., Companion of the Most Distinguished Order of St. Michael and St. George, whose full powers have been found in due and proper form, and His Majesty Emperor Menelek, negotiating in his own name as the King of Kings of Ethiopia, they have agreed upon and do conclude the following Articles, which shall be binding on themselves, their heirs and successors:-

Article 1

The subjects of or persons protected by each of the Contracting Parties shall have full liberty to come and go and engage in commerce in the territories of the other, enjoying the protection of the Government within whose jurisdiction they are; but it is forbidden for armed bands from either side to cross the frontier of the other on any pretext whatever without previous authorization from the competent authorities.

Article II

The frontiers of the British Protectorate on the Somali Coast recognized by the Emperor Menelek shall be determined subsequently by exchange of notes between James Rennell Rodd, Esq., as representative of Her Majesty the Queen, and Ras Maconen, as representative of His Majesty the Emperor Menelek, at Harar. These notes shall be annexed to the present Treaty, of which they will form an integral part, as soon as they have received the approval of the High Contracting Parties, pending which the *status quo* shall be maintained.

Article III

The caravan route between Zeyla and Harrar by way of Gildessa shall remain open throughout its whole extent to the commerce of both nations.

Article IV

His Majesty the Emperor of Ethiopia, on the one hand, accords to Great Britain and her Colonies, in respect of import duties and local taxation, every advantage which he may accord to the subjects of other nations.

On the other hand, all material destined exclusively for the service of the Ethiopian State shall, on application from His Majesty the Emperor, be allowed to pass through the port of Zeyla into Ethiopia free of duty.

Article V

The transit of fire-arms and ammunition destined for His Majesty the Emperor of Ethiopia through the territories depending on the Government of Her Britannic Majesty is authorized, subject to the conditions prescribed by the General act of the Brussels Conference, signed the 2nd July, 1890.

Article VI

His Majesty the emperor Menelek II, King of Kings of Ethiopia, engages himself towards the Government of Her Britannic Majesty to do all in his power to prevent the passage through his dominions of arms and ammunition to the Mahdists, whom he declares to be the enemies of his Empire.

The present Treaty shall come into force as soon as its ratification by Her Britannic Majesty shall have been notified to the Emperor of Ethiopia, but it is understood that the prescriptions of Article VI shall be put into force from the date of its signature.

In faith of which His Majesty Menelek II, King of Kings of Ethiopia, in his own name, and James Rennell Rodd, Esq., on behalf of Her Majesty Victoria, Queen of Great Britain and Ireland, Empress of India, have signed the present Treaty, in duplicate, written in the English and Amharic languages identically, both texts being considered as official, and have thereto affixed their seals.

Done at Addis Ababa, the 14th Day of May, 1897.

(L.S)

[Signed] JAMES RENNEL RODD.

[Seal of His Majesty the Emperor Menelek II]

Annexes to Treaty signed at Addis Ababa on the 14th May
1897, by His Majesty the Emperor Menelek, and by Mr. James Rennel
Rodd

Annex 1
Mr Rodd to the Emperor Menelek

Addis Ababa, May 14, 1897.

Your Majesty,

With reference to Article II of the treaty which we are to sign to-day,
I am instructed by my Government, in the event of a possible occupation
by Ethiopia of territories inhabited by tribes who have formally accepted
and enjoyed British Protection in the districts excluded from the limits
of the British Protectorate on the Somali Coast, as recognised by your
Majesty, to bring to your knowledge the desire of Her Majesty the Queen
to receive from your Majesty an assurance that it will be your special care
that these tribes receive equitable treatment, and are thus no losers by
this transfer of suzerainty.

In expressing the hope that your Majesty will enable me to give this
assurance, I have, & c.

[Signed]
RENNEL RODD

The Emperor Menelek to Mr. Rodd

[Translation]

The Conquering Lion of the Tribe of Judah, Menelek II, by the grace
of God, King of Kings of Ethiopia, to Mr. Rennel Rodd, Envoy of the
Kingdom of England.

Peace be unto you.

YOUR letter, written in Genbot 1889, respecting the Somalis, has
reached me. With regard to the question you have put to me, I give you
the assurance that the Somalis who may by boundary arrangements
become subjects of Ethiopia shall be well treated and have orderly
government.

Written at Addis Ababa, on the 6th Genbot, 1889 (14th May, 1897)

[Seal of His majesty the Emperor Menelek II]

Annex 2

The Emperor Menelek to Mr. Rodd

[Translation]

From Menelek II, by the grace of God, King of Kings of Ethiopia, Conquering Lion of theTribe of Judah.

May this reach James Rennel Rodd.

Peace be unto you.

WITH reference to the Treaty which we have written in the Amharic and English languages at Addis Ababa, as I have no interpreters with me who understands the English language well enough to compare the English and Amharic version, if by any possibility in the future there should ever be found any misunderstanding between the Amharic and English versions in any of the Articles of this Treaty, let this translation, which is written in French language, and which I enclose in this letter, be the witness between us, and if you accept this proposal, send me word of your acceptance by letter.

Dated 7th Genbot, 1889 (14th May, 1897)

[Seal of His Majesty the Emperor Menelek II]

Mr.Rodd to the Emperor Menelek

Addis Ababa, May 14, 1897

Your Majesty

I HAVE the honour to acknowledge the receipt of your Majesty's letter enclosing the French translation of the Treaty which we are to sign this day in English and Amharic, and I agree, on behalf of my Government, to the proposal of your Majesty, that, in case a divergency of opinion should arise hereafter as to the correct interpretation to be given either to the English or Amharic text, the French translation, which has been agreed to on both sides as adequate, should be accepted as furnishing a solution of the matter under dispute.

In recording this assurance, I have, &c.

[Signed] RENNELL RODD.

Annex 3

Mr. Rodd to Ras Makunan

Harrar, June 4, 1897 (28 Genbot 1889)

Peace be unto you.

AFTER friendly discussion with your Excellency, I have understood that His Majesty the Emperor of Ethiopia will recognize as a frontier of the British Protectorate on the Somali Coast the line which, starting from the sea at the point fixed in the Agreement between Great Britain and France on the 9th February, 1888, opposite the wells of Hadou, follows the caravan-road, described in that Agreement, through Abbassouen till it reaches the hill of Somadou. From this point on the road the line is traced by the Saw Mountains and the hill of Egu to Moga Medir; from Moga Medir it is traced by Eylinta Kaddo to Arran Arrhe, near the intersection of latitude 44° east of Greenwich with longitude 9°north. From this point a straight line is drawn to the intersection of 47° east of Greenwich with 8° north. From here the line will follow the frontier laid down in the Anglo-Italian Protocol of the 5th May, 1894, until it reaches the sea.

The tribes occupying either side of the line shall have the right to use the grazing-grounds on the other side, but during their migration it is understood that they shall be subject to the jurisdiction of the territorial authority. Free access to the nearest wells is equally reserved to the tribes occupying either side of the line.

This understanding, in accordance with article II of the treaty signed on the 14th May, 1897 (7th Genbot, 1889), by His Majesty the Emperor Menelek and Mr. Rennel Rodd, at Addis Ababa, must be approved by the two High Contracting Parties.

I have, &c.
[Signed] RENNEL RODD

Ras Makunan to Mr. Rodd
[Translation]
Sent from Ras Makunan, Governor of Harrar and its dependencies:
May this reach the honourable Mr. Rennell Rodd Envoy of the British Kingdom.

I INFORM you to-day that, after long friendly discussion, the boundary of the British Somali Protectorate upon which we have agreed is as follows:-

Starting from the sea-shore opposite the wells of Hadou (as on which the French and the English Governments agreed in February 1888,) it follows the caravan-road by Abbassouen till mount Somadou; from mount Somadou to mount Saw; from mount Saw to mount Egu; from mount Egu to Moga Medir; starting from Moga Medir it goes in a direct line to Eylinta Kaddo and Arran Arrhe on 44° east of Greenwich and 9° north, and again a in direct line until 47° east and 8° north. After this the boundary follows the line on which the English and the Italians agreed on the 5th May, 1894, until the sea.

The subjects of both the Contracting Parties are at liberty to cross their frontiers and graze their cattle, but these people, in every place where they go, must obey the Governor of the country in which they are, and the wells which are in the neighbourhood shall remain open for the two parties.

These two letters in which we have agreed according to Article II of the Treaty of His Majesty the Emperor of Ethiopia and Mr. Rennell Rodd of the 7th Genbot, 1889 (14th May, 1897), the two Sovereigns having seen them, if they approve them shall be sealed again (ratified).

Written at Harrar, the 28th Genbot, 1889 (4th June, 1897).

[Signed] RAS MAKUNAN

Mr. Rodd to the Emperor Menelek II

Cairo, August 30th 1897

From Mr. Rennell Rodd, Special Envoy of Her Majesty Queen Victoria, to His Majesty Menelek II, by the grace of God, King of Kings of Ethiopia.

Peace be unto your Majesty.

I HAVE the honour to announce that the Queen, my gracious Sovereign, has been pleased to approve and ratify the Treaty which I had the honour to sign with your Majesty on the 14th May last.

Her Majesty has also been pleased to approve of the arrangement which, in accordance with the terms of Article II of the Treaty, was agreed upon between Ras Makunan, as representative of your Majesty, and myself by exchange of notes relative to the frontier of the British Protectorate in the Somali Coast; and it is presumed by Her Majesty's Government that your Majesty has also approved of it, as they have received no notification to the contrary.

The notes exchanged have accordingly been annexed to the Treaty which has received ratification, signifying Her Majesty's approval of all these documents.

I have now the honour to return herewith the copy of the Treaty intrusted to me by your Majesty, with its ratification in due form.

When I shall have received from your Majesty a letter signifying that this Treaty, thus ratified and approved, has come safely to your Majesty's hands, it will be made public by the Government of the Queen, that all her subjects may observe it and abide by it, and that it may strengthen the ties of friendship between our countries, and increase the feelings of esteem and good-will towards your Majesty which the reception of the British Mission in Ethiopia has awakened in my country.

I pray that your Majesty's life and health may long be preserved, and that your people may have peace and prosperity.

[Signed] RENNEL RODD

The Emperor Menelek to the Queen

[Translation]

Menelek II, Elect of God, King of Kings of Ethiopia, to Her Most gracious Majesty Queen Victoria, Queen of Great Britain and Ireland, and Empress of India, Upholder and Keeper of the Christian Religion.

May peace be unto you.

YOUR Majesty's letters of the 28th Hamlé (3rd August) and 22nd (23rd) Mascarem (1st (2nd) October), 1897, and the Treaty with the Great Seal, dated the 28th hamlé (3rd August), 1897, have reached me, and We received it with joy. The Treaty of peace which is now between your Government and our Government. We hope it will ever increase in firmness and last for ever.

We ask God to give your Majesty health, and to your Kingdom quietness and peace.

Written at Addis Ababa, the 8th December, 1897, AD.

[Seal of His Majesty the Emperor Menelek II]

II. Treaty between Italy and Abyssinia, signed at Addis Ababa, 26 OCTOBER 1896

[Ratified by the King of Italy, 1 January 1897]

In the name of the Most Holy Trinity

His Majesty Umberto I, King of Italy, and His Majesty Menelek II, Emperor

Of Ethiopia, being desirous of ending the state of war and of reviving their former friendship, have concluded the following Treaty:

For the purpose of concluding this Treaty, His Majesty the King of Italy appointed, as his Envoy Plenipotentiary, Major Doctor Cesare Nerazzini, Knight of Saint Maurice and Saint Lazarus, Officer of the Crown of Italy. The full powers of Major Nerazzini having been found to be in good and due form, His Excellency Major Nerazzini, in the name of his Majesty the King of Italy, and His Majesty Menelek II, Emperor of Ethiopia and of the Galla Countries, in his own name, have met and agreed the following Articles:

Art. I – [End of state of war. Perpetual Peace and Friendship.]

Art. II – [Treaty of 2nd May, 1889, annulled]

Art. III – [Recognition by Italy of Ethiopia as a Sovereign and Independent State]

Frontiers

Art. IV. – The two contracting Powers having been unable to agree on the question of frontiers, but desiring to conclude a peace without delay and thus to bring to their Countries the benefit of peace, it has been agreed that within one year from today's date, Commissioner of His Majesty the King of Italy and of His Majesty the Emperor of Ethiopia will establish the definitive frontiers by mutual agreement. Until the frontiers have been thus fixed, the two Contracting Parties agree to observe the statu quo ante, and mutually refraining strictly from breaching the provisional frontier, delimited by the courses of the Mareb, Belessa, and Mouna Rivers.

Non-cession of Territory by Italy to any other Power

Art. V. –Until the Italian Government and the Ethiopian Government have by mutual agreement fixed their definitive frontiers, the Italian Government undertakes not to make any cession whatsoever of territory to any other Power. If the Italian Government of its own volition wishes to abandon a part of the territory which it holds, such territory will be transferred to Ethiopia.

Art. VI. – [Commercial agreements to the concluded.)

Art. VII. – [Treaty to be brought to notice of other Powers.)

Art. VIII. – Ratification of Treaty

This treaty shall be ratified by the Italian Government within three months of today's date.

Art. IX. – This Treaty of Peace concluded today shall be drawn up in Amharic and in French, the two texts being in absolute conformity, made in duplicate, signed by the two Parties; one copy shall remain in the hands of His Majesty the king of Italy and the other in the hands of His Majesty the Emperor of Ethiopia.

Being in agreement on the terms of this treaty, His Majesty Menelek II, Emperor of Ethiopia, in his own name, and his Excellency Major Doctor Nerazzini, in the name of His Majesty the king of Italy, have approved the same and affixed their seals.

Done at Addis Ababa, 17 Tekemt 1889 (corresponding to 26 October 1896).

[L.S.] Major CESARE NERAZZINI
Envoy plenipotentiary of His
Majesty the King of Italy.
[Seal of His Majesty Emperor Menelek II.]

III. Convention between Ethiopia and Italy settling the frontier between the Italian possesions of Somalia and the Ethiopian empire. – signed at Addis Ababa, may 16, 1908 [Sanctioned by royal Italian decree of July 17, 1908]

[Translation]

His Majesty King Victor Emmanuel III of Italy, in his own name and the name of his successors, by means of his representative in Addis Ababa, Cavalier Giuseppe Colli

di Felizzano, Captain of Cavalry, and His Majesty Menelek II, King of Kings of Ethiopia, in his own name and that of his successors, desiring to settle definitively the frontier between the Italian possession of Somalia and the provinces of the Ethiopian Empire, have determined to sign the following Convention:-

ART.I. The line of frontier between the Italian possession of Somalia and the provinces of the Ethiopian Empire starts from Dolo at the confluence of the Daua and the Ganale, proceeds eastwards by the source of the Maidaba and continues as far as the Uebi scebeli following the territorial boundaries between the tribes of Rahanuin, which remains dependent on Italy, and all the tribes to its north, which remains dependent on Abyssinia.

II. The frontier on the Uebi scebeli shall be point where the boundary between the territory of the Baddi-Addi tribe, which remains dependent on Italy, and the territory of the tribes above the Baddi-Addi, which remains dependent on Abyssinia, touches the river.

III. The tribes on the left of the Juba, that of Rahamuin and those on the Uebi scebeli below the frontier point, shall be dependent on Italy. The tribes of Digodia, of Afgab of Djedjedi and all the others to the north of the frontier line shall be dependent on Abyssinia.

IV. From the Uebi scebeli the frontier proceeds in a north-easterly direction, following the line accepted by the Italian government in 1897: all the territory belonging to the tribes towards the coast shall remain dependent on Italy: all the territory of Ogaden and all that of tribes towards the Ogaden shall remain dependent on Abyssinia.

V. The two governments undertake to delimit on the spot and as soon as possible the actual line of the frontier as above mentioned.

VI. The two governments formally undertake not to exercise any interference beyond the frontier line, and not to allow the tribes dependent on them to cross the frontier in order to commit acts of violence to the detriment of the tribes on the other side of the line; but should questions or incidents arise between or on account of the limitrophe tribes, the two Governments shall settle this by common accord.

VII. The two Governments mutually undertake to take no action and to allow their dependents to take no action which may give rise to questions or incidents or disturb the tranquillity of the frontier tribes.

VIII. The present Convention shall, as regards Italy, be submitted to the approval of the Parliament and ratified by His Majesty the King.

Done in duplicate and identic terms in the languages, Italian and Amharic.

One copy remains in the hands of the Italian Government, and the other in the hands of the Ethiopian Government.

Given in the city of Addis Ababa, the 16th day of the month of May of the Year 1908.

GIUSEPPE COLLI di FELIZZANO

[Seal of Menelek]

Appendix 5

Some un charter articles about the application of the principle of self-determination to non-self-governing people

Article 55

With a view to the creation of conditions of stability and well-being which are necessary for peaceful and friendly relations among nations based on respect for the principle of equal rights and self-determination of peoples, the United Nations shall promote:

a. higher standards of living, full employment, and conditions of economic and social progress and development;

b. solutions of international economic, social, health, and related problems; and international cultural and educational co-operation; and

c. universal respect for, and observance of, human rights and fundamental freedoms for all without distinction as to race, sex, language, or religion.

Article 73

Members of the United Nations which have or assume responsibilities for the administration of territories whose peoples have not yet attained a full measure of self-government recognize the principle that the interests of the inhabitants of these territories are paramount, and accept as a sacred trust the obligation to promote to the utmost, within the system of international peace and security established by the present Charter, the well-being of the inhabitants of these territories, and, to this end:

a. to ensure, with due respect for the culture of the peoples concerned, their political, economic, social, and educational advancement, their just treatment, and their protection against abuses;

b. to develop self-government, to take due account of the political aspirations of the peoples, and to assist them in the progressive development of their free political institutions, according to the particular circumstances of each territory and its peoples and their varying stages of advancement;[6]

c. to further international peace and security;

d. to promote constructive measures of development, to encourage research, and to co-operate with one another and, when and where appropriate, with specialized international bodies with a view to the practical achievement of the social, economic, and scientific purposes set forth in this Article; and

e. to transmit regularly to the Secretary-General for information purposes, subject to such limitation as security and constitutional considerations may require, statistical and other information of a technical nature relating to economic, social, and educational conditions in the territories for which they are respectively responsible other than those territories to which Chapters XII and XIII apply.

Article 74

Members of the United Nations also agree that their policy in respect of the territories to which this Chapter applies, no less than in respect of their metropolitan areas, must be based on the general principle of good-neighbourliness, due account being taken of the interests and well-being of the rest of the world, in social, economic, and commercial matters.

Notes

Chapter 1

David D. Laitin & Said S. Samatar, 1987, *Somalia, A Nation in Search of a State*, Westview Press, page 12.

Taddesse Tamrat, 1977, *Ethiopia, the Red Sea and the Horn, the Cambridge History of Africa*, Cambridge University Press, Volume3, pages 143-1454, 148–149, 154–155, 156.

Paul B. Henze, 1991, *The Horn of Africa, from War to Peace*, pages 18–38.

Ronald Oliver and Anthony Atmore, 2001, Medieval Africa (1250-1800), Cambridge University Pres, page 118.

M. Abir, 1975, *Ethiopia and the Horn of Africa, the Cambridge History of Africa*, pages 538–542, 552–555.

Paul B. Henze, 2000, *Layers of Time, A History of Ethiopia*, pages 64–67, 85–91, 154.

Sheikh Ibrahim Abdallah, 2001, *Tuhfatul Awfiya, Limasirati Atahriri Wata'ribi, Fil Qarnil Ifriqi*, Horn of Africa studies, pages 59–62.

Chapter 2

I.M. Lewis, 2002, *A Modern History of the Somali*, James Currey, pages 40–62.

Paul B. Henze, 1991, *The Horn of Africa, from War to Peace*, Macmillan Academic and Professional Ltd, pages 33–35.

Mohamed Osman Omar, 2001, *The Scramble in the Horn of Africa*, Somali Publications, pages 105–166.

Paul B. Henze, 2000, *Layers of time, A History of Ethiopia*, Hurst & Co Ltd, pages 145–173, 189–199.

David D. Laitin & Said S. Samatar, 1987, *Somalia, A Nation in Search of a State*, page 49–65.

Bahru Zewde, 1991, *A History of Modern Ethiopia (1855–1974)*, pages 85–129, 179–81.

John Drysdale, 1964, *The Somali Dispute*, pages 25-70.

Chapter 3

Ray Beachey, 1990, *The Warrior Mullah*, pages 1–160.

Chapter 4

David D. Laitin & Said S. Samatar, 1987, *Somalia, A Nation in Search of a State*, Westview Press, pages 68–139.

M.M. Abdi, 1996, *The Performance of the Structural Adjustment Programme of the International Monetary Fund in Somalia*, Norwegian University of Science and

Technology, page 7.

Christopher Clapham, 1984, *The Horn of Africa, the Cambridge History of Africa*, pages 473–475.

I.M. Lewis, 2002, *A Modern History of the Somali*, James Currey, pages 178–183.

John Drysdale, 1964, *The Somali Dispute*, pages 88–121.

Chapter 5

Sheikh Ibrahim Abdallah, 2001, *Tuhfatul Awfiya, Limasirati Atahriri Wata'ribi Fil Qarnil Ifriqi, Horn of Africa Studies*, pages 59–62. Other sources of information about the formation of the Ogaden Liberation Front/Nasrullah included interviews with Garad Makhtal and other veteran liberation activists.

Department of State, 1964–68, Central files, POL 321 ETH-SOMALI (Declassified Files).

David D. Laitin & Said S. Samatar, 1987, *Somalia, A Nation in Search of a State*, Westview Press, pages 129–136.

Christopher Clapham, 1984, *The Horn of Africa, the Cambridge History of Africa*, Cambridge University Press, Volume 8, page 480-85.

Paul B. Henze, 2000, *Layers of Time, A History of Ethiopia*, pages 176–185.

I. M. Lewis, 2002, *A Modern History of the Somali*, James Currey, pages 195–204.

Louis FitzGibbon, 1982, *The Betrayal of the Somalis*, Rex Collins, pages 41–51.

Chapter 6

Sheikh Ibrahim Abdallah, 2001, *Tuhfatul Awfiya, Limasirati Atahriri Wata'ribi Fil Qarnil Ifriqi*, Horn of Africa Studies, page 142.

I.M. Lewis, 2002, *A Modern History of the Somali*, pages 228–231.

M.M. Abdi, 1996, *The Performance of Structural Adjustment Programme of the International Monetary Fund in Somalia*, Norwegian University of Science and Technology, pages 8–11.

David D. Laitin & Said S. Samatar, 1987, *Somalia, A Nation in Search of a State*, Westview Press, pages 135–140.

Paul B. Henze, 2000, *Layers of Time, A History of Ethiopia*, Hurst & Co Ltd pages 295–302.

Chapter 7

Ermias Abebe, 1995, *The Horn, the Cold War, and new documents from the former East bloc: An Ethiopian View*, Ethiopian Review Com. page 5. The document was part of a collection of declassified documents from the former Eastern bloc on the Horn of Africa crises 1977–78.

Harold G. Marcus, 1994, *A History of Ethiopia*, pages 196–197

Louis FitzGibbon, 1982, *The Betrayal of the Somalis*, Rex Collins Ltd, pages 52–62.

Chapter 8

Louis FitzGibbon, 1985, *The Evaded Duty*, page 15–17 and 85–91.

Sheikh Ibrahim Abdallah, 2001, *Tuhfatul Awfiya, Limasirati Atahriri Walta'ribi Fil Qarinil Ifriqi*, Horn of Africa Studies, pages 137–183, 193–194.

Louis FitzGibbon, 1985, *The Evaded Duty*, pages 76–77.

David D. Laitin & Said S. Samatar, 1987, *Somalia, a Nation in Search of a State*, Westview Press, page143–151.

Louis FitzGibbon, 1982, *The Betrayal of the Somalis*, pages 62–76

M.M. Abdi, 1996, *The Performance of the Structural Adjustment Programme of the International Monetary Fund (IMF) in Somalia*, Norwegian University of Science and Technology, pages 12–20.

I.M. Lewis, 2002, *A Modern History of the Somali*, James Currey, pages 239–248

Chapter 9

Al-Itihad Foreign Bureau 1997, *Information bulletin, Al-Itihad*, pages 5–6.

Sheikh Ibrahim Abdallah, 2001, *Tuhfatul Awfiya, Limasirati Atahriri watta'ribi Fil Qarinil Ifriqi*, pages 223–259.

I.M. Lewis, 2002, *A Modern History of the Somali*, James Currey, pages 289 and 251–254.

Chapter 10

Ogaden Human Rights Committee, 2006, *Mass killing in the Ogaden*, OHRC, page1.

Paul B. Henze, 2000, *Layers of Time, A History of Ethiopia*, Hurst & Co Ltd, pages 309–333.

Harold G. Marcus, 1994, *A History of Ethiopia*, pages 202–207.

M.M. Abdi, 1998, *Human Rights Promotion and Environmental Protection in Ethiopia and the Occupied Ogaden Region*, Abdi, pages 1–8.

Ogaden Natural Resources and Environmental Organization 1998, ONREO Report I, pages 1–10.

Various unpublished press reports.

Chapter 11

Al-Itihad Foreign Bureau 1998, Information Bulletin, *Al-Itihad*, pages 6–8.

Ogaden Natural Resources and Environmental Organization, 1998 Report I, pages 1–8.

Ogaden Human Rights Committee Reports, 1996–2006, OHRC.

Alliance for Freedom and Democracy, 22 May 2006, Press Statement.

Unpublished sources, including interviews with ONLF officials.

Chapter 12

Louis FitzGibbon, 1985, *The Evaded Duty*, pages 20–155.
UNESCO, (1975–2006), United Nations Human Development Reports.
AU Constitutive Act, AU website(www.africa-union.org).
OAU Charter, AU website(www.africa-union.org).

Appendices

Mohamed Osman Omar, 2001, *The Scramble in the Horn of Africa*, Somali publications, pages 106, 122–130.
Louis FitzGibbon, 1982, *The Betrayal of the Somalis*, Rex Collins Ltd, pages 23–24.
Louis FitzGibbon, 1985, *The Evaded Duty*, Rex Collins Ltd, pages 125–134.
UN charter, UN website (www.un.org).
Foreign Office Archives, 1897, Concerning the Mission of Mr. James Rennel Rodd to Emperor Menelik, file Reference FO. 1/32 & 33.
British and Foreign State Papers 1884–1886, Concerning Agreements Concluded between Britain and Various Somali Tribes, Volumes 76 & 77.

Index

Printed in the USA
CPSIA information can be obtained
at www.ICGtesting.com
LVHW092251211023
761780LV00006BA/98

9 781906 342395